Climate Change and Energy Transition

This book series is a collaborative initiative between the *International Society for Energy Transition Studies (ISETS)* and *Springer*. It aims to provide a comprehensive collection of works addressing key topics on climate change and energy transition from a global perspective, with an emphasis on the interdisciplinary nature of this field. By exploring theoretical, empirical, and policy-relevant research, the series focuses on the critical challenges and opportunities in the climate-driven energy transition.

The objective of the series is to deliver diverse and accessible content to a broad audience, including policymakers, researchers, and the general public. Covering the latest advancements in the area, it seeks to offer a toolbox of vital information, a platform for knowledge sharing, and a forum for discussing pertinent issues related to the global energy transition.

Mengmeng Guo · Dayong Zhang · Yixiang Yu

Social-Economic Impacts of Air Pollution

Risks, Responses, and Resilience

Springer

Mengmeng Guo
School of Finance
Nanjing Agricultural University
Nanjing, China

Yixiang Yu
School of Finance and Public Administration
Anhui University of Finance and Economics
Bengbu, China

Dayong Zhang
Research Institute of Economics and Management
Southwestern University of Finance and Economics
Chengdu, China

ISSN 2731-9903 ISSN 2731-9911 (electronic)
Climate Change and Energy Transition
ISBN 978-981-96-7857-0 ISBN 978-981-96-7858-7 (eBook)
https://doi.org/10.1007/978-981-96-7858-7

This Springer imprint is published by the registered company Springer Nature Singapore Pte Ltd.
The registered company address is: 152 Beach Road, #21-01/04 Gateway East, Singapore 189721, Singapore

To all those who are working tirelessly to reduce air pollution and to create a cleaner, healthier world for future generations. This book is dedicated to the environmental warriors, policymakers, and innovators who strive for a sustainable and resilient future.

Foreword

Air pollution is one of the most pressing global challenges of our time, affecting millions of lives every day. From its direct impact on human health to its indirect effects on economies and markets, the consequences of air pollution are far-reaching and often underestimated. This book, *Social-Economic Impacts of Air Pollution: Risks, Responses, and Resilience*, delves into the multi-dimensional impacts of air pollution and explores how individuals, corporations, and societies can respond to and mitigate these risks. Each chapter examines a different aspect of the problem, from its health implications to its role in shaping market dynamics and driving green innovation.

The contributions in this book offer valuable insights into how we can create resilient systems in the face of environmental threats. The interdisciplinary nature of the book reflects the urgency and complexity of the issue, making it an essential resource for researchers, policymakers, and practitioners in the fields of economics, public health, and environmental science.

Preface

Air pollution remains one of the most pervasive environmental challenges, with profound effects on both human health and economic performance. This book aims to bring attention to the social and economic dimensions of air pollution, highlighting its impact on industries, markets, and societal well-being. Each chapter addresses a distinct area of concern, from the effects of air pollution on stock market performance and tourism to its role in reshaping corporate behavior and spurring innovation.

The aim of this book is not only to deepen our understanding of the diverse ways in which air pollution shapes our world but also to provide actionable insights for mitigating its impact. By analyzing the multifaceted nature of air pollution, we hope to encourage more effective responses from both policymakers and industry leaders.

As the world faces the growing threat of environmental degradation, it is our collective responsibility to foster resilience and implement sustainable practices that ensure a healthier future. I am honored to contribute to this important discourse through this work.

Nanjing, China
Chengdu, China
Bengbu, China

Mengmeng Guo
Dayong Zhang
Yixiang Yu

Competing Interests The authors have no competing interests to declare that are relevant to the content of this manuscript.

Contents

Chapter 1
A Silent Threat with Loud Consequences

Air pollution is one of the most pervasive yet underestimated threats of our time. It is invisible to the naked eye, yet it silently reshapes societies, economies, and ecosystems. Every year, millions of people worldwide suffer from its consequences, with low- and middle-income countries bearing the brunt of its impact. Beyond its well-documented health effects, air pollution disrupts economic stability, exacerbates social inequalities, and challenges our ability to build resilient communities.

This book, Social-Economic Impacts of Air Pollution: Risks, Responses, and Resilience, explores the complex interplay between air pollution and human societies. It examines not only the risks but also the responses and resilience-building strategies needed to address this multifaceted crisis. By integrating insights from public health, economics, environmental science, and social justice, the book offers a holistic perspective on how air pollution affects—and is affected by—global economic dynamics.

Air pollution is not merely an environmental issue; it is a systemic challenge with profound social and economic repercussions. As reported by the World Health Organization, 99% of the global population breathes air that exceeds recommended safety thresholds, with East Asia, South Asia, and sub-Saharan Africa experiencing the most severe impacts. In 2016 alone, outdoor air pollution caused 4.2 million premature deaths, while household air pollution claimed an additional 3.8 million lives. These statistics, however, only scratch the surface of the problem.

The economic toll is equally staggering. Air pollution costs the global economy trillions of dollars annually in lost labor income, healthcare expenses, and reduced productivity. In low- and middle-income countries, these costs strain already fragile healthcare systems and hinder economic growth. Meanwhile, marginalized communities face disproportionate exposure to pollutants, perpetuating cycles of poverty and inequality.

While the health impacts of air pollution are well-documented, its broader societal effects often go overlooked. Air pollution degrades ecosystems, diminishes quality of life, and disrupts social cohesion. It accelerates climate change, threatens food and

M. Guo et al., *Social-Economic Impacts of Air Pollution*, Climate Change and Energy Transition, https://doi.org/10.1007/978-981-96-7858-7_1

water security, and forces governments to divert resources from critical investments like education and infrastructure.

Perhaps most concerning is its role in deepening social inequities. Low-income communities, often located near industrial zones or busy roads, face higher exposure risks and limited access to healthcare. Children, the elderly, and those with preexisting conditions are particularly vulnerable, creating intergenerational cycles of disadvantage.

Despite these challenges, air pollution is not an insurmountable crisis. It is a problem shaped by human choices—and one that can be addressed through collective action. This book emphasizes the importance of resilience: the capacity of societies to mitigate, adapt to, and recover from air pollution's impacts. From policy reforms and technological innovations to community-led initiatives, resilience-building offers pathways to a healthier, more equitable future.

In the following sections, we explore the impacts of air pollution on society and the economy from three perspectives: health, economic costs, and broader societal effects.

1.1 Health Impacts of Air Pollution

Air pollution is a major contributor to a range of health problems, from respiratory and cardiovascular diseases to cancer and neurological disorders. Data from the World Health Organization (WHO) indicate that ambient (outdoor) air pollution accounted for approximately 4.2 million premature deaths worldwide in 2016. These fatalities were primarily linked to conditions such as stroke, cardiovascular disease, lung cancer, and chronic respiratory illnesses. Household air pollution, primarily from cooking with solid fuels, was responsible for an additional 3.8 million premature deaths in the same year.

Air pollution represents a major environmental risk factor contributing to the development of both respiratory and cardiovascular illnesses. Among the various pollutants, fine particulate matter (PM2.5) and nitrogen dioxide (NO_2) are particularly detrimental due to their ability to infiltrate deep pulmonary tissues and enter the circulatory system, where they induce inflammation and oxidative stress. Prolonged exposure to these substances has been associated with a heightened incidence of respiratory conditions such as chronic obstructive pulmonary disease (COPD), asthma, and related disorders. Moreover, compelling evidence links air pollution to cardiovascular morbidity, with ischemic heart disease and stroke among the most affected outcomes. According to estimates from the World Health Organization (WHO), approximately one-quarter of all deaths resulting from heart disease and stroke can be attributed to exposure to polluted air.

The International Agency for Research on Cancer (IARC) classifies air pollution as a Group 1 carcinogen, indicating sufficient evidence of its carcinogenicity in humans. Long-term exposure, especially to PM2.5, has been strongly correlated with an elevated risk of lung cancer. WHO data suggest that air pollution is implicated in nearly 29% of global lung cancer fatalities. In addition to lung cancer, an expanding body of evidence suggests that air pollution may also be linked to the development of other malignancies, such as bladder and breast cancers.

Recent research has highlighted the potential impact of air pollution on neurological health. Exposure to air pollution, particularly PM2.5, has been associated with an increased risk of neurodegenerative diseases such as Alzheimer's disease and Parkinson's disease. Children exposed to high levels of air pollution may also experience cognitive deficits and developmental delays. The WHO has recognized the growing evidence of the neurological effects of air pollution and has called for further research to better understand these risks.

1.2 Economic Costs of Air Pollution

The health impacts of air pollution translate into significant economic costs, both direct and indirect. These costs include healthcare expenditures, lost productivity, and reduced economic growth. The WHO estimates that air pollution costs the global economy trillions of dollars annually in lost labor income and increased healthcare spending.

Air pollution places a substantial burden on healthcare systems worldwide. Managing diseases associated with air pollution—particularly respiratory and cardiovascular conditions—places a substantial demand on healthcare systems. This burden is especially pronounced in low- and middle-income countries, where medical infrastructure is often limited and already under pressure. According to the World Health Organization (WHO), the annual global healthcare costs attributable to air pollution amount to several hundred billion dollars.

Air pollution further exerts a notable influence on labor productivity, contributing to economic inefficiencies through its adverse effects on worker health and performance. Workers who suffer from air pollution-related illnesses are more likely to take sick leave, reducing their productivity and earning potential. In severe cases, chronic illnesses may force workers to leave the labor market altogether, resulting in long-term economic losses. The WHO estimates that air pollution-related lost labor income amounts to hundreds of billions of dollars annually, with the highest costs borne by low- and middle-income countries.

The cumulative impact of healthcare expenditures and lost productivity can hinder economic growth. Air pollution can reduce the overall productivity of a workforce, leading to lower GDP growth rates. In addition, the costs associated with air pollution can divert resources away from other productive investments, such as education and infrastructure. The WHO has warned that the economic costs of air pollution could undermine efforts to achieve sustainable development goals, particularly in developing countries.

1.3 Broader Societal Impacts of Air Pollution

Beyond the direct health and economic impacts, air pollution has broader societal effects that can exacerbate social inequalities and hinder sustainable development. These impacts include environmental degradation, reduced quality of life, and social inequities.

Air pollution contributes to environmental degradation, including acid rain, eutrophication, and damage to ecosystems. The formation of acid rain, primarily resulting from atmospheric deposition of sulfur dioxide (SO_2) and nitrogen oxides (NO_x), poses serious threats to forested areas, soil quality, and freshwater ecosystems. Eutrophication, resulting from the deposition of nitrogen compounds, can lead to the overgrowth of algae in water bodies, disrupting aquatic ecosystems and reducing biodiversity. The degradation of ecosystems can have cascading effects on human well-being, including reduced availability of clean water and food.

Air pollution substantially diminishes quality of life at both individual and community levels, affecting physical health, well-being, and overall environmental livability. Poor air quality can limit outdoor activities, reduce visibility, and create unpleasant odors. In urban areas, where air pollution levels are often highest, residents may experience a lower overall quality of life due to the constant exposure to polluted air. Vulnerable populations-including children, the elderly, and those with underlying health conditions-are disproportionately affected by air pollution, thereby intensifying existing social and health inequities.

Air pollution often disproportionately affects marginalized and low-income communities. These populations are often concentrated in environments with elevated pollution levels—such as those adjacent to major roadways or industrial zones—where exposure risks are particularly high. Compounding their vulnerability, limited access to healthcare and other mitigating resources further restricts their ability to cope with pollution-related health challenges. The World Health Organization (WHO) has emphasized the importance of implementing targeted policies to address the socio-environmental disparities linked to air pollution, especially in low- and middle-income countries.

Despite the clear evidence of air pollution's harmful effects, less attention has been given to how it reshapes broader economic dynamics. From influencing stock market performance to altering consumption patterns, the economic consequences of air pollution are vast and multifaceted. Understanding these economic and social impacts is crucial for policymakers, businesses, and investors, as it can drive more informed decisions, particularly regarding climate change, sustainable development, and corporate strategies.

This volume investigates the multifaceted and far-reaching connections between air pollution and the global economy, offering a comprehensive examination of its impacts across social and economic domains, as well as the responses they elicit. The book is structured into ten chapters, beginning with an introductory overview and concluding with a synthesis of key findings and implications. Below is a brief introduction to the content of the eight chapters in between.

In Chap. 2, we explore the link between environmental risks—particularly air pollution—and stock market performance. As environmental concerns increasingly shape investor decision-making, the influence of air quality on financial markets has become more pronounced. We analyze empirical evidence indicating that cities with elevated pollution levels tend to exhibit reduced stock returns and trading activity, especially among firms with a strong local market focus or limited institutional ownership. The analysis identifies that investors in these areas—especially those with local biases—are more sensitive to environmental conditions. The study suggests that while environmental awareness is growing among investors, stock markets have started to adapt over time, incorporating air pollution data into their assessments. Over time, the direct influence of air pollution on market performance has exhibited a declining pattern, suggesting that investors are increasingly incorporating environmental risks into their investment strategies and pricing mechanisms.

The chapter also emphasizes the growing importance of environmental, social, and governance (ESG) factors, which have gained increasing attention in recent years amid the heightened salience of climate-related risks. The analysis presents empirical evidence showing how air pollution contributes to fluctuations in stock market returns, and the emerging trend of socially responsible investing, where investors prioritize sustainability and environmental impact.

In Chap. 3, this chapter examines how air pollution influences the decision-making and behavioral patterns of individual investors. While previous studies have predominantly focused on institutional investors, this chapter emphasizes the decision-making process of individual investors who may be more emotionally influenced by their local environment. Using transaction data, the study finds that air pollution significantly affects individual investors' trading behavior. Specifically, individuals are less likely to purchase stocks on days with high pollution levels and are more inclined to sell. This behavior indicates that environmental factors—specifically pollution—can lead to market inefficiencies. The chapter also investigates how factors such as investor experience, regional pollution levels, and the type of stocks being traded interact with air pollution to shape investor behavior.

The analysis uncovers new insights into the inefficiencies that pollution can introduce into financial markets, especially concerning individual decision-making. The findings suggest that environmental policies aimed at reducing pollution could not only improve public health but also enhance market efficiency by reducing investor biases driven by local environmental factors. In addition, this chapter adds to the behavioral economics literature by illustrating how air pollution functions as an exogenous factor that shapes financial decision-making within the investment landscape.

In Chap. 4, we shift focus to the capital markets, specifically the initial public offering (IPO) market. The study investigates how air pollution influences the performance of companies seeking to list on the stock exchange, particularly in regions that experience significant air quality challenges. The findings indicate that in cities with elevated air pollution, the performance of initial public offerings (IPOs) tends to be adversely affected. However, interestingly, IPOs in the environmental and clean-tech sectors exhibit stronger performance despite high pollution levels. These results imply that investors exhibit a stronger preference for firms that prioritize environmental sustainability and actively pursue strategies to address air pollution challenges.

Furthermore, this chapter examines the influence of institutional investors on IPO performance, emphasizing their growing sensitivity to environmental conditions. It contends that IPOs launched in areas with relatively cleaner air are more likely to attract institutional capital, reflecting a broader trend of integrating environmental risk assessments into investment strategies. The analysis reinforces the critical role environmental considerations play in shaping capital market dynamics, especially in the realm of initial public offerings.

In Chap. 5, this chapter offers a detailed examination of the impact of air pollution on consumer behavior, with particular attention to its effects on online review patterns within service-oriented sectors such as the restaurant industry. The study finds that higher levels of air pollution lead to lower customer ratings, which is particularly pronounced when pollution levels exceed certain thresholds, such as an AQI of 200 or more. The chapter explores how air pollution affects consumers' dining experiences and their willingness to provide positive feedback. The analysis underscores the importance of perceived air quality—shaped by local pollution conditions—in influencing customer satisfaction, which in turn affects the public image and reputational standing of businesses.

The chapter explores strategic responses that firms can adopt to counteract the reputational risks posed by air pollution, aiming to preserve consumer trust and brand value. Strategies such as improving indoor air quality and providing transparent information about pollution levels may help businesses retain customer loyalty, even during periods of high pollution. This chapter offers new insights into the direct link between air quality and consumer satisfaction, which has important implications for businesses and the service industry.

In Chap. 6, this chapter investigates the effects of air pollution on domestic tourism in China, drawing on panel data from 2006 to 2016. The findings demonstrate that elevated pollution levels exert a significant negative influence on tourism revenues, with the impact being especially pronounced in areas experiencing persistent air quality issues. As air pollution worsens, tourists are less likely to travel to affected areas, leading to declines in both the number of visitors and the amount of money spent in local economies.

The chapter further examines the amplifying role of public awareness—proxied by online search activity on platforms such as Baidu—in intensifying the adverse impact of air pollution on domestic tourism demand. The study demonstrates that tourism is highly sensitive to environmental factors, and cities with high pollution are likely to see reduced tourist numbers and, consequently, lower economic output from the tourism sector. This chapter underscores the economic consequences of air pollution for the tourism sector—one of the world's largest industries—and proposes potential mitigation strategies, including the promotion of clean air initiatives and the diversification of tourism products to sustain visitor engagement in the face of environmental challenges.

In Chap. 7, the chapter centers on the healthcare sector, with a particular focus on the rising demand for health insurance as a response to deteriorating air quality. Empirical evidence from China reveals a substantial increase in health insurance uptake during periods characterized by elevated pollution levels, indicating a behavioral shift driven by heightened health risk awareness. This demand is particularly strong in cities with chronic pollution issues, where residents are more concerned about the potential health risks associated with poor air quality. The chapter analyzes how air pollution drives up the cost of healthcare and influences the market for health insurance products, offering new insights into the intersection of environmental risk and health insurance markets.

As public concern over air pollution grows, insurance providers are increasingly including environmental risk assessments in their offerings, adjusting premiums to account for the heightened health risks in polluted areas. The chapter discusses how insurance companies can adapt to these changes and how policymakers can incentivize the industry to incorporate environmental factors into their pricing models.

There is growing global recognition among governments of the substantial economic and societal burdens imposed by air pollution, prompting a wave of policy initiatives designed to curb emissions and alleviate their broader economic consequences. This chapter explores the policy tools available to governments to tackle air pollution and their effectiveness in both environmental and economic terms.

In Chap. 8, the chapter begins by examining the role of regulatory measures, such as emission standards, pollution caps, and urban planning, in curbing air pollution. A detailed analysis is provided on the economic costs and benefits of these policies, considering both the short-term costs (such as enforcement and regulatory compliance) and the long-term gains (including improved public health and productivity). The chapter also delves into the economic mechanisms behind air pollution taxation, tradable permits, and subsidies for green technologies, showing how these policy instruments can be designed to incentivize companies and individuals to reduce their environmental footprint.

Furthermore, the chapter addresses the role of international cooperation in addressing transnational air pollution issues. Given the transboundary nature of air pollution, international accords—such as the Paris Agreement—and regional collaborative mechanisms are crucial for addressing air quality challenges on a global scale. The chapter discusses how such agreements can enhance coordination between nations to mitigate the economic impacts of pollution through shared technologies, resources, and best practices.

The chapter concludes by emphasizing the critical role of local governments in deploying air quality monitoring infrastructures and initiating public health measures to address pollution-related risks. By adopting air quality indices (AQI) and promoting public awareness campaigns, local governments can help mitigate the economic impact of air pollution on consumers and businesses. The chapter offers practical recommendations for policymakers, emphasizing the need for a comprehensive, multi-level approach to managing air pollution.

In Chap. 9, the book focuses on the business sector and how companies can adapt to the growing economic challenges posed by air pollution. Businesses are often on the frontline when it comes to dealing with air pollution's economic effects, both directly through costs such as healthcare and employee absenteeism, and indirectly through changes in consumer preferences and regulatory pressure.

The chapter opens with an examination of how air pollution affects worker productivity and broader labor market dynamics. High pollution levels have been shown to lead to increased absenteeism and reduced work performance, especially in industries requiring outdoor labor or in locations with chronic air pollution. The chapter examines the economic costs businesses face due to these impacts and presents strategies to mitigate these effects. For instance, businesses can implement flexible working hours, remote work options, or invest in air filtration systems to improve indoor air quality. In addition, the chapter highlights the potential for businesses to enhance employee engagement by supporting environmental initiatives and contributing to air quality improvement projects.

Subsequently, the chapter investigates how firms operating in industries such as manufacturing, agriculture, and transportation adjust their operational strategies to reduce environmental externalities and mitigate their ecological impact. For example, manufacturing companies can invest in cleaner production technologies, while transportation companies can shift toward electric or hybrid fleets to reduce their emissions. Such initiatives contribute not only to the reduction of a firm's environmental footprint but also yield long-term economic advantages, including enhanced energy efficiency and strengthened corporate reputation.

The chapter also discusses how air pollution affects consumer preferences and purchasing behavior, particularly in the context of industries such as real estate, retail, and tourism. As consumer awareness of the environmental consequences of consumption continues to grow, firms that do not align with evolving sustainability preferences risk a reduction in market demand. This chapter explores how corporate social responsibility (CSR) initiatives contribute to fostering consumer trust and brand loyalty, highlighting the strategic use of sustainability practices as a means of differentiation in increasingly competitive markets.

In Chap. 10, we provide the conclusion and a vision of future with clean air. Creating a future with clean air and sustainable development requires a multifaceted approach that combines policy reforms, technological innovation, economic strategies, and cultural shifts. By transitioning to renewable energy sources, revolutionizing transportation systems, and leveraging green finance, we can significantly reduce emissions and improve air quality. Strengthening regulations, promoting corporate responsibility, and empowering communities through education and awareness are essential steps in building resilience against air pollution. Global cooperation and equity must underpin these efforts, ensuring that all nations, particularly low- and middle-income countries, have the resources and support to participate fully in this transition. Through collective action and a commitment to sustainability, we can create a world where clean air is a universal right, ecosystems thrive, and economic prosperity is achieved without compromising the health and well-being of future generations.

Chapter 2
Choking Returns: Air Pollution and Stock Market Performance

Abstract Drawing on prior research that links environmental conditions to investor sentiment, along with insights from the literature on local bias, we propose a negative association between air pollution and stock market performance. Empirical results are consistent with this expectation, indicating that firms located in more polluted cities exhibit lower stock returns and reduced trading activity. Supporting our core hypothesis, the effects are especially pronounced among firms with a predominantly regional investor base—characterized by limited institutional ownership and sparse analyst coverage. Moreover, the influence of air pollution on market outcomes appears to have weakened over time, suggesting that investors gradually adapt their trading behavior as they assimilate environmental risks into their decision-making processes.

Keywords Air pollution · Stock return · Local bias

2.1 Introduction

It has long been recognized in psychology that environmental conditions can shape individuals' moods, cognition, and judgment. Building on these insights, financial researchers have explored the extent to which such factors contribute to behavioral patterns in asset pricing. Nonetheless, the empirical link between environmental variables and stock returns remains contested. A substantial body of literature has investigated how weather-related elements influence investor behavior and market outcomes, yet the findings are mixed. Notably, studies by Saunders (1993) and Hirshleifer and Shumway (2003) report that stock returns tend to be lower on overcast days compared to sunny ones, offering direct evidence that investor sentiment can affect

This chapter is an extension of the paper titled "Air pollution, local bias and stock return", by Ding, X. Guo, M*., and Yang, T. (2021), Finance Research Letters, 39:101576.

M. Guo et al., *Social-Economic Impacts of Air Pollution*, Climate Change and Energy Transition, https://doi.org/10.1007/978-981-96-7858-7_2

market performance. Beyond sunshine and cloud cover, additional research highlights the influence of other meteorological and temporal factors—such as temperature fluctuations, wind conditions, daylight saving time adjustments, and even lunar phases—on financial markets (Cao and Wei 2005; Kamstra et al. 2000, 2003; Yuan et al. 2006). In contrast, some researchers provide evidence that the findings in support of the causal relationship of weather conditions and stock returns is either weak (Loughran and Schultz 2004) or can be explained by other variables that exhibit strong seasonal patterns (Jacobsen and Marquering 2008; Kelly and Meschke 2010).

Departing from prior studies that primarily infer investor behavior from transient weather conditions, this research contributes to the ongoing discourse on environmental influences by examining the relationship between air pollution and stock returns. Specifically, we analyze how air quality in a firm's host city correlates with its stock performance in the Chinese market. There are several reasons for focusing on Chinese firms and air pollution as the environmental variable of interest. First, the psychological effects of air pollution are generally more consistent and less ambiguous than those associated with other environmental factors such as weather. A substantial body of psychological literature has documented that acute exposure to ambient air pollutants can exert both direct and indirect impacts on emotional and cognitive functioning (e.g., Bullinger 1990), often resulting in elevated levels of depression, anxiety, and irritability (Evans 1987; Cohen 1986; Bullinger 1989; Schiffman 1995). Second, there is high heterogeneity in air quality within China. Over our 8-year sample period, the mean air quality index (AQI) ranges from 111.11 for the most polluted city Shijiazhuang to 39.11 for the least polluted city Haikou. Third, the Chinese equity market is heavily influenced by individual investors, who tend to exhibit pronounced behavioral biases (Chen 2004; Tan et al. 2008) and demonstrate a marked preference for geographically proximate firms (Feng and Seasholes 2004). These characteristics are likely to amplify the sensitivity of stock performance to local environmental conditions, such as air pollution. As such, China provides a particularly suitable context for investigating how environmental stressors influence investor sentiment and, by extension, stock returns.

Building on prior research linking air pollution to mood disturbances, and mood to financial decision-making, we hypothesize a negative association between air pollution and firm-level stock returns. Employing a comprehensive dataset encompassing all A-share firms listed on the Shanghai and Shenzhen Stock Exchanges from 2009 to 2016, we document that companies headquartered in more polluted cities experience both lower stock returns and reduced trading activity. This effect of air pollution is not only statistically robust but also economically meaningful. Specifically, a one-standard-deviation increase in the Air Quality Index (AQI) is associated with a 1.86 basis point decline in daily returns, translating to an annualized reduction of approximately 4.6%. Consistent with our main hypothesis, we observe that the effect of air pollution is particularly significant for firms that are more prone to local investor ownership—specifically, those with lower institutional investor presence and fewer analysts covering them. This evidence strongly suggests that investor sentiment, influenced by exposure to air pollution, may be a key factor driving the negative relationship between pollution levels and stock returns. Additionally, we find that the strength of this effect diminishes over time, indicating that investors are progressively incorporating environmental factors into their decision-making processes. The robustness of our findings is further supported by various empirical checks using different proxies for air pollution, such as overall pollution levels, fluctuations in pollution, and pollution data adjusted for seasonal patterns and city-specific characteristics. These results remain consistent even after controlling for a broad set of weather-related variables, as well as fixed effects for city, year, month, and weekday.

This study adds to the expanding body of research exploring the intersection of environmental influences, investor sentiment, and asset pricing. By capitalizing on the considerable variation in air quality across Chinese cities and the dominance of retail investors in the domestic equity market, we uncover a notable negative relationship between local air pollution and firm-level stock returns. Our results are consistent with previous studies, such as Saunders (1993), Hirshleifer and Shumway (2003), and Goetzmann (2015), which highlight the impact of weather conditions on market performance. Crucially, our findings suggest that local ambient air pollution can influence the behavior of less informed retail investors, indicating that mood-driven biases may significantly contribute to the formation of asset prices. Our study is also closely related to the study by Loughran and Schultz (2004). Although they confirm the existing findings that investors are more likely to trade nearby stocks, they find cloud cover around a firm's location has little impact on stock trading volume. Instead, we find that a firm is more likely to have lower returns and lower trading volume on heavily polluted days.

Our research distinguishes itself from earlier studies exploring the connection between air pollution and stock market performance. For instance, Levy and Yagil (2011) investigate the relationship between air quality in Philadelphia and Kings County, New York, and daily returns across several U.S. stock exchanges, including the NYSE, AMEX, NASDAQ, and the Philadelphia Stock Exchange. In a similar vein, Lepori (2016) investigates the impact of air pollution on trading behavior by analyzing the transition from traditional floor trading to electronic systems at the Milan Stock Exchange. While both studies offer evidence of a negative correlation between air pollution and stock returns, their primary emphasis is on the behavior of professional traders and the overall performance of exchanges. In contrast, our study highlights the influence of retail investors—who play a dominant role in China's equity market—on price formation, thereby offering a distinct perspective on how environmental factors affect investor behavior and market outcomes. We show that local air pollution associates with retail investors' trading behavior and hence negatively relates to stock trading and stock returns.

Our study also makes a significant contribution to the growing body of research on environmental challenges in China. As the world's second-largest economy and a major player in global markets, China faces severe environmental degradation and is among the most polluted nations worldwide (Diao 2009; Xu et al. 2012; Jiang et al. 2014; Tanaka 2015). While the negative health effects of air pollution are well-documented, its broader economic consequences—particularly its impact on firm-level financial outcomes—remain underexplored. This study fills that gap by providing evidence of a significant negative relationship between air pollution and stock returns in China. This finding is of particular economic relevance, as stock prices are closely linked to a firm's cost of capital, which, in turn, shapes corporate investment decisions, financing strategies, and long-term competitive positioning.

The remainder of the paper is organized as follows: Sect. 2.2 presents the theoretical framework and hypotheses; Sect. 2.3 details the data sources and empirical methodology; Sect. 2.4 discusses the key findings; and Sect. 2.5 offers concluding remarks.

2.2 Hypothesis Development

The existing literature indicates that environmental conditions can impact an investor's mood, and investor mood can impact stock trading behaviors. Among others, Saunders (1993) documents a significant association between the New York Stock Exchange's daily returns and weather conditions in New York City. Hirshleifer and Shumway (2003) investigate 26 stock exchanges worldwide and find similar results. Goetzmann (2015) find that investor optimism based on cloud cover affects institutional investors' perceptions about market mispricing and their propensities to buy. Cao and Wei (2005) analyze global stock markets and report a significant inverse relationship between ambient temperature and stock returns, implying that temperature-induced mood changes may influence investor behavior. Similarly, Kamstra et al. (2000, 2003) provide evidence that Seasonal Affective Disorder (SAD) can lead to increased depressive symptoms among investors, subsequently affecting their risk preferences and trading decisions. In addition, studies by Keef and Khaled (2011) and Yuan et al. (2006) reveal a consistent association between lunar cycles and stock market performance across 48 international markets, further highlighting the role of environmental and psychological factors in shaping financial outcomes. The overarching conclusion from this line of research is that weather-related variables, by influencing investor psychology, can exert a substantial effect on stock market index fluctuations.

In contrast, Loughran and Schultz (2004) report limited evidence that cloud cover in the vicinity of a firm's headquarters has any meaningful impact on its stock returns, thereby raising skepticism about the extent to which weather-related factors influence return patterns. Jacobsen and Marquering (2008) find that the results in Kamstra et al. (2000, 2003) and Cao and Wei (2005) can also be explained by other variables with strong seasonal patterns, such as the Sell-in-May effect and the Halloween effect. Kelly and Meschke (2010) further find there is no relation between the prevalence of Seasonal Affective Disorder (SAD) and stock returns and that the SAD effect is driven by an overlapping dummy-variable specification and higher returns around the turn of the year. Therefore, whether environmental factors can affect stock returns is subject to debate.

This paper argues that air pollution may negatively affect stock returns through its psychological impact on investors. Several psychological studies have demonstrated a positive correlation between exposure to air pollution and increased cortisol levels, a stress hormone released by the adrenal cortex (Raff et al. 1985; Hsieh et al. 1991; Tomei 2003). Elevated cortisol is linked to adverse emotional states, including increased depression, anxiety, irritability, and feelings of helplessness. These negative emotional conditions, in turn, affect individuals' decision-making and risk-taking behavior. For instance, Morris (2000) finds that individuals in positive (negative) emotional states are more likely to make optimistic (pessimistic) judgments. Similarly, Slovic and Peters (2006) show that negative moods can heighten risk aversion by influencing individuals' subjective evaluation of future uncertainties. Recent findings from the financial literature provide further empirical support for the mood-based mechanism. de Haan et al. (2017) demonstrate that analysts exposed to adverse weather conditions exhibit weaker responses to earnings announcements, an effect attributed to mood alterations. Complementing this, Dong (2019) show that air pollution during corporate site visits negatively influences subsequent analyst earnings forecasts. These results suggest that negative affect leads investors to assign greater weight to unfavorable outcomes in their subjective probability assessments, thereby shaping risk attitudes and market behavior. Therefore, when air quality is good (bad), investors are more optimistic (pessimistic) and they are more likely to buy (sell), which in turn drives up (down) the stock price. Therefore, we contend that elevated levels of air pollution can deteriorate investor mood, which in turn dampens trading activity and exerts a negative impact on stock returns.

The potential relationship between air pollution and firm-level stock returns may be influenced by local bias in investor behavior. Previous research consistently demonstrates that investors tend to favor firms located geographically close to them (e.g., Huberman 2001; Grinblatt and Keloharju 2001; Massa and Simonov 2006; Coval and Moskowitz 1999, 2001; Ivković and Weisbenner 2005). In the context of Mainland China, Feng and Seasholes (2004) find that retail investors allocate approximately 8% more of their portfolio to firms based in their home province than would be predicted by a capitalization-weighted benchmark. These results suggest that local sentiment, influenced by environmental factors like air pollution, may directly shape trading behavior and, in turn, impact the pricing of local equities. Consequently, we hypothesize that the negative relationship between air pollution and stock returns will be more pronounced for firms with a predominantly local investor base.

Thus, our primary testable hypothesis is as follows:

H1 A firm's stock return is negatively associated with the level of air pollution in the city where the firm is headquartered.

Furthermore, unlike the U.S. equity market—which is largely driven by sophisticated institutional investors with extensive expertise—the Chinese A-share market is predominantly composed of retail investors. Existing research has shown that individual investors are particularly prone to behavioral biases, which can significantly influence their trading decisions and market outcomes (e.g., Odean 1998; Barber and

Odean 2000; Barber et al. 2008; Barberis and Huang 2001; Cohen et al. 2002).[1] China started the Shanghai and Shenzhen Stock Exchanges in 1990, with a relatively young history, Chinese individual investors by and large lack significant knowledge about investments in financial markets (China Securities and Futures Statistical Yearbook 2004). They show a strong tendency of herding (Tan 2008), tend to be overconfident and are inclined to exhibit the disposition effect and representative bias (Chen 2004). Given the substantial influence of behavioral biases among individual investors in the Chinese stock market, we posit that investor mood—shaped by environmental conditions such as air pollution—can meaningfully affect local financial outcomes. This perspective informs our second testable prediction:

H2 The negative association between air pollution and stock returns is more pronounced for firms whose shares are predominantly held by individual investors.

2.3 Data and Methodology

2.3.1 Data Description

The empirical analysis draws on data from three main sources. Air quality data, specifically the Air Quality Index (AQI), is obtained from the official website of the Ministry of Environmental Protection of the People's Republic of China (MEPC). Financial and stock market data are sourced from the China Stock Market and Accounting Research (CSMAR) database. In line with prior research (Coval and Moskowitz 1999; Ivković and Weisbenner 2005), we use the location of a firm's headquarters as a proxy for its geographic presence, based on the assumption that corporate headquarters are generally located near the firm's primary business operations (Pirinsky and Wang 2006). To avoid the possible distortion by the financial crisis in year 2008, our sample spans the post-crisis years 2009–2016. To control for potential confounding effects from other meteorological variables, such as temperature, precipitation, sunshine duration, wind speed, and humidity, we source weather data from the China Meteorological Administration (CMA). All the data represent daily frequency information.

To reduce the impact of extreme values, all variables are winsorized at the 1st and 99th percentiles. Panel A of Table 2.2 provides the descriptive statistics for

[1] For example, individual investors tend to hold their losers and sell their winning investments, hence exhibiting a disposition effect (Odean 1998); individual investors tend to speculate on small stocks and high risky stocks and are over confident causing them to trade stocks frequently, resulting in a poor performance (Barber and Odean 2000). Further, individual investors are unduly influenced by familiarity and salience (Barber et al. 2008), are vulnerable to errors in assessing risk (Barberis and Huang 2001), tend to use "heuristics" in making financial decisions (Tversky and Kahneman 1973, 1975), engage in attention-based buying activities (Barber et al. 2008), and last, but not the least, are slow to incorporate news into security prices (Cohen et al. 2002).

the key variables utilized in the analysis, including stock returns, the logarithm of trading volume, quarterly return on assets (ROA), and several weather-related control variables. For each variable, we report the mean, standard deviation, as well as the 25th and 75th percentiles. On average, the daily return during the study period is approximately 0.1%, with a standard deviation of 3.1%. However, the logarithm of trading volume varies relatively slightly. Panel B provides the distribution of the sample across different years and industries, illustrating the temporal and sectoral composition of the dataset. We need to mention here that after 2013, more cities started to disclose their air quality index, which produced more cities for inclusion in our sample. Therefore, our sample contains unbalanced panel data. The increasing tendency of firms is clearly described in Panel B of Table 2.2. We also summarize the detailed allocation information of the firms among the 13 different industries (according to the classifications of CSRC2001). One can note that more than the half of the sample belongs to the manufacturing industry, followed by wholesale and retail and the IT industries. More detailed information is presented in Panel B of Table 2.2. In panel C of Table 2.2, we provide the correlation matrix for all control variables, including the air quality index and weather conditions. It is intuitive to observe that the weather variables are negatively related to the AQI index.

2.3.2 *Empirical Strategy*

To precisely estimate the effect of the Air Quality Index (AQI) on daily stock returns, we employ an empirical specification that incorporates the first lag of returns as a control variable, effectively addressing potential nonsynchronous trading effects (Saunders 1993; Kamstra et al. 2003; Cao and Wei 2005). Moreover, according to different measures of AQI, we separately run the following several models:

1. First, we introduce the baseline model, which is directly used to measure the effect of the local AQI on stock return:

$$\begin{aligned} \mathrm{RET_{ijt}} &= \mathrm{a} + \mathrm{b_1} * \mathrm{AQI}_{jt} + \mathrm{b_2} * \mathrm{RET_{ijt-1}} + \text{Weather Conditions} \\ &\quad + \text{Year Fixed} + \text{Month Fixed} + \text{Weekday Fixed} \end{aligned} \tag{2.1}$$

   Here, i represents the firm, j represents the city, and t denotes the date. We control for the lag of the firm's stock return, as well as all temporal effects, including year fixed effects, month fixed effects, and weekday fixed effects. The coefficient b_1 captures the effect of local air pollution on the local stock return, which is the key variable of interest in this study.
2. In addition to the local AQI, we also control for the AQI of the firm's headquarters and the AQI of the two stock exchanges:

$$\mathrm{RET_{ijt}} = \mathrm{a} + \mathrm{b_1} * \mathrm{AQI_{jt}} + \mathrm{b_2} * \text{Exchange } \mathrm{AQI_t} + \mathrm{b_3} * \mathrm{RET_{ijt-1}}$$

Table 2 Summary statistics

Panel A Descriptive statistics for dependent and control variables

Variable	Obs	Mean	Std. Dev	Q1	Median	Q3
Return	2,912,935	0.001	0.031	−0.014	0.001	0.016
Lnvolume	2,912,935	15.631	1.254	14.777	15.619	16.470
AQI	245,108	75.861	40.791	51.000	66.000	90.000
Temperature	245,108	15.355	10.640	8.000	17.400	23.900
Precipitation	245,108	225.962	826.428	0.000	0.000	0.300
Sunshine	245,108	5.442	4.198	0.000	6.200	9.000
Wind	245,108	2.183	1.121	1.400	1.900	2.700
Humidity	245,108	68.304	18.849	58.000	72.000	82.000

Panel B Sample breakdown by year and industry

Year	N	%	Industry	N	%
2009	266,382	9.140	Agriculture & Farming	36,685	1.26
2010	288,421	9.900	Mining	89,829	3.08
2011	346,857	11.91	Manufacturing	1,492,103	51.22
2012	369,817	12.70	Electricity & Gas & Water	131,512	4.51
2013	379,223	13.02	Building	94,478	3.24
2014	387,085	13.29	Transportation & Warehousing	130,602	4.48
2015	416,628	14.30	IT	215,906	7.41
2016	458,522	15.74	Wholesale & Retail	227,473	7.81
Total	2,912,935	100	Finance & Insurance	84,914	2.92
			Real Estate	205,613	7.06
			Social Services	117,615	4.04
			Communication & Culture	49,971	1.72
			General	36,234	1.24
			Total	2,912,935	100.00

Panel C Correlation matrix of all control variables

	AQI	Temperature	Precipitation	Sunshine	Wind	Humidity
AQI	1.000					
Temperature	−0.3096***	1.000				
Precipitation	−0.0364***	0.0370***	1.000			
Sunshine	−0.0238***	0.1219***	−0.1560***	1.000		
Wind	−0.2010***	0.001	0.0112***	0.0558***	1.000	
Humidity	−0.1501***	0.2389***	0.1029***	−0.4961***	−0.0876***	1.000

$$+ \text{Weather Conditions} + \text{Year Fixed} + \text{Month Fixed} + \text{Weekday Fixed} \quad (2.2)$$

Since the firms in the sample are listed on either the Shanghai or Shenzhen Stock Exchange, we define the Exchange AQI as the air quality index corresponding to the location of the exchange where each firm is listed.

3. In the third model specification, we replace AQI by AQI change and Lag AQI, where AQI change is the difference of the AQI at time t and the AQI at time t − 1, and Lag AQI represents the AQI of time t − 1. The model can be written as:

$$\begin{aligned} RET_{ijt} = {} & a + b_1{*}\text{AQI Change}_{jt} + b_2{*}\text{Lag AQI}_{jt} + b_3{*}RET_{ijt-1} \\ & + \text{Weather Condition} + \text{Year Fixed} + \text{Month Fixed} \\ & + \text{Weekday Fixed} \end{aligned} \quad (2.3)$$

Two phenomena can be explained by this model. First, investors may show adaptive behavior, which means that they may adapt to the air pollution today if the air pollution today is similar to that of yesterday. Hence, the two variables AQI change and lag AQI are used to capture the effect, and the coefficient in front of AQI change then stands for the adaptive effect of investors. However, if the AQI today and AQI yesterday are quite different, then the investor's mood will be influenced by the change, which further changes their trading strategy. In other words, this model measures how investors immediately respond if the AQI of the two continuous days change significantly. We suspect the change of AQI will have a negative effect on the stock return.

4. To identify the abnormal impact of air pollution on stock returns and explore potential adaptive responses from investors, we incorporate the demeaned AQI—calculated relative to the city-specific average—into our regression framework. Specifically, we demean the AQI by calculating the average AQI for each month in that city of that year and subtracting the month's AQI of each day. The empirical model turns to replace AQI by the demeaned AQI, which is expressed as follows:

$$\begin{aligned} RET_{ijt} = {} & a + b_1{*}\text{demeaned AQI}_{jt} + b_2{*}RET_{ijt-1} + \text{Weather Conditions} \\ & + \text{Year Fixed} + \text{Month Fixed} + \text{Weekday Fixed} \end{aligned} \quad (2.4)$$

The demeaned AQI represents the excess AQI of that month beyond the average monthly AQI. Hence, the coefficient in front of the demeaned AQI measures the effect of the daily excess AQI on the stock return.

5. To ensure that our findings reflect the effect of air pollution rather than confounding seasonal patterns, we apply a deseasonalization procedure to the air quality data. The daily air quality in any particular city is highly seasonal. Meantime, the stock return data also shows a significant seasonal pattern as well. This provides us an explicit measure of the effect of air pollution. Following similar

methods used by Hirshleifer and Shumway (2003), we implement monthly deseasonality rather than weekly deseasonality. We argue that investors probably can predict more accurately how bad the air quality is each month rather than how bad it is each week. The model is written as follows:

$$\mathrm{RET}_{\mathrm{ijt}} = \mathrm{a} + \mathrm{b}_1{*}\text{deseasoned } \mathrm{AQI}_{\mathrm{jt}} + \mathrm{b}_2{*}\mathrm{RET}_{\mathrm{ijt}-1} + \text{Weather Conditions} + \text{Year Fixed} + \text{Month Fixed} + \text{Weekday Fixed} \quad (2.5)$$

More precisely, we construct the deseasonalized air pollution measure by first calculating the monthly average AQI for each city over the sample period and then subtracting this monthly mean from the corresponding daily AQI values.

In all empirical specifications, we include a thorough set of weather controls. Variables such as local temperature, precipitation, sunshine duration, wind speed, and humidity are included to account for their potential correlation with air pollution levels, as well as their possible impact on investor sentiment and, in turn, trading behavior. To address unobserved heterogeneity, we apply firm fixed effects alongside year, month, and weekday fixed effects, effectively controlling for both time-invariant and temporal factors that could introduce bias into the estimation. Given that the primary variation in our analysis arises from the city level, we cluster standard errors at the city level to account for potential intra-city correlation.

Additionally, to verify the consistency of the observed relationship between air pollution and stock returns, we conduct a series of robustness checks. These tests incorporate insights from the literature on local bias to further substantiate our empirical findings. More specifically, we will separately investigate whether the effects display heterogeneity due to the different characteristics of the firms. Moreover, to address some possible effects of local regulations on stock market, we further implement the city-year two-way fixed effect to capture the potential issues.

2.4 Empirical Results

2.4.1 Firm Stock Return and Air Pollution

We separately investigate how the air pollution index influences the stock market performance through the following three measures: the individual stock return, the city portfolio returns and the logarithm of individual stock trading volume.

Table 2.3 presents the regression results examining the impact of the AQI on individual stock returns. We regress stock returns on the air quality of the corresponding firm headquarters and other AQI measures. To ensure accurate estimations, we also control for potential weather factors in the relevant city. Column (1) reports the baseline results, showing the direct effect of the Air Quality Index (AQI) on firm-level stock returns. The regression reveals a strong positive serial correlation between current and lagged daily returns, which aligns with the presence of nonsynchronous trading effects. More importantly, the results demonstrate a statistically significant negative relationship between air pollution and stock performance. In terms of economic significance, an increase in the AQI from the 25th to the 75th percentile corresponds to a decline of about 1.77 basis points in daily returns, which translates to an annualized reduction of 4.43%. Furthermore, the effect is even more pronounced in cities like Beijing, where AQI levels exhibit considerable variation. When we add the exchange AQI in the subsequent columns, the results remain similar, though slightly smaller in magnitude. Column (3) further shows that the day-over-day change in AQI, rather than the AQI level itself from the previous day, significantly affects stock returns. The AQI level from the previous day is not statistically significant once the lagged return is included in the model. This suggests that any delayed effects of air pollution are largely captured by the lagged stock return variable. In Column (4), we assess the impact of the demeaned AQI—constructed by subtracting the monthly city-level mean—and find that the coefficient remains significantly negative at the 1% level. This result suggests that even after accounting for monthly average patterns, elevated pollution levels continue to negatively impact stock performance. We further extend the analysis by examining the effect of deseasonalized AQI on stock returns. The results are consistent with the demeaned analysis, but the effect of the deseasonalized AQI is even more pronounced. One possible reason is that the deseasoned AQI summarizes the pattern of AQI for the whole sample period in the total 8 years, while the demeaned AQI captures the pattern only in that year rather than in other years. Therefore, it is reasonable that the deseasoned effect is larger than the demeaned effect. Overall, the negative relationship between AQI and stock returns remains robust across various specifications of air quality measures. Furthermore, the associated decline in stock performance attributable to air pollution is both statistically significant and economically substantial.

2.4.2 City Portfolio Return and Stock Return

To further assess the impact of air pollution on stock performance, we construct an equally weighted daily stock portfolio for each city in the sample. Following the same empirical strategy as the individual stock returns, we test whether on average air quality relates to firms' stock returns in that city. For ease of implementation, we construct city-level portfolios by assigning equal weights to the daily returns of all constituent firms. This portfolio-based approach helps mitigate the idiosyncratic noise associated with individual trading behaviors and more accurately captures the aggregate impact of air pollution at the city level. Table 2.4 presents the corresponding regression results. In line with the firm-level analysis, we observe a significantly negative relationship between AQI and city-level portfolio returns. Notably, the magnitude of the effect is even more pronounced at the portfolio level. Specifically, an increase in the AQI from the 1st to the 3rd quartile corresponds to a decline of approximately 2.95 basis points in daily returns, which translates to an annualized loss of 7.38%.

Table 2.3 Firm stock returns and air pollution

	(1)	(2)	(3)	(4)	(5)
AQI	−4.549*** (−4.105)	−3.753*** (−2.969)			
Exchange AQI		−4.123*** (−3.316)			
AQI change			−7.912*** (−3.830)		
Lag AQI			−2.383 (−1.420)		
AQI monthly demean				−3.515*** (−2.979)	
AQI monthly Deseason					−5.016*** (−4.361)
N	2,265,600	2,265,600	2,265,600	2,265,600	2,265,600
Adj.R^2	0.010	0.010	0.010	0.010	0.010

Notes This table presents the fixed effect regression results examining the relationship between daily individual stock returns and the Air Quality Index (AQI). Column (1) shows the effect of the raw AQI on local stock returns; Column (2) includes both the raw AQI and the AQI of the exchange; Column (3) examines the effect of the change in AQI and lagged AQI; Column (4) reports the results for the demeaned AQI; and Column (5) presents the results for the deseasonalized AQI. ***, **, * indicate significance at the 1%, 5%, and 10% levels, respectively. All standard errors are clustered at the city level, with robust t-statistics reported in parentheses. The regressions include all control variables, as well as year, month, weekday, and city fixed effects

Similar patterns emerge across alternative pollution specifications, with the overall impact on city portfolios exceeding that observed for individual stocks.

2.4.3 Stock Trading Volume and Air Pollution

We further investigate whether air pollution influences investor trading behavior—specifically, whether heightened pollution levels lead to increased pessimism and a corresponding reduction in trading activity. To test this hypothesis, we regress local trading volume on contemporaneous air pollution levels while controlling for the lagged trading volume to account for autocorrelation in trading behavior. Before the estimation, we run the panel unit root test of the logarithm of trading volume. The testing results show that all sequences are stationary. The estimation results support this statement empirically, as shown in Table 2.5. It is obvious that the AQI has a significantly negative effect on trading volume, as described in Column (1) of Table 2.5. First, we observe a strong autocorrelation in trading volume, with the coefficient on the lagged logarithm of volume estimated at 0.824. Second, the AQI exhibits a statistically significant negative effect on the log of trading volume at the 1% significance level. From an economic perspective, this effect is also meaningful:

Table 2.4 City portfolio return and air pollution

	(1)	(2)	(3)	(4)	(5)
AQI	−7.573** (−2.519)	−6.923** (−2.287)			
Exchange AQI		−6.639 (−1.466)			
AQI change			−14.789*** (−3.973)		
Lag AQI			−3.459 (−1.002)		
AQI monthly demean				−6.976 (−1.622)	
AQI monthly Deseason					−4.693 (−1.464)
N	66,442	66,442	66,442	66,442	66,442
Adj.R^2	0.009	0.009	0.009	0.009	0.009

Notes This table presents the fixed effect regression results examining the relationship between daily equally weighted city portfolio returns and the Air Quality Index (AQI). Column (1) shows the effect of the raw AQI on local stock returns; Column (2) includes both the raw AQI and the AQI of the exchange; Column (3) examines the effect of the change in AQI and lagged AQI; Column (4) reports the results for the demeaned AQI; and Column (5) presents the results for the deseasonalized AQI. ***, **, * denote significance at the 1%, 5%, and 10% levels, respectively. All standard errors are clustered at the city level, with robust t-statistics reported in parentheses. The regressions include all control variables, as well as year, month, weekday, and city fixed effects

an increase in the AQI from the 1st to the 3rd quartile corresponds to an average decline of approximately 0.45% in daily trading volume. According to the large trading volume in the whole stock market, the decreasing trading volume is a huge number, which can significantly influence the whole stock market. We sequentially investigate the effects of other AQI measures on the trading volume, and this effect also holds for other air pollution measures except for the demeaned AQI. Moreover, the regression results are similar to the one from the stock return results, providing consistently empirical evidence for our study.

2.4.4 *Subsample Analysis Based on Local Bias Evidence*

Previous literature shows that certain firm characteristics significantly influence local bias, which may further influence the investors' trading strategy. For instance, Coval and Moskowitz (1999) show that the local bias of fund managers is more severe for small capitalization stocks than it is for large ones, which provides us the evidence to separate the firm into small and large sizes. We investigate the local bias effect from several dimensions, mainly focusing on the factors that may contribute to local bias.

Table 2.5 Trading volume and air pollution

	(1)	(2)	(3)	(4)	(5)
AQI	−115.989*** (−5.835)	−85.366*** (−4.838)			
Exchange AQI		−158.855*** (−8.730)			
AQI change			−127.248*** (−4.234)		
Lag AQI			−108.733*** (−5.621)		
AQI monthly demean				12.867 (0.882)	
AQI monthly Deseason					−112.035*** (−4.807)
N	2,265,600	2,265,600	2,265,600	2,265,600	2,265,600
Adj.R^2	0.782	0.782	0.782	0.781	0.782

Notes This table presents the fixed effect regression results examining the relationship between the logarithm of the daily individual stock trading volume and the Air Quality Index (AQI). Column (1) shows the effect of the raw AQI on local stock returns; Column (2) includes both the raw AQI and the AQI of the exchange; and Column (3) examines the effect of the change in AQI and lagged AQI; Column (4) presents the results of the demeaned AQI; Column (5) presents the results of the deseasoned AQI. ***, **, * denote significance at 1%, 5%, 10% levels, respectively. All the standard errors are clustered at city level. The robust t statistics are reported in the parenthesis. The regressions include all control variables, year FE, month FE, weekday FE and city FE

First, we argue that firms with high institutional ownership perform differently than do firms with low institutional ownership. We separate the whole sample by the median of institutional ownership. If the firm's institutional ownership is higher than the median, then it belongs to the high institutional ownership group, denoting it as high IO. If the institutional ownership is below the median, then the firm is a low-institutional ownership firm, denoting it as low IO. Given that firms with lower institutional ownership tend to have a higher proportion of individual investors, they may exhibit greater sensitivity to air pollution. Columns (1) and (2) of Table 2.6 present the regression results for firms with low and high levels of institutional ownership, respectively. The results support our hypothesis: the negative impact of AQI on stock returns is more pronounced for firms with lower institutional ownership, even after controlling for all relevant confounding factors. Additionally, a formal test confirms that the difference between the two coefficients is statistically significant at the 5% level.

Second, firms that were established earlier may be better known nationally, while young firms may receive more attention from the local investors than from the national sources. To further explore heterogeneity in the impact of air pollution, we examine whether the effect of AQI differs between younger and more established firms. Firms are categorized into 'young' and 'old' groups based on the median firm age within the sample. If the firm's age is above the median, then the firm belongs to the old group;

Table 2.6 Local bias effect

	(1)	(2)	(3)	(4)	(5)	(6)
	High IO	Low IO	Old	Young	More Analyst	Less Analyst
AQI	−9.355***	−11.304***	−4.618***	−4.333***	−3.706***	−5.289***
	(−7.403)	(−8.840)	(−3.981)	(−2.960)	(−2.884)	(−3.772)
L.Return	0.075***	0.078***	0.054***	0.083***	0.050***	0.068***
	(28.250)	(28.009)	(29.089)	(31.958)	(24.431)	(24.977)
N	777,294	752,478	1,542,353	723,191	854,470	890,692
Adj.R^2	0.010	0.010	0.008	0.010	0.006	0.009

Notes This table presents a subsample analysis based on the local bias effect. We examine different scenarios across various subsamples. Column (1) reports the results for firms with high institutional ownership; Column (2) presents the results for firms with low institutional ownership; Column (3) shows the results for older firms; Column (4) presents the results for younger firms; Column (5) describes the results for firms with more analysts; and Column (6) presents the results for firms with fewer analysts. ***, **, * indicate significance at the 1%, 5%, and 10% levels, respectively. All standard errors are clustered at the city level, with robust t-statistics reported in parentheses. The regressions include all control variables, as well as year, month, weekday, and city fixed effects

otherwise, it is placed in the young group. The results also align with our expectations, as presented in Columns (3) and (4) of Table 2.6. The estimated coefficient for AQI is −4.333 for young firms and −4.618 for older firms. However, the difference between these two estimates is not statistically significant, with a p-value of 0.826. This suggests that firm age does not significantly moderate the relationship between air pollution and stock returns.

We further divide the sample into two subsamples based on the level of analyst coverage. Specifically, firms are classified into the "high analyst coverage" group if the number of analysts following the firm exceeds the median number of analysts within its industry for a given year; otherwise, the firm is assigned to the "low analyst coverage" group. We argue that in firms with more analysts there may be discourse on more public and formal information; therefore, these firms may be influenced less by local selection biases than are the firms with less analysts. The empirical results tell the same story. Columns (5) and (6) show that the coefficient of AQI is −3.706 for firms with high analyst coverage, compared to −5.289 for those with low analyst coverage, with both estimates statistically significant at the 1% level. On average, when the AQI increases from the 1st quantile to the 3rd quantile, the daily stock returns of firms with high (low) analyst coverage decrease by 1.44 (2.06) basis points, which corresponds to an annualized return reduction of 3.60% (5.15%). The two coefficients are also statistically different at 5% level.

In all, the empirical results provide strong support for the local bias assumption and are consistent with our hypothesis.

2.4.5 *Robustness Checks*

2.4.5.1 Free Float

Wang and Xu (2004) demonstrate that free float is a useful predictor of stock returns in the Chinese market. Therefore, we add the free float factor into our model to check if our core results still hold. Free Float is defined as the daily tradable share capital divided by total share capital.[2] Table 2.7 presents the estimation results, demonstrating that the core variables maintain their statistical significance with coefficient magnitudes aligning closely with the baseline specifications. It is arguable that the free float effect is insignificant in our test. The sample period in Wang and Xu (2004) is from 1996 to 2002 and the mean of the free float measure is around 0.3. As noted in their paper, the Chinese listed companies were characterized by dual classes of shares—majority non-tradable shares owned by the government and minority tradable shares held by private owners, therefore, free float plays an essential role on a firm's stock returns. However, in April of 2005, the China Securities Regulatory Commission (CSRC) implemented the split equity reform (Green et al. 2010). The reform was to eliminate the dualistic structured stock market by gradually converting non-tradable shares into tradable shares. Indeed, in our sample period, the mean of free float is around 0.745, indicating most shares are tradable. Therefore, the role of free float has diminished since 2005 and we find the free float effect is insignificant in our sample period.

2.4.5.2 Time Trend

We further test whether investors learn from the market over time and whether the market tends to be efficient in China. We define 2009 as the base year and add interactions between year dummy and the air pollution index to the baseline regression. The coefficients of the interaction should reflect the time trend as well as how investor react over years. The results are displayed in Fig. 2.1. The solid black line stands for the coefficients, and the two red dashed lines represent their 5–95% point-wise confidence intervals. The results indicate that the negative AQI effect has become less substantial over time since 2011, which supports the conjecture that investors could potentially observe the air pollution effect and adjust their trading behaviors accordingly. It is also noteworthy that the negative AQI effect is the strongest in 2011. In 2011, the USA Embassy in Beijing for the first time released the PM2.5 index indicating that the PM2.5 concentration in Beijing was "beyond index" based on the United States Environmental Protection Agency (US EPA)'s air quality index. The news sparked significant concerns both internationally and domestically regarding the severe air pollution in China, while also raising public awareness about the issue (Wang 2018). In the same year, Baidu started to publish search index for both PCs

[2] We also use an alternative annual measure provide in the document of the Equity Structure of The Listed Firms by CSMAR.

Table 2.7 Robustness check with free float

	(1)	(3)	(2)	(4)	(5)
AQI	0.064*** (39.611)	0.064*** (39.604)	0.064*** (39.635)	0.064*** (39.584)	0.064*** (39.618)
Exchange AQI	−4.549*** (−4.104)	−3.753*** (−2.969)			
AQI Change		−4.123*** (−3.320)			
Lag AQI			−7.911*** (−3.831)		
AQI Monthly Demean			−2.383 (−1.419)		
AQI Monthly Deseason				−3.515*** (−2.979)	
Temperature					−5.016*** (−4.361)
N	2,265,600	2,265,600	2,265,600	2,265,600	2,265,600
Adj.R^2	0.010	0.010	0.010	0.010	0.010

Notes This table reports the fixed-effects regression estimates analyzing the relationship between daily individual stock returns and air quality index (AQI), with adjustments for free float effects. Column (1) presents baseline results for raw AQI's impact on local stock returns. Column (2) extends the specification by incorporating both raw AQI and exchange-location AQI. Column (3) evaluates the effects of contemporaneous AQI changes and one-period lagged AQI. Columns (4) and (5) report estimates using demeaned and deseasonalized AQI measures, respectively. Statistical significance at the 1%, 5%, and 10% levels is denoted by ***, **, and. Standard errors are clustered at the city level, with robust t-statistics provided in parentheses. All regressions control for the full set of covariates, including year, month, weekday, and city fixed effects

and mobiles for words such as air pollution and smog (Zhang et al. 2013). Therefore, the strongest AQI effect in 2011 is possibly due to the unpreceded amount of attention to air pollution and in that year.

2.4.5.3 Two-Way Fixed Effect

Local environmental regulations and policies may differ across regions due to varying levels of development and environmental priorities, which could, in turn, influence the relationship between air pollution and stock returns. In order to comprehensively capture the cross-regional and cross-time variations, we control for the two-way city-year fixed effects. We allow each city-year combination to be different from other cities and even the same city in a different year. The city-year fixed effects not only capture the regulation effect but also other potential factors that may differ across time and city. Even after accounting for city-year fixed effects and other control variables, the results remain statistically significant. The economic magnitude of the

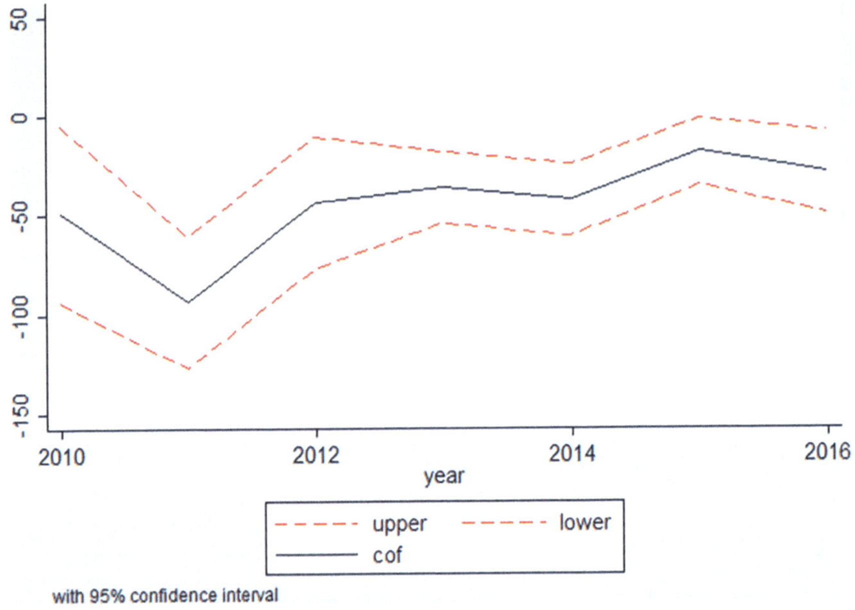

Fig. 2.1 The time trend effect of air pollution on stock returns. *Note* The solid black line stands for the coefficients of the interaction between AQI and year dummy; the two red dashed lines represent their 5%-95% point-wise confidence intervals

effect is also consistent with the findings in the baseline model. Due to the constraint of space, the results are available upon request.

2.5 Conclusions

Psychological studies have long established that environmental factors impact individuals' moods, cognition, and decision-making. Researchers in finance have extended these insights to explore behavioral influences on stock prices. However, the question of whether environmental factors directly affect stock returns remains contentious. Building on prior research that establishes a connection between environmental conditions, investor sentiment, and local bias, we posit an inverse relationship between air pollution and firm-level stock returns.

Analyzing a comprehensive sample of all A-shares listed on the Shanghai and Shenzhen Stock Exchanges from 2009 to 2016, we document that firms headquartered in cities with elevated air pollution exhibit significantly depressed stock returns and diminished trading activity. In line with our primary hypothesis, the adverse effect of pollution is particularly acute for firms with greater local investor ownership. Furthermore, we identify a temporal attenuation of this effect, implying behavioral adaptation as investors gradually internalize persistent pollution signals. Our findings contribute novel evidence to the growing literature on environmental determinants of financial markets, while also underscoring the broader economic ramifications of pollution in emerging economies like China.

References

Barber BM, Odean T (2000) Trading is hazardous to your wealth: the common stock investment performance of individual investors. J Financ 55(2):773–806

Barber BM, Odean T, Zhu N (2008) Do retail trades move markets? Rev Financ Stud 22(1):151–186

Barberis N, Huang M (2001) Mental accounting, loss aversion, and individual stock returns. J Financ 56(4):1247–1292

Bullinger M (1989) Psychological effects of air pollution on healthy residents—a time-series approach. J Environ Psychol 9(2):103–118

Bullinger M (1990) Environmental stress: effects of air pollution on mood, neuropsychological function and physical state. In: Psychobiology of stress. Springer, pp 241–250

Cao M, Wei J (2005) Stock market returns: a note on temperature anomaly. J Bank Financ 29(6):1559–1573

Chen G (2004) Behavior and performance of emerging market investors: evidence from China. Unpublished Working Paper. Washington State University

China Securities and Futures Statistical Yearbook (2004) China Financial & Economic Publishing House, Beijing

Cohen S (1986) Stress processes and the costs of coping. In: Behavior, health, and environmental stress. Plenum Press, pp 1–23

Cohen RB, Gompers PA, Vuolteenaho T (2002) Who underreacts to cash-flow news? Evidence from trading between individuals and institutions. J Financ Econ 66(2–3):409–462

Coval JD, Moskowitz TJ (1999) Home bias at home: local equity preference in domestic portfolios. J Financ 54(6):2045–2073

Coval JD, Moskowitz TJ (2001) The geography of investment: informed trading and asset prices. J Polit Econ 109(4):811–841

de Haan E, Madsen J, Piotroski JD (2017) Do weather-induced moods affect the processing of earnings news? J Account Res 55(3):509–550

Diao XD (2009) EKC analysis for studying economic growth and environmental quality: a case study in China. J Clean Prod 17(5):541–548

Dong R (2019) Air pollution, affect, and forecasting bias: evidence from Chinese analysts. J Financ Econ

Evans GW (1987) The interaction of stressful life events and chronic strains on community mental health. Am J Community Psychol 15(1):23–34

Feng L, Seasholes MS (2004) Correlated trading and location. J Financ 59(5):2117–2144

Goetzmann WN (2015) Weather-induced mood, institutional investors, and stock returns. Rev Financ Stud 28(1):73–111

Green W, Morris R, Tang H (2010) The split equity reform and corporate financial transparency in China. Account Res J 23(1):20–48

Grinblatt M, Keloharju M (2001) How distance, language, and culture influence stockholdings and trades. J Financ 56(3):1053–1073

Hirshleifer D, Shumway T (2003) Good day sunshine: stock returns and the weather. J Financ 58(3):1009–1032

Hsieh GC, Sharma RP, Parker RDR (1991) Hypothalamic-pituitary-adrenocortical axis activity and immune function after oral exposure to benzene and toluene. Immunopharmacology 21(1):23–32

Huberman G (2001) Familiarity breeds investment. Rev Financ Stud 14(3):659–680

Ivković Z, Weisbenner S (2005) Local does as local is: information content of the geography of individual investors' common stock investments. J Financ 60(1):267–306
Jacobsen B, Marquering W (2008) Is it the weather? J Bank Financ 32(4):526–540
Jiang L, Lin C, Lin P (2014) The determinants of pollution levels: firm-level evidence from Chinese manufacturing. J Comp Econ 42(1):118–142
Kamstra MJ, Kramer LA, Levi MD (2000) Losing sleep at the market: the daylight saving anomaly. Am Econ Rev 90(4):1005–1011
Kamstra MJ, Kramer LA, Levi MD (2003) Winter blues: a SAD stock market cycle. Am Econ Rev 93(1):324–343
Keef SP, Khaled MS (2011) Are investors moonstruck? Further international evidence on lunar phases and stock returns. J Empir Financ 18(1):56–63
Kelly PJ, Meschke F (2010) Sentiment and stock returns: the SAD anomaly revisited. J Bank Financ 34(6):1308–1326
Lepori GM (2016) Air pollution and stock returns: evidence from a natural experiment. J Empir Financ 35:25–42
Levy T, Yagil J (2011) Air pollution and stock returns in the US. J Econ Psychol 32(3):374–383
Loughran T, Schultz P (2004) Weather, stock returns, and the impact of localized trading behavior. J Financ Quant Anal 39(2):343–364
Massa M, Simonov A (2006) Hedging, familiarity and portfolio choice. Rev Financ Stud 19(2):633–685
Morris WN (2000) Some thoughts about mood and its regulation. Psychol Inq 11(3):200–202
Odean T (1998) Are investors reluctant to realize their losses? J Financ 53(5):1775–1798
Pirinsky C, Wang Q (2006) Does corporate headquarters location matter for stock returns? J Financ 61(4):1991–2015
Raff H, Goldmann RW, Kindwall EP (1985) Adrenocortical function after acute carbon monoxide exposure in humans. Arch Environ Health 40(2):88–90
Saunders EM (1993) Stock prices and Wall Street weather. Am Econ Rev 83(5):1337–1345
Schiffman SS (1995) The effect of environmental odors emanating from commercial swine operations on the mood of nearby residents. Brain Res Bull 37(4):369–375
Slovic P, Peters E (2006) Risk perception and affect. Curr Dir Psychol Sci 15(6):322–325
Tan L (2008) Herding behavior in Chinese stock markets: an examination of a and B shares. Pac Basin Financ J 16(1):61–77
Tan L, Chiang TC, Mason JR, Nelling E (2008) Herding behavior in Chinese stock markets: an examination of A and B shares. Pac Basin Financ J 16(1):61–77
Tanaka S (2015) Environmental regulations on air pollution in China and their impact on infant mortality. J Health Econ 42:90–103
Tomei F (2003) Plasma cortisol levels and workers exposed to urban pollutants. Ind Health 41(4):320–326
Tversky A, Kahneman D (1973) Availability: a heuristic for judging frequency and probability. Cogn Psychol 5(2):207–232
Tversky A, Kahneman D (1975) Judgment under uncertainty: heuristics and biases. In: Utility, probability, and human decision making. Springer, Dordrecht, pp 141–162
Wang L (2018) Taking action on air pollution control in the Beijing-Tianjin-Hebei (BTH) region: progress, challenges and opportunities. Int J Environ Res Public Health 15:306
Wang F, Xu Y (2004) What determines Chinese stock returns? Financ Anal J 60(6):65–77
Xu XD, Zeng SX, Tam CM (2012) Stock market's reaction to disclosure of environmental violations: evidence from China. J Bus Ethics 107(2):227–237
Yuan K, Zheng L, Zhu Q (2006) Are investors moonstruck? Lunar phases and stock returns. J Empir Financ 13(1):1–23
Zhang W, Shen D, Zhang Y, Xiong X (2013) Open source information, investor attention, and asset pricing. Econ Model 33:613–619

Chapter 3
Trading on Thin Air: Pollution, Behavior, and Market Efficiency

Abstract Extending prior work on environmental influences in financial decision-making, this study hypothesizes an adverse association between air pollution and individual investors' trading behavior. Leveraging a proprietary dataset of granular transaction records, we demonstrate that elevated pollution levels significantly reduce individuals' propensity to buy stocks while increasing their disposition to sell. These effects exhibit pronounced heterogeneity across investor sophistication, security characteristics, and regional pollution exposure—with particularly strong impacts among novice investors and residents of high-pollution urban centers. Our findings provide the first micro-level evidence linking air quality to retail trading strategies, thereby advancing the literature on environmental finance and behavioral biases.

Keywords Air pollution · Investor trading behavior · Investor mood

3.1 Introduction

Air pollution has emerged as a critical environmental challenge, attracting substantial public and academic scrutiny. While extensive research has documented its adverse health and socioeconomic consequences—including mortality risk (Chen et al. 2013), mental health deterioration (Chen et al. 2018), cognitive impairment (Zhang et al. 2018), labor supply reductions (Hanna and Oliva 2015), and productivity losses (Graff Zivin and Neidell 2012; Chang et al. 2016a, b; Guo and Fu 2019)—only recently have finance scholars begun examining its capital market effects. Pioneering work by Levy and Yagil (2011), Heyes et al. (2016), Lepori (2016), Ding et al. (2021), and Huang et al. (2020) has established pollution's detrimental impact on aggregate stock performance. Yet the micro-level behavioral mechanisms -particularly how pollution shapes individual trading decisions-remain unexplored.

This chapter is an extension of the paper titled "Does air pollution influence investor trading behavior? Evidence from China", by Guo, M., Wei, M. and Huang, L. (2022), Emerging Markets Review, 50:100822.

M. Guo et al., *Social-Economic Impacts of Air Pollution*, Climate Change and Energy Transition, https://doi.org/10.1007/978-981-96-7858-7_3

Our study addresses this gap by investigating pollution-induced trading patterns across heterogeneous investors and securities.

This inquiry builds on robust psychological evidence demonstrating environmental factors' capacity to alter affective states and subsequent decision-making (Cunningham 1979; Schwarz and Clore 1983). Financial researchers have operationalized these insights through weather-based studies: seminal findings by Saunders (1993) and Hirshleifer and Shumway (2003) reveal depressed equity returns during overcast conditions, while Cao and Wei (2005), Kamstra et al. (2003), and Yuan et al. (2006) identify temperature, wind, daylight, and lunar cycles as return predictors. Notably, Goetzmann et al. (2015) extend this literature to institutional trading. Our work advances this paradigm by examining how air pollution, a persistent environmental factor, systematically distorts retail investment behavior.

Prior research has established air pollution's market effects through mood-mediated channels. Levy and Yagil (2011) demonstrated that pollution-induced mood deterioration heightens risk aversion, depressing returns across four U.S. exchanges. Similarly, Lepori (2016) identified mood alteration as the primary mechanism driving pollution's trading effects on the Italian Stock Exchange. Contemporary work by Dong et al. (2021) reveals how haze during corporate site visits impairs analyst forecasts through mood impairment, while Ding et al. (2021) confirm pollution's adverse localized market impacts. These findings collectively underscore mood as a critical transmission channel between environmental conditions and financial outcomes.

China presents an ideal natural laboratory for extending this research. Three distinctive features motivate our focus: (1) Extreme pollution exposure, with PM2.5 concentrations ranking second globally (World Bank 2016); (2) Substantial intra-national AQI variation (9–500 in our sample); and (3) A retail-dominated equity market where individual investors' documented behavioral sensitivities (Chen et al. 2004; Tan et al. 2008) likely amplify pollution effects. Building on the mood-mediation framework, we posit that pollution exacerbates risk aversion, prompting divestment. We test this using 372,310 investor transactions (2016–2018), offering unprecedented granularity in behavioral environmental finance research.

Consistent with the notion that higher pollution levels foster pessimistic sentiments, our findings reveal that investors tend to reduce their stock holdings and sell stocks during periods of significant air pollution. Specifically, a 1% increase in the daily AQI results in a 0.453% decline in the propensity to buy stocks and a 0.528% increase in the propensity to sell. Drawing on behavioral finance literature (Dhar and Zhu 2006; Barber and Odean 2008; Chuang and Susmel 2011), We find that individual investors, particularly non-professional ones, are more susceptible to behavioral biases. Our results show that air pollution has a stronger effect on less active investors (those with lower trading frequencies) and those with smaller social networks (fewer followers). Additionally, the impact is more pronounced in smaller cities and in areas with higher pollution levels.

This study further investigates the dynamics of stock trading under conditions of elevated pollution. Building on the work of Baker and Wurgler (2006), which identifies heightened investor sensitivity to returns in stocks that are smaller, younger, highly volatile, unprofitable, non-dividend-paying, and high-growth, we assess the differential impact of air pollution on investor behavior across various stock categories. Our empirical results suggest that stocks of smaller firms are more prone to being sold during periods of intense pollution. Additionally, those with lower book-to-market ratios and firms with shorter operating histories are found to be especially vulnerable to the negative consequences of hazy environmental conditions. We also investigate whether the stocks traded during hazy days are associated with pollution-related industries, finding significant differences in selling propensities between pollution and non-pollution industries, suggesting the presence of behavioral biases.

To validate the robustness of our results, we perform several robustness checks. First, we vary the air quality measures by examining the effects of daytime AQI, AQI during trading hours, and the prolonged impact of AQI on stock returns. Our results remain consistent with the baseline model. Second, we introduce alternative measures of trading behavior, constructing city-level and stock-date panel data to account for investor preferences and market noise. These additional analyses further support our main conclusions.

This study contributes to the expanding literature exploring the relationship between air pollution, investor sentiment, and stock returns. We offer direct evidence that ambient air pollution influences investor trading behavior, thereby corroborating the findings of Levy and Yagil (2011), Heyes et al. (2016), and Lepori (2016). Our results suggest that air pollution increases risk aversion among investors, leading to reduced holdings of high-risk assets and ultimately lower stock returns. By examining account-level data, we offer insights into how air pollution manifests in the daily trading activities of individual investors, addressing a gap in the existing literature. Our findings align with recent studies by Huang et al. (2020) and Li et al. (2020), which investigate the effects of air pollution on investor trading behavior. In this regard, our research adds to the growing body of evidence highlighting the negative economic impacts of air pollution.

The structure of the remainder of the paper is as follows: Sect. 3.2 provides the scientific background; Sect. 3.3 outlines the data and empirical methodology; Sect. 3.4 presents the empirical results; and Sect. 3.5 concludes the paper.

3.2 Scientific Background

A significant body of psychological research has highlighted the impact of acute exposure to ambient air pollution on individuals' psychological and mental well-being, both directly and indirectly (Bullinger 1990). Such exposure has been linked to increased levels of depression, stress, and annoyance (Cohen et al. 1986; Evans et al. 1987; Bullinger 1989; Schiffman et al. 1995). Empirical studies indicate that ambient air pollution can elevate cortisol production, a hormone associated with stress responses (Hsieh et al. 1991; Tomei et al. 2003). Cortisol plays a critical role in psychological and behavioral reactions to both physical and psychological stressors (Coates and Herbert 2008). Given that stock trading is a psychologically taxing activity, elevated cortisol levels may notably influence trading behavior by reducing risk-taking (Rosenblitt et al. 2001).

Beyond its biophysical effects, air pollution has been shown to significantly affect individuals' emotional states. Levy and Yagil (2011) conducted a review of the literature on the relationship between air pollution and negative emotional states, highlighting that exposure to pollution is associated with elevated levels of anxiety and depression (Evans et al. 1988; Lundberg 1996). Sagar et al. (2007) found a strong connection between air quality and symptoms such as fatigue, low mood, and exhaustion. Empirical studies have also shown that individuals experiencing negative moods tend to exhibit heightened pessimism and overestimate the likelihood of negative outcomes, influencing their risk preferences (Johnson and Tversky 1983; Mayer et al. 1992; Wright et al. 1992; Mittal and Ross 1998; Kliger and Levy 2003, 2008). This phenomenon, known as the "availability heuristic" (Kahneman and Tversky 1973), posits that emotional shifts enhance the recall of memories consistent with the current emotional state, thus increasing the perceived likelihood of negative events during periods of low mood.

Building on this concept, we hypothesize that air pollution exacerbates risk aversion among investors, resulting in a reduction in stock holdings and an increase in selling activity. The primary aim of this study is to investigate the negative relationship between air pollution and investor trading behavior. However, the data utilized in this study do not permit a direct identification of the mechanisms through which air pollution affects investor behavior, leaving this as a critical avenue for future research.

3.3 Data and Empirical Strategy

3.3.1 Data Sources

Our primary dataset on investor trading behavior comes from Snowball, a popular Chinese platform for sharing trading-related information. Snowball has over 12 million registered users, with more than 7.84 million active users as of June 24, 2018, representing approximately 25% of China's active individual traders. Our sample includes 3592 users with observable locations and trading performance, covering 104 Chinese cities from June 24, 2016, to November 7, 2018. The dataset comprises 372,310 transaction records, providing detailed insights into investor trading behavior, including buy and sell transactions, transaction volumes, and the number of followers.

We obtained daily AQI data from the Ministry of Environmental Protection of China (MEPC) and city-level weather information from the China Meteorological Administration (CMA). Additionally, stock characteristics and market indicators were sourced from the China Stock Market and Accounting Research (CSMAR) database.

3.3.2 Variable Construction

Definition of Trading Behavior. The main outcome variable in this study is investor trading behavior, which is measured using several indicators. At the outset, we conceptualize trading behavior in terms of portfolio adjustments. Inspired by the framework of Goetzmann et al. (2015), we treat an individual investor's stock holdings as a consolidated portfolio and monitor its reallocation whenever the investor engages in buying or selling. These reallocations are quantified as ratios relative to the overall portfolio composition.

To capture these dynamics, we construct several specific metrics that reflect trading intensity and direction for individual stocks within a portfolio:

Buy: the cumulative percentage of a stock acquired by an investor, measured on a scale from 0% to 100%.

Sell: the total percentage of a stock liquidated by the investor, also ranging from 0% to 100%.

Abs_imb: the absolute trading imbalance, calculated as the sum of the absolute values of buy and sell activities. This measure spans from 0% to 200%, with higher values denoting more vigorous trading engagement.

Recognizing that investors may execute multiple trades within a single day, we further align our approach with standard portfolio theory, which posits that stocks are riskier compared to cash. Emotional states influence risk preferences—negative moods can elevate risk aversion and prompt selling, while positive moods may encourage risk-taking and buying. As such, purchases often signal investor optimism, whereas sales imply pessimism.

To synthesize these behaviors into daily sentiment-oriented metrics, we introduce two additional variables:

Net_buy: the net positive proportion of stock purchases (i.e., when buy volume exceeds sell volume), ranging from 0% to 100%, representing bullish investor sentiment.

Net_sell: the net negative proportion of stock sales (i.e., when sell volume exceeds buy volume), also between 0% and 100%, reflecting bearish sentiment.

Lastly, we incorporate a market variable to account for both intraday and overnight information influencing investor decisions. This includes the daily market return and the logarithmic change between the opening index and the previous day's closing index. Together, these elements capture market volatility and help explain investors' inclination to initiate trades on a given day.

3.3.3 Summary Statistics of All Related Variables

To minimize the influence of extreme values, all continuous variables in our dataset are winsorized at the 1st and 99th percentiles. Table 3.1 presents the summary statistics for the key variables employed in our analysis, including those related to trading behavior (e.g., abs_imb, net_buy, net_sell), market performance, and environmental conditions. For each variable, we report the mean, standard deviation, interquartile range (25th and 75th percentiles), along with the observed minimum and maximum values. Panel A in Table 3.1 presents a detailed overview of these statistics.

A noteworthy observation is the substantial variability across most of the primary variables, which facilitates credible identification strategies. Trading behavior indicators, in particular, vary significantly across investors and time periods, reinforcing the richness of the dataset. Similarly, the air quality index (AQI)—our main explanatory variable—exhibits wide dispersion, with values ranging from 9 to 500 and an average of approximately 73, ensuring meaningful variation for empirical analysis.

Panel B of Table 3.1 shifts the focus to user-level characteristics from the Snowball platform, including trading frequency and the number of followers per user. These characteristics are instrumental in enabling heterogeneity analysis, offering a lens into investor activity levels, sophistication, and their role in the information-sharing ecosystem. The distribution of followers is highly skewed: while some users have none, others are followed by over 300,000 individuals, suggesting varied degrees

Table 3.1 Summary statistics

Variable	Obs	Min	Mean	Std.Dev.	P25	P50	P75	Max
Panel A: Summary statistics of dependent variable and control variables								
abs_imb	143,354	0.01	40.57	48.50	7.28	20.21	54.55	200.00
net_sell	62,126	0.00	17.25	23.76	1.94	7.63	21.63	100.00
net_buy	83,074	0.01	18.65	25.61	1.61	7.44	24.12	100.00
AQI	142,992	9.00	73.10	51.98	40.00	59.00	87.00	500.00
Precipitation	143,354	0.00	3.38	11.67	0.00	0.00	0.40	275.50
Pressure	143,354	651.10	1000.60	30.87	997.60	1006.60	1015.80	1038.60
Humidity	143,336	11.00	68.93	17.58	58.00	72.00	82.00	100.00
Sunshine	143,354	0.00	5.60	4.15	1.00	6.40	9.00	14.20
Temperature	143,336	−29.40	16.42	11.13	8.20	18.70	25.70	36.50
Wind	143,301	0.00	2.03	1.06	1.30	1.80	2.60	14.10
Market	143,354	−4.27	−0.07	1.02	−0.59	0.01	0.47	3.01
$Market_{overnight}$	143,354	−0.031	−0.001	0.005	−0.002	−0.001	0.001	0.019
Panel B: Summary statistics of investor characteristics								
Trans.No.	3592	1	103.650	71.187	38	92	184	204
Followers	3592	0	549.57	7459.33	2	8	31	312,752

of market influence and expertise. Notably, users with more followers often exhibit traits associated with greater financial knowledge and trading experience.

Lastly, meteorological conditions are closely tied to AQI fluctuations and may indirectly affect investor sentiment. Recognizing their dual role—as both correlated variables and potential mood influencers—we incorporate these weather indicators into our models to control for their confounding effects on trading behavior.

3.4 Empirical Strategy

3.4.1 Logit Model

To initially assess the direct impact of air pollution on investor trading behavior, we employ a logit model to investigate its effect on investor position adjustments. Within this framework, buying a stock signifies an optimistic stance, whereas selling a stock denotes a pessimistic trading behavior. Consequently, we define the variable y as equal to one if *net_buy* exceeds 0; otherwise, it is set to 0. Our expectation is that the coefficient associated with air pollution will be negative, reflecting the potential influence of air pollution on inducing negative trading behavior. The logit regression model, denoted as model (3.1) below, is as follows:

$$\Pr\left(y_{ijt} = 1\right) = F\left(\alpha_i + \beta_1 AQI_{jt} + \beta_2 W_{jt} + \gamma market_t + \lambda_t\right) \tag{3.1}$$

where we employ a logistic function denoted as F(.), with i representing the individual, j the city, and t the date. The variable AQI_{jt} denotes the air quality index of city j on date t, while W_{jt} accounts for the weather conditions of city j on date t. Furthermore, the variable *market* characterizes stock market information on the date t, as previously defined. To further account for time effects, denoted as λ_t, encompassing year, month, and weekday variations, and thereby eliminate potential time-invariant influences, such as seasonality or calendar effects, we introduce α_i as the individual fixed effect. Eventually, our coefficient of interest is β_1, which captures the impact of air pollution on investor trading behavior.

Incorporating weather-related variables into the analysis fulfills two essential objectives. On the one hand, meteorological factors such as temperature, rainfall, sunshine hours, wind velocity, humidity, and atmospheric pressure are closely linked to fluctuations in air quality and therefore serve as relevant covariates. On the other hand, these environmental elements may also shape investor sentiment, indirectly influencing their trading decisions.

To further account for potential market-driven effects, we introduce measures that capture both intra-day and overnight market dynamics. Specifically, we include the logarithmic differences between the opening and closing indices on the same trading day, as well as between the current day's opening index and the previous day's closing index, thereby reflecting broader market volatility and informational spillovers across trading sessions.

Our empirical framework also includes individual-level fixed effects, along with year, month, and weekday fixed effects, to control for unobserved heterogeneity and cyclical patterns that might otherwise bias our estimations. Furthermore, standard errors are clustered at the city level to address potential cross-sectional dependence among investors. Our methodology for assessing the impact of air pollution on trading behavior capitalizes on both temporal and spatial variations in air quality across different urban environments and trading days.

3.4.2 Individual-City-Date Panel Data

To comprehend the accurate effect of air pollution on trading behavior, we further introduce the fixed effect regression model as follows:

$$\text{trading}_{ijt} = \alpha_i + \beta_1 AQI_{jt} + \beta_2 W_{jt} + \gamma market_t + \lambda_t + \varepsilon_{ijt} \tag{3.2}$$

In this model, all independent variables, including the control variables and the key variable of interest, are defined in the same manner as in Model (3.1). We utilize variations in investor trading behavior and the Air Quality Index (AQI) across the temporal dimension. Specifically, we explore three distinct measures of trading behavior, namely *abs_imb*, *net_buy*, and *net_sell*, as defined in the previous section, with our primary focus on the coefficient β_1.

To strengthen the robustness and reliability of our findings regarding the impact of air pollution on investor trading behavior, we conduct a comprehensive set of heterogeneity analyses. These are designed to capture differential responses based on investor profiles, stock characteristics, and city-level contextual factors. Specifically, we divide investors into subgroups based on characteristics such as trading activity, transaction frequency, and geographic location, assuming that different investor types may respond uniquely to changes in air quality. Similarly, we stratify the sample according to stock attributes, including company size, book-to-market ratio, and firm age. Given the well-documented phenomenon of local bias in investment behavior, we also examine whether pollution effects differ when investors trade stocks from local firms versus those headquartered elsewhere. Additionally, we factor in urban-level variables, including the extent of air pollution and regional economic development, to assess their role in shaping investor behavior. These contextual elements are expected to influence risk preferences and, by extension, trading decisions.

To bolster the credibility of our findings, we perform a series of robustness checks. First, we examine alternative measures of the Air Quality Index (AQI). While our main specification relies on the daily mean AQI, we introduce supplementary indicators—such as the average AQI during daytime hours (6:00 a.m. to 6:00 p.m.) and AQI observed during active trading windows (9:30–11:30 a.m. and 1:00–3:00 p.m.)—to explore intra-day variations. Moreover, we assess the lagged impact of pollution by incorporating moving averages of AQI over the preceding 3-day, 5-day, and 7-day intervals, which help reveal any delayed or persistent behavioral effects.

In a second robustness strategy, we redefine the measurement of trading behavior. Rather than relying solely on individual-level panel data, we restructure our dataset to reflect city-level activity across trading dates. Specifically, we calculate the average number of trades per investor for each city on a given day. This method is similarly applied to disaggregate buying and selling activity. The result is a new dependent variable, termed city trading, which serves as the basis for an alternative model specification designed to test the consistency of our original results under different empirical frameworks. Eventually, our novel dependent variable, referred to as "city trading," is formed, and our model is expressed as follows:

$$citytrading_{jt} = \alpha_j + \beta_1 AQI_{jt} + \beta_2 W_{jt} + \gamma market_t + \lambda_t + \varepsilon_{jt} \tag{3.3}$$

In this model, represents the city, and denotes the date. The dependent variable is the city-averaged trading behavior. For example, to compute the number of sell transactions, we first aggregate all sell transactions and then divide the total by the number of investors in the city. The total number of transactions and the number of buy transactions are calculated in the same manner. All other variables, including the Air Quality Index (AQI) and weather conditions, are defined as in Model (3.1). We account for the time-invariant city fixed effect in Model (3.3).

3.4.3 Stock-City-Date Panel Data

As a further refinement, our third measure of trading behavior constructs a three-dimensional panel dataset defined by stock, city, and date. This structure is motivated by the possibility that investors may respond similarly to shared information about a specific stock. However, earlier measures do not adequately reflect stock-specific characteristics and may be confounded by price fluctuations that are themselves influenced by air pollution levels. By adopting this more granular panel design, we are able to incorporate stock-level heterogeneity and better isolate the effects of external shocks—such as pollution—on trading decisions across both geographic and temporal dimensions. The model employing this stock-date panel structure is presented as follows:

$$stocktrading_{sjt} = \alpha_s + \beta_1 AQI_{jt} + \beta_2 W_{jt} + \gamma market_t + \lambda_t + \varepsilon_{sjt} \tag{3.4}$$

where s represents the stock, j represents the city and t is the date. The dependent variable *stocktrading* represents the average proportion of buying or selling a specific stock in city j on date t. Furthermore, all the other control variables are the same as defined in model (3.1).

3.5 Empirical Results

3.5.1 Univariate Analysis

To initiate our analysis of the impact of air pollution on investor trading behavior, we first conduct a univariate analysis. Specifically, we utilize paired t-tests to compare trading patterns under differing air quality conditions, distinguishing between high and low AQI environments. Building on the methodology of Goetzmann et al. (2015), investors are ranked daily based on the AQI levels in their respective cities. Based on their ranking position, they are classified as either high- or low-AQI investors, with cutoffs defined by the top and bottom x percentiles, where x takes values of 10, 25, and 50.

We evaluate and compare the net_buy and net_sell behaviors across these groups. Table 3.2 presents the statistically significant outcomes of these comparisons. Panel A highlights that investors exposed to higher AQI levels tend to have consistently lower net_buy values than those experiencing better air quality, with differences significant at the 1% level. Moreover, the gap widens as the percentile threshold becomes more extreme—for example, the net_buy difference is −0.502 for the 50th percentile split and expands to −1.373 for the 10th percentile comparison.

A mirror pattern is observed for net_sell, as shown in Panel B: poorer air quality is associated with a marked increase in selling activity. These findings indicate that elevated pollution levels may negatively affect investor sentiment, resulting in more conservative trading behavior characterized by reduced purchases and heightened sales. Overall, our findings indicate a clear and progressively negative effect of deteriorating air quality on investor trading behavior.

Table 3.2 Univariate test

	Hight AQI	Low AQI	Hight AQI – Low AQI
Panel A: Net_buy			
50th percentile split	16.824	17.326	−0.502***
25th percentile split	16.587	17.678	−1.091***
10th percentile split	16.518	17.891	-1.373***
Panel B: Net_sell			
50th percentile split	17.629	17.017	0.612***
25th percentile split	17.507	16.654	0.853***
10th percentile split	17.794	16.288	1.506***

*** $p < 0.01$, ** $p < 0.05$, * $p < 0.1$

3.5.2 Baseline Model

To obtain a deeper understanding of how air pollution influences investor trading behavior, we conduct a series of multivariate regression analyses. The primary empirical results are summarized in Table 3.3. Column (1) reports the outcome from the Logit model, which assesses whether deteriorating air quality affects the likelihood of investors choosing to buy versus sell. The analysis reveals a statistically significant and negative association, suggesting that higher pollution levels dampen investors' willingness to engage in stock purchases.

In Column (2), we present the results from a fixed-effects model that accounts for weather-related confounders, stock market dynamics, and time-specific effects.

Table 3.3 Baseline regression results

	Logit	abs_imb	net_buy	net_sell
	(1)	(2)	(3)	(4)
ln_AQI	−0.031***	−0.355***	−0.453*	0.528**
	(0.010)	(0.132)	(0.250)	(0.210)
Precipitation	0.001**	0.002	0.019*	0.005
	(0.000)	(0.005)	(0.011)	(0.009)
Pressure	−0.001	0.000	−0.030	−0.018
	(0.001)	(0.019)	(0.035)	(0.027)
Humidity	−0.001	−0.002	−0.016	0.004
	(0.000)	(0.007)	(0.013)	(0.011)
Sunshine	0.000	0.041**	−0.001	−0.017
	(0.002)	(0.020)	(0.041)	(0.032)
Temperature	−.007***	0.034	0.081**	−0.012
	(0.002)	(0.024)	(0.040)	(0.037)
Wind	−0.012	−0.146*	−0.154	0.051
	(0.008)	(0.078)	(0.146)	(0.128)
$Market_t$	−1.243***	−16.522***	−21.163***	5.293*
	(0.121)	(1.927)	(2.917)	(2.803)
$Market_{overnight}$	−14.061***	−26.057	−4.482	15.992
	(1.511)	(21.979)	(22.180)	(21.708)
Individual F.E.	Yes	Yes	Yes	Yes
Year F.E.	Yes	Yes	Yes	Yes
Month F.E.	Yes	Yes	Yes	Yes
Weekday F.E.	Yes	Yes	Yes	Yes
Observations	142,344	142,880	82,729	61,790
R^2	–	0.282	0.207	0.542

Robust standard errors in parentheses. *** $p < 0.01$, ** $p < 0.05$, * $p < 0.1$

This specification confirms that air pollution suppresses overall trading activity, as reflected by reduced trading intensity. To further disentangle investor sentiment, Columns (3) and (4) focus on the net buying and net selling behaviors, captured by the variables net_buy and net_sell, respectively.

The findings consistently show that worsening air quality decreases the tendency to buy and increases the inclination to sell. These effects are statistically significant—at the 10% level for net_buy and at the 5% level for net_sell. Concretely, a 1% uptick in pollution levels is linked to a 0.453% drop in buying propensity and a 0.528% rise in selling activity. Considering an average AQI of 73, a one standard deviation increase in pollution translates into an approximate 32% decrease in buying likelihood and a 37% increase in selling tendency—figures that carry substantial economic relevance, especially in a market dominated by retail investors.

These results align well with previous research, such as Levy and Yagil (2011) and Huang et al. (2020), which document the detrimental effect of air pollution on stock performance. More importantly, our study provides behavioral evidence explaining this link: heightened pollution appears to intensify investor risk aversion, echoing findings by Tauni et al. (2017) and Bian et al. (2016) on the role of risk attitudes in shaping investment choices.

We also examine how broader market indicators influence investor behavior. Both same-day and overnight returns are included in our models. The former exhibits a significant relationship with trading behavior, in line with the findings of Abbas and Wang (2020). However, the impact of overnight returns proves statistically insignificant. Specifically, we observe that positive market returns during the day suppress trading volume and reduce buying, while modestly encouraging sales—a pattern that may reflect the well-known disposition effect, wherein individual investors tend to lock in gains by selling when markets perform well.

3.5.3 Heterogeneity Analysis

To further refine our understanding of the baseline results, we perform a series of heterogeneity analyses across three key dimensions. The first dimension examines variations in investor sophistication, with the aim of determining whether investor experience and behavioral characteristics affect the relationship between air pollution and trading activity. To this end, we classify investors into two broad categories—sophisticated and unsophisticated—based on observable attributes such as trading frequency, follower count, and geographic location. The second dimension explores the impact of stock-specific characteristics, including firm size, book-to-market ratio, age, and industry classification. Finally, we examine whether the severity of air pollution across different urban areas results in heterogeneous effects on trading behavior.

3.5.3.1 Heterogeneity Analysis Across Investors

Prior studies provide relevant insights into how expertise shapes responses to environmental stressors. For example, Dong et al. (2021) demonstrate that the negative impact of pollution on analyst performance is more pronounced among seasoned professionals. Similarly, studies such as Dhar and Zhu (2006), Barber and Odean (2008), and others consistently show that individual investors are more susceptible to cognitive and emotional biases compared to institutional participants. Inspired by this body of work, we begin our heterogeneity analysis by exploring how investor expertise moderates the behavioral response to pollution shocks. We hypothesize that less experienced or casual investors are more likely to react emotionally to adverse environmental conditions, amplifying the influence of air quality on their trading decisions.

To test this premise, we segment our sample according to trading frequency. Investors with transaction volumes above the median are deemed "active" and serve as a proxy for higher sophistication, while those below the median are classified as "non-active." Descriptive statistics support this classification: active investors record a mean return of 4.721%, while their non-active counterparts incur an average loss of −1.238%, yielding a statistically significant gap of 5.959%. Our regression results further validate this distinction as shown in Table 3.4. When controlling for confounding factors, we observe that air pollution significantly affects non-active traders—reducing their trading intensity, discouraging purchases, and prompting more frequent sales. In contrast, the impact on active investors is muted and statistically insignificant.

Table 3.4 Heterogeneity results based on the investor trading frequency

	abs_imb		net_buy		net_sell	
	Active	Non_active	Active	Non_active	Active	Non_active
	(1)	(2)	(3)	(4)	(5)	(6)
ln_AQI	−0.040	−0.583***	−0.163	−0.507**	0.174	0.874***
	(0.171)	(0.195)	(0.263)	(0.243)	(0.279)	(0.315)
Controls	Yes	Yes	Yes	Yes	Yes	Yes
Individual F.E.	Yes	Yes	Yes	Yes	Yes	Yes
Year F.E.	Yes	Yes	Yes	Yes	Yes	Yes
Month F.E.	Yes	Yes	Yes	Yes	Yes	Yes
Weekday F.E.	Yes	Yes	Yes	Yes	Yes	Yes
Observations	67,052	75,828	36,882	45,847	31,180	30,610
R^2	0.241	0.272	0.167	0.156	0.543	0.492

t-test of returns between active and non-active investors

	Active	Non-active	Active-Non-active	*p*-values
Mean	4.721	−1.238	5.959	0.0000

Robust standard errors in parentheses. *** $p < 0.01$, ** $p < 0.05$, * $p < 0.1$

As an illustrative example, a 1% rise in AQI leads to a 0.5% decline in net_buy among non-active traders, compared to only a −0.16% change for active ones, which lacks statistical significance. Notably, the impact of pollution on non-active traders is stronger than the effect observed in the overall baseline model. Moreover, statistical tests indicate that the difference in coefficients between the two investor groups is statistically significant at the 1% level, providing further evidence that investor sophistication plays a crucial role in shaping behavioral responses to environmental factors (Table 3.4).

Secondly, we use the number of followers associated with each investor as an alternative proxy for sophistication. A larger follower count is assumed to reflect greater financial acumen and market experience, likely derived from more frequent engagement and influence within the investment community on the platform. Given the skewed nature of the distribution, we define "sophisticated" investors as those falling above the 75th percentile, which corresponds to having at least 38 followers.

We posit that investors with fewer followers may be more emotionally reactive under high air pollution conditions, making their trading behavior more susceptible to mood-related fluctuations. Table 3.5 reports the empirical outcomes. As shown in columns (2), (4), and (6), air pollution significantly impacts the behavior of investors with lower follower counts, while those with more followers exhibit no statistically meaningful response. This pattern mirrors the earlier findings related to trading frequency, suggesting that lower sophistication levels correlate with greater vulnerability to environmental stressors.

Moreover, statistical tests confirm that the differences in estimated coefficients between the two subgroups are significant, generally at or above the 5% level. These

Table 3.5 Heterogeneity analysis based on the number of followers

	abs_imb		net_buy		net_sell	
	More	Fewer	More	Fewer	More	Fewer
	(1)	(2)	(3)	(4)	(5)	(6)
ln_AQI	−0.292	−0.382**	−0.352	−0.501*	0.371	0.893**
	(0.234)	(0.160)	(0.454)	(0.300)	(0.253)	(0.375)
Controls	Yes	Yes	Yes	Yes	Yes	Yes
Individual F.E.	Yes	Yes	Yes	Yes	Yes	Yes
Year F.E.	Yes	Yes	Yes	Yes	Yes	Yes
Month F.E.	Yes	Yes	Yes	Yes	Yes	Yes
Weekday F.E.	Yes	Yes	Yes	Yes	Yes	Yes
Observations	38,652	104,228	22,403	60,326	16,669	45,121
R^2	0.296	0.276	0.209	0.207	0.574	0.530

t-test of returns between more and fewer investors

	More	Fewer	More-Fewer	*p*-values
Mean	9.121	−0.716	9.837	0.0000

Robust standard errors in parentheses. *** $p < 0.01$, ** $p < 0.05$, * $p < 0.1$

findings strengthen our-broader conclusion that investor heterogeneity—particularly in terms of experience and platform influence—plays a key role in moderating behavioral responses to pollution shocks.

Third, we examine whether the effect of air pollution on trading behavior differs across regions with varying levels of economic development. Specifically, we differentiate between investors in China's Tier 1 cities—Beijing, Shanghai, Guangzhou, and Shenzhen—and those residing in other regions. These major metropolitan centers are characterized by leading GDP performance, rapid economic growth, high income levels, mature financial markets, and the presence of key stock exchanges. These cities also represent the largest concentration of active users in our dataset, indicating a higher likelihood of investor sophistication.

Based on this classification, we divide the sample into two groups: investors from Tier 1 cities and those from Non-Tier 1 cities. The results, presented in Table 3.6, show a marked asymmetry. Among investors in less developed cities, air pollution significantly suppresses trading activity and alters their propensity to buy or sell stocks. In contrast, investors in Tier 1 cities appear largely unaffected by fluctuations in air quality, as the estimated effects are statistically insignificant.

This divergence supports our initial conjecture: market participants in Tier 1 cities—due to their proximity to financial institutions and greater exposure to market information—are likely more professional and resilient to mood swings induced by environmental stress. Conversely, investors in smaller or less developed cities may be more emotionally reactive, rendering them more vulnerable to pollution-driven behavioral changes.

Table 3.6 Heterogeneity analysis based on the development of cities

	abs_imb		net_buy		net_sell	
	Non-tier 1	Tier 1	Non-tier 1	Tier 1	Non-tier 1	Tier 1
	(1)	(2)	(3)	(4)	(5)	(6)
ln_AQI	−0.445**	−0.312	−0.645**	−0.156	0.746**	0.595**
	(0.168)	(0.221)	(0.318)	(0.306)	(0.350)	(0.267)
Controls	Yes	Yes	Yes	Yes	Yes	Yes
Individual F.E.	Yes	Yes	Yes	Yes	Yes	Yes
Year F.E.	Yes	Yes	Yes	Yes	Yes	Yes
Month F.E.	Yes	Yes	Yes	Yes	Yes	Yes
Weekday F.E.	Yes	Yes	Yes	Yes	Yes	Yes
Observations	67,683	75,197	43,258	39,471	32,856	28,934
R^2	0.286	0.278	0.207	0.208	0.536	0.547

t-test of returns between more and fewer investors

	Tier 1	Non-tier 1	Tier 1-Non-tier 1	*p*-values
Mean	3.195	0.555	2.639	0.0001

Robust standard errors in parentheses, *** $p < 0.01$, ** $p < 0.05$, * $p < 0.1$

In conclusion, our three heterogeneous analyses confirm that sophisticated investors are better able to absorb higher risks and are less influenced by air pollution than their unsophisticated counterparts.

3.5.3.2 Heterogeneity Analysis Across Stocks

Previous studies suggest that investor sentiment exerts a stronger influence on certain types of stocks, particularly those characterized by smaller size, limited profitability, higher volatility, lack of dividends, extreme growth potential, or financial distress (Baker and Wurgler 2006; Wu et al. 2018). Building on this body of literature, we further investigate whether the behavioral effects of air pollution differ depending on the characteristics of the assets held by investors. Specifically, we examine heterogeneity based on firm attributes such as size, book-to-market ratio, and age. In addition, informed by earlier findings, we examine how air pollution influences trading decisions in relation to firms' environmental classifications and geographic proximity (Levy and Yagil 2013; Wu et al. 2018).

Our first heterogeneity test examines firm size, categorizing companies into large-cap and small-cap groups based on the median market capitalization. As shown in Table 3.7, the negative impact of air pollution is more pronounced for smaller firms, especially in terms of decreased trading intensity and increased selling activity. While the statistical significance of the effects on trading volume and buying behavior is marginal (around the 10% level), the disparity between the two size groups is robust. Specifically, the differences in coefficients between small and large firms are statistically significant at or above the 5% threshold, as highlighted in the bottom row of Table 3.7.

Table 3.7 Heterogeneity analysis based on firm size

	abs_imb		net_buy		net_sell	
	Small	Big	Small	Big	Small	Big
	(1)	(2)	(3)	(4)	(5)	(6)
ln_AQI	−0.359*	−0.143	−0.454*	−0.276	0.474**	0.041
	(0.189)	(0.133)	(0.240)	(0.249)	(0.240)	(0.201)
Controls	Yes	Yes	Yes	Yes	Yes	Yes
Individual F.E.	Yes	Yes	Yes	Yes	Yes	Yes
Year F.E.	Yes	Yes	Yes	Yes	Yes	Yes
Month F.E.	Yes	Yes	Yes	Yes	Yes	Yes
Weekday F.E.	Yes	Yes	Yes	Yes	Yes	Yes
Observations	108,554	105,622	57,770	63,992	47,542	44,277
R^2	0.482	0.475	0.408	0.406	0.495	0.504

Robust standard errors in parentheses. *** $p < 0.01$, ** $p < 0.05$, * $p < 0.1$

The second dimension of heterogeneity we investigate centers on firms' book-to-market (BE/ME) ratios. We categorize the stock sample into two groups based on whether a firm's BE/ME ratio is above or below the median. As shown in Table 3.8, the results reveal that air pollution exerts a more pronounced negative effect on trading behavior when investors hold low BE/ME (growth-oriented) stocks. This effect is evident across several dimensions, including reduced trading intensity, lower buying activity, and increased selling tendencies.

More specifically, investors appear more inclined to dispose of low book-to-market stocks under polluted conditions, whereas their behavior is less affected when holding high BE/ME (value) stocks. The difference in responses between the two groups is statistically significant, with the differences in coefficients reaching at least the 5% significance level, as indicated in the final row of Table 3.8.

The third layer of analysis distinguishes firms based on their age. Drawing from extensive literature on initial public offerings (e.g., Ljungqvist and Wilhelm Jr 2003), we classify companies as "young" if they have been publicly listed for fewer than 5 years, and as "mature" if their listing history exceeds this threshold. Table 3.9 summarizes the corresponding results.

After controlling for relevant variables, we find that the negative impact of air pollution on investor behavior is especially pronounced for younger firms. Specifically, trading activity declines, buying interest weakens, and selling pressure increases in response to poor air quality for these firms. In contrast, no statistically significant effect is observed for older firms.

Furthermore, the magnitude of the pollution-induced impact is clearly larger in the younger firm group, with the differences in response between the two categories reaching statistical significance at the 5% level, as shown in the bottom panel of Table 3.9.

Table 3.8 Heterogeneity analysis based on book-to-market ratio

	abs_imb		net_buy		net_sell	
	High BE/ME	Low BE/ME	High BE/ME	Low BE/ME	High BE/ME	Low BE/ME
	(1)	(2)	(3)	(4)	(5)	(6)
ln_AQI	−0.097	−0.421**	−0.122	−0.368*	0.049	0.382*
	(0.148)	(0.169)	(0.190)	(0.221)	(0.212)	(0.231)
Controls	Yes	Yes	Yes	Yes	Yes	Yes
Individual F.E.	Yes	Yes	Yes	Yes	Yes	Yes
Year F.E.	Yes	Yes	Yes	Yes	Yes	Yes
Month F.E.	Yes	Yes	Yes	Yes	Yes	Yes
Weekday F.E.	Yes	Yes	Yes	Yes	Yes	Yes
Observations	118,716	95,445	68,693	53,130	49,853	42,012
R^2	0.499	0.481	0.431	0.408	0.513	0.500

Robust standard errors in parentheses. *** $p < 0.01$, ** $p < 0.05$, * $p < 0.1$

Table 3.9 Heterogeneity analysis based on firm age

	abs_imb		net_buy		net_sell	
	Old	Young	Old	Young	Old	Young
	(1)	(2)	(3)	(4)	(5)	(6)
ln_AQI	−0.117	−0.684**	−0.134	−0.575**	0.014	0.900**
	(0.128)	(0.288)	(0.160)	(0.261)	(0.177)	(0.387)
Controls	Yes	Yes	Yes	Yes	Yes	Yes
Individual F.E.	Yes	Yes	Yes	Yes	Yes	Yes
Year F.E.	Yes	Yes	Yes	Yes	Yes	Yes
Month F.E.	Yes	Yes	Yes	Yes	Yes	Yes
Weekday F.E.	Yes	Yes	Yes	Yes	Yes	Yes
Observations	176,218	37,739	102,091	19,800	74,550	17,159
R^2	0.487	0.533	0.431	0.471	0.514	0.574

Robust standard errors in parentheses. *** $p < 0.01$, ** $p < 0.05$, * $p < 0.1$

The fourth dimension of heterogeneity is based on firm industry classification. Certain sectors may be directly associated with environmental issues, and prior research—such as Levy and Yagil (2013)—has shown that pollution-related industries tend to experience stronger negative effects of air pollution on stock returns. To test whether the observed behavioral changes in our study stem from such industry-specific exposure, we categorize stocks according to their sectoral affiliation.

We rely on the classification framework published by the Ministry of Environmental Protection of China (MEPC) in 2008, which identifies industries considered to be heavy polluters. Under this system, firms operating in these sectors are labeled as "polluting," while all others are classified as "non-polluting." If investor responses were driven purely by industry exposure to pollution, we would expect substantial behavioral divergence between these two groups. However, if the effect arises from shifts in risk perception, the impact would likely extend across all equities, regardless of industry.

As reported in Table 3.10, air pollution significantly influences trading behavior for both polluting and non-polluting firms. Nonetheless, the magnitude of this influence differs notably between the two categories. In particular, investor activity—measured through trading volume, buying inclination, and selling behavior—shows stronger responses for polluting firms. These findings suggest that heightened air pollution amplifies risk aversion among investors, especially when dealing with firms perceived to be more environmentally exposed.

The final dimension of our heterogeneity analysis is grounded in the theory of local bias in investor behavior. Prior studies, such as Wu et al. (2018) and Ding et al. (2021), have highlighted the tendency of Chinese investors to favor firms headquartered in their own regions. Motivated by this pattern, we explore whether the behavioral response to air pollution differs depending on whether an investor holds local or

Table 3.10 Heterogeneity analysis based on industry categories

	abs_imb		net_buy		net_sell	
	Polluting	Non polluting	Polluting	Non polluting	Polluting	Non polluting
	(1)	(2)	(3)	(4)	(5)	(6)
ln_AQI	−0.391**	−0.369**	−0.327**	−0.216	0.512**	0.486*
	(0.171)	(0.173)	(0.153)	(0.201)	(0.251)	(0.289)
Controls	Yes	Yes	Yes	Yes	Yes	Yes
Individual F.E.	Yes	Yes	Yes	Yes	Yes	Yes
Year F.E.	Yes	Yes	Yes	Yes	Yes	Yes
Month F.E.	Yes	Yes	Yes	Yes	Yes	Yes
Weekday F.E.	Yes	Yes	Yes	Yes	Yes	Yes
Observations	100,637	99,628	60,120	45,306	39,875	44,005
R^2	0.423	0.420	0.385	0.325	0.521	0.503

Robust standard errors in parentheses. *** $p < 0.01$, ** $p < 0.05$, * $p < 0.1$

non-local stocks. Earlier research has also indicated that the impact of air pollution on stock performance tends to be stronger for locally headquartered firms compared to firms located elsewhere.

Building on this insight, we categorize a stock as "local" when its registered headquarters align with the investor's location; otherwise, it is classified as "non-local." Table 3.11 presents the detailed results of this analysis. Our findings indicate that air pollution significantly impacts trading behavior in both categories, influencing both trading intensity and the willingness to buy or sell. However, the effect is notably more pronounced when investors trade in local firms.

This outcome aligns with previous literature, reinforcing the view that psychological proximity and personal attachment to local assets may amplify the behavioral effects of environmental stressors such as pollution.

3.5.3.3 Heterogeneity Analysis Across Cities

In addition to the differentiated responses observed across various investor types and stock characteristics, the influence of air pollution may also depend on the overall pollution severity in a given region. To explore this possibility, we incorporate regional air quality levels into our heterogeneity analysis by distinguishing between cities with high and low pollution intensity. Specifically, a city is identified as "heavily polluted" if its Air Quality Index (AQI) exceeds 150; otherwise, it is classified as "lightly polluted."

The findings, summarized in Table 3.12, reveal that investor behavior in more polluted cities is more strongly affected by air quality deterioration. Significant

Table 3.11 Heterogeneity analysis based on local bias

	abs_imb		net_buy		net_sell	
	Yes	No	Yes	No	Yes	No
	(1)	(2)	(3)	(4)	(5)	(6)
ln_AQI	−0.487**	−0.285**	−0.291**	−0.248*	0.630***	0.313*
	(0.220)	(0.131)	(0.144)	(0.157)	(0.221)	(0.198)
Controls	Yes	Yes	Yes	Yes	Yes	Yes
Individual F.E.	Yes	Yes	Yes	Yes	Yes	Yes
Year F.E.	Yes	Yes	Yes	Yes	Yes	Yes
Month F.E.	Yes	Yes	Yes	Yes	Yes	Yes
Weekday F.E.	Yes	Yes	Yes	Yes	Yes	Yes
Observations	15,998	198,169	8937	112,761	6412	85,372
R^2	0.575	0.486	0.528	0.425	0.617	0.514

Robust standard errors in parentheses. *** $p < 0.01$, ** $p < 0.05$, * $p < 0.1$

effects are observed across key dimensions of trading behavior, including overall activity, willingness to buy, and selling propensity. As pollution becomes more severe, investors exhibit increasingly pessimistic sentiment, which in turn suppresses their inclination to engage in buying activity.

Furthermore, the differences in behavioral responses between heavily and lightly polluted cities are statistically robust, consistently reaching significance across the examined measures. These results suggest that the ambient level of pollution in a city serves as an important contextual factor in shaping the behavioral impact of environmental conditions on financial decision-making.

Table 3.12 Heterogeneity analysis based on air pollution severity

	abs_imb		net_buy		net_sell	
	Severely	Lightly	Severely	Lightly	Severely	Lightly
	(1)	(2)	(3)	(4)	(5)	(6)
ln_AQI	−0.567***	−0.430	−0.801**	−0.564	0.802**	0.358
	(0.195)	(0.442)	(0.372)	(0.908)	(0.320)	(0.761)
Controls	Yes	Yes	Yes	Yes	Yes	Yes
Individual F.E.	Yes	Yes	Yes	Yes	Yes	Yes
Year F.E.	Yes	Yes	Yes	Yes	Yes	Yes
Month F.E.	Yes	Yes	Yes	Yes	Yes	Yes
Weekday F.E.	Yes	Yes	Yes	Yes	Yes	Yes
Observations	27,454	115,071	15,821	66,466	11,393	49,881
R^2	0.287	0.354	0.220	0.294	0.548	0.607

Robust standard errors in parentheses. *** $p < 0.01$, ** $p < 0.05$, * $p < 0.1$

3.5.4 Robustness Check

3.5.4.1 Different Measures of AQI

To ensure the robustness of our key empirical findings, we conduct a thorough series of checks, including alternative measures of air pollution and revised indicators of investor trading behavior. The first set of tests focuses on refining how pollution is measured. Although our main analysis relies on the 24-h average AQI as the benchmark for pollution exposure, We acknowledge that investor sentiment and behavior are more likely to be affected by air quality during the day, particularly within trading hours.

To account for this, we introduce two supplementary pollution indicators: (1) the average AQI recorded between 6:00 a.m. and 6:00 p.m., and (2) the AQI observed specifically during market hours (i.e., 9:30–11:30 a.m. and 1:00–3:00 p.m.). These measures are used in our initial robustness checks.

The results, presented in Panels A and B of Table 3.13, are in line with our baseline findings. Interestingly, the estimated coefficients for both the daytime and trading-period AQI measures are slightly larger than those based on the full-day average, suggesting that investors are particularly sensitive to pollution levels during active trading times. The similarity in effect size between the two refined AQI measures provides additional support for the robustness of our conclusions.

In addition to its immediate effects, air pollution may exert a lasting influence on investor sentiment, thereby affecting trading decisions over an extended horizon. To account for potential persistence in the effects, we include lagged measures of

Table 3.13 Robustness check with AQI from the day time

	Logit	abs_imb	net_buy	net_sell
	(1)	(2)	(3)	(4)
Panel A: The AQI from daytime: 6:00 a.m–6:00 p.m				
ln_AQI_6	−0.042***	−0.338**	−0.366	0.624***
	(0.012)	(0.148)	(0.279)	(0.232)
All controls	Yes	Yes	Yes	Yes
Observations	142,704	143,240	82,938	61,945
R^2	–	0.282	0.207	0.542
Panel B: The AQI from the trading time: 9:30–11:30 a.m & 1:00–3:00 p.m				
ln_AQI_trade	−0.037***	−0.327**	−0.374	0.609***
	(0.012)	(0.140)	(0.263)	(0.219)
All controls	Yes	Yes	Yes	Yes
Observations	142,700	143,236	82,935	61,944
R^2	–	0.282	0.207	0.542

Robust standard errors in parentheses. *** $p < 0.01$, ** $p < 0.05$, * $p < 0.1$

air quality by calculating the average AQI over the preceding 3, 5, and 7 days, and re-estimate the baseline regression model. The results are reported in Table 3.14.

Our findings indicate that these lagged AQI variables have a significant impact on investor behavior, particularly in relation to trading activity levels and the likelihood of making purchases. Interestingly, while past pollution levels continue to influence buying behavior and trading intensity, their effect on the inclination to sell diminishes and loses statistical significance over time.

These observations are consistent with prior work, such as Dong et al. (2021), and may be attributed to the asymmetry in investor risk preferences. Since holding equities typically involves greater perceived risk compared to holding cash, prolonged exposure to poor air quality may reinforce cautious behavior, making investors more hesitant to initiate new positions rather than prompting immediate liquidation.

3.5.4.2 Different Measures of Trading Behavior

Beyond the primary metrics used to assess investor trading behavior, our second set of robustness checks incorporates two alternative measures designed to capture trading dynamics from both a city-level and stock-level perspective. Drawing upon the framework established by Goetzmann et al. (2015), we construct two panel datasets—one organized by city and date, and the other by stock and date.

The first indicator, referred to as citytrading, represents the average number of transactions at the city-date level. This aggregated approach helps mitigate individual-level noise, facilitating a clearer identification of pollution-related effects at a broader scale. To construct this variable, we first calculate the total number of transactions initiated by all investors in a given city on a specific trading day, and then divide it by the number of active investors to obtain the average transaction count, denoted as total_num. Similarly, we compute buy_num and sell_num by calculating the average number of buy and sell transactions per investor at the city-date level.

These variables are then incorporated into regression Model (3.3), with controls for weather conditions, market trends, and time-fixed effects. Additionally, we utilize a fixed-effects specification to account for time-invariant characteristics at the city level. Table 3.15 presents the estimation results: Column (1) reports the influence of AQI on overall transaction volume; Column (2) presents the effect on buying activity; and Column (3) details the impact on selling behavior.

Our analysis reveals that higher levels of air pollution are associated with an increase in both total transaction volume and selling frequency. However, the relationship between AQI and buying activity is statistically insignificant. A likely interpretation is that worsening air quality induces a more pessimistic sentiment among investors, prompting them to reduce exposure by selling off assets. Since each sell order is recorded as an individual transaction, elevated sell-side activity

Table 3.14 Robustness check with previous average AQI

	abs_imb	net_buy	net_sell	abs_imb	net_buy	net_sell	abs_imb	net_buy	net_sell
	(1)	(2)	(3)	(4)	(5)	(6)	(7)	(8)	(9)
ln_AQI_L3	−0.348*	−0.346*	0.210						
	(0.010)	(0.132)	(0.250)						
ln_AQI_L5				−0.587**	−0.521**	0.137			
				(0.266)	(0.262)	(0.410)			
ln_AQI_L7							−0.766**	−0.757**	0.363
							(0.320)	(0.360)	(0.486)
Controls	Yes	Yes	Yes	Yes	Yes	Yes	Yes	Yes	Yes
Individual F.E.	Yes	Yes	Yes	Yes	Yes	Yes	Yes	Yes	Yes
Year F.E.	Yes	Yes	Yes	Yes	Yes	Yes	Yes	Yes	Yes
Month F.E.	Yes	Yes	Yes	Yes	Yes	Yes	Yes	Yes	Yes
Weekday F.E.	Yes	Yes	Yes	Yes	Yes	Yes	Yes	Yes	Yes
Observations	125,851	72,820	54,431	113,109	65,425	48,908	99,607	57,583	43,065
R^2	0.282	0.213	0.547	0.287	0.218	0.549	0.291	0.228	0.555

Robust standard errors in parentheses. *** $p < 0.01$, ** $p < 0.05$, * $p < 0.1$

Table 3.15 Robustness check with the city-date panel data

	total_num	buy_num	sell_num
	(1)	(2)	(3)
ln_AQI_L3	0.032**	0.018*	−0.014*
	(0.016)	(0.011)	(0.008)
Controls	Yes	Yes	Yes
Individual F.E.	Yes	Yes	Yes
Year F.E.	Yes	Yes	Yes
Month F.E.	Yes	Yes	Yes
Weekday F.E.	Yes	Yes	Yes
Observations	33,559	33,559	33,559
R^2	0.218	0.148	0.149

Robust standard errors in parentheses. *** $p < 0.01$, ** $p < 0.05$, * $p < 0.1$

under polluted conditions could explain the rise in total transaction counts, even in the absence of increased buying.

The second alternative measure of investor trading behavior is constructed using a stock-date panel dataset. This approach acknowledges the possibility that investors' actions may be influenced by stock-specific volatility—potentially correlated with air pollution—rather than purely by shifts in sentiment. The stock-date structure enables us to capture variations associated with individual securities over time, providing a more detailed view of trading dynamics.

To further refine this analysis, we expand the framework into a three-dimensional panel that includes stock, city, and date dimensions, as previously outlined. This richer data structure enables us to better account for heterogeneity at both the asset and regional levels. Using Model (3.4), we re-estimate the relationships while controlling for a range of confounding factors, consistent with the specifications in Models (3.1) through (3.3).

The empirical results, presented in Table 3.16, align closely with our baseline findings. These results support the conclusion that air pollution has a significant behavioral impact on investors, decreasing their willingness to buy and increasing their tendency to sell. These outcomes provide further evidence supporting the robustness and generalizability of our main argument.

Table 3.16 Robustness check with the stock-city-date panel data

	Logit	abs_imb	net_buy	net_sell
	(1)	(2)	(3)	(4)
ln_AQI	−0.013**	−0.147**	−0.146**	0.136*
	(0.005)	(0.066)	(0.070)	(0.073)
Controls	Yes	Yes	Yes	Yes
Individual F.E.	Yes	Yes	Yes	Yes
Year F.E.	Yes	Yes	Yes	Yes
Month F.E.	Yes	Yes	Yes	Yes
Weekday F.E.	Yes	Yes	Yes	Yes
Observations	236,042	236,042	133,367	103,025
R^2	–	0.145	0.158	0.142

Robust standard errors in parentheses. *** $p < 0.01$, ** $p < 0.05$, * $p < 0.1$

3.6 Conclusion

This study investigates the impact of air pollution on investor trading behavior using a unique dataset encompassing over 3000 individual investors and 372,310 transaction records from June 24, 2016, to November 7, 2018. After controlling for weather conditions and temporal effects, our analysis reveals a distinct negative relationship between deteriorating air quality and trading activity. Specifically, higher pollution levels are associated with decreased investor engagement and a reduced likelihood of purchasing stocks, while simultaneously increasing the propensity to sell. We observe significant heterogeneity across investor profiles, stock characteristics, and geographic locations. These findings remain robust across a variety of pollution measures and alternative definitions of trading behavior, including city- and stock-level perspectives.

A plausible explanation for these behavioral shifts is that poor air quality induces negative mood states, which in turn reduce risk-taking and dampen market participation.

Our research contributes to the growing body of literature on environmental factors in financial markets. It provides new insights into the economic consequences of pollution within the Chinese context, highlighting the intersection between environmental conditions and economic behavior. Second, the study provides novel insights for psychology and labor economics by documenting how environmental stressors, specifically air pollution, can impair performance among a distinct group of professionals, namely individual investors. Third, we establish a behavioral linkage between environmental quality, trading decisions, and ultimately stock returns.

Although we do not directly measure mood in this study, we hypothesize that mood changes induced by pollution play a central role in shaping trading outcomes. Future research may benefit from incorporating sentiment analysis—such as extracting emotional tone from investor commentary—to more precisely capture the psychological mechanisms underlying these observed patterns.

References

Abbas G, Wang S (2020) Does macroeconomic uncertainty really matter in predicting stock market behavior? A comparative study on China and USA. China Financ Rev Int 10(4):393–427

Baker M, Wurgler J (2006) Investor sentiment and the cross-section of stock returns. J Financ 61(4):1645–1680

Barber BM, Odean T (2008) All that glitters: the effect of attention and news on the buying behavior of individual and institutional investors. Rev Financ Stud 21(2):785–818

Bian Y, Xu L, Li J, Liu X (2016) Dynamical evolution of trading behavior on anti-coordination game in complex networks. China Financ Rev Int 6(4):367–379

Bullinger M (1989) Psychological effects of air pollution on healthy residents—a time-series approach. J Environ Psychol 9(2):103–118

Bullinger M (1990) Environmental stress: effects of air pollution on mood, neuropsychological function and physical state. In: Psychobiology of stress. Springer

Cao M, Wei J (2005) Stock market returns: a note on temperature anomaly. J Bank Financ 29(6):1559–1573

Chang T, Graff Zivin J, Gross T, Neidell M (2016a) Particulate pollution and the productivity of pear packers. Am Econ J Econ Pol 8:141–169

Chang T, Graff Zivin J, Gross T, Neidell M (2016b) The effect of pollution on worker productivity: evidence from call-center workers in China. NBER Working Paper, (22328)

Chen GM, Kim KA, Nofsinger JR, Rui OM (2004) Behavior and performance of emerging market investors: evidence from China. Washington State University

Chen Y, Ebenstein A, Greenstone M, Li H (2013) Evidence on the impact of sustained exposure to air pollution on life expectancy from China's Huai River policy. Proc Natl Acad Sci 110(32):12936–12941

Chen S, Guo C, Huang X (2018) Air pollution, student health, and school absences: evidence from China. J Environ Econ Manag 92:465–497

Chuang W-I, Susmel R (2011) Who is the more overconfident trader? Individual vs. institutional investors. J Bank Financ 35(7):1626–1644

Coates JM, Herbert J (2008) Endogenous steroids and financial risk taking on a London trading floor. Proc Natl Acad Sci 105(16):6167–6172

Cohen S, Evans GW, Stokols D, Krantz DS (1986) Stress processes and the costs of coping. In: Behavior I (ed) Health, and environmental stress. Plenum Press, New York, pp 1–23

Cunningham MR (1979) Weather, mood, and helping behavior: quasi experiments with the sunshine samaritan. J Pers Soc Psychol 37(11):1947–1956

Dhar R, Zhu N (2006) Up close and personal: investor sophistication and the disposition effect. Manag Sci 52(5):726–740

Ding X, Guo M, Yang T (2021) Air pollution, local bias and stock returns. Financ Res Lett 39:101576

Dong R, Fisman R, Wang Y, Xu N (2021) Air pollution, affect, and forecasting bias: evidence from Chinese analysts. J Financ Econ 139(3):971–984

Evans GW, Jacobs SV, Dooley D, Catalano R (1987) The interaction of stressful life events and chronic strains on community mental health. Am J Community Psychol 15(1):23–34

Evans GW, Colome SD, Shearer DF (1988) Psychological reactions to air pollution. Environ Res 45(1):1–15

Goetzmann WN, Kim D, Kumar A, Wang Q (2015) Weather-induced mood, institutional investors, and stock returns. Rev Financ Stud 28(1):73–111

Graff Zivin J, Neidell M (2012) The impact of pollution on worker productivity. Am Econ Rev 102(7):3652–3673
Guo M, Fu S (2019) Running with a mask? The effect of air pollution on marathon runners' performance. J Sports Econ 20(7):903–928
Hanna R, Oliva P (2015) The effect of pollution on labor supply: evidence from a natural experiment in Mexico city. J Public Econ 122:68–79
Heyes AM, Neidell M, Saberian S (2016) The effect of air pollution on investor behavior: evidence from the S&P 500. NBER Working Paper, (22753)
Hirshleifer D, Shumway T (2003) Good day sunshine: stock returns and the weather. J Financ 58(3):1009–1032
Hsieh GC, Sharma RP, Parker RDR (1991) Hypothalamic-pituitary-adrenocortical axis activity and immune function after oral exposure to benzene and toluene. Immunopharmacology 21(1):23–32
Huang J, Xu N, Yu H (2020) Pollution and performance: do investors make worse trades on hazy days? Manag Sci 66(10):4455–4476
Johnson EJ, Tversky A (1983) Affect, generalization, and the perception of risk. J Pers Soc Psychol 45(1):20–31
Kahneman D, Tversky A (1973) Availability: a heuristic for judging frequency and probability. Cogn Psychol 5(2):207–232
Kamstra MJ, Kramer LA, Levi MD (2003) Winter blues: a SAD stock market cycle. Am Econ Rev 93(1):324–343
Kliger D, Levy O (2003) Mood-induced variation in risk preferences. J Econ Behav Organ 52(4):573–584
Kliger D, Levy O (2008) Mood impacts on probability weighting functions: "large-gamble" evidence. J Soc Econ 37(4):1397–1411
Lepori GM (2016) Air pollution and stock returns: evidence from a natural experiment. J Empir Financ 35:25–42
Levy T, Yagil J (2011) Air pollution and stock returns in the US. J Econ Psychol 32(3):374–383
Levy T, Yagil J (2013) Air pollution and stock returns—extensions and international perspective. Int J Eng Bus Enterp Appl 4(1):1–14
Li J, Massa M, Zhang H, Zhang J (2020) Behavioral bias in haze: evidence from air pollution and the disposition effect in China. J Financ Econ 142:641–673
Ljungqvist A, Wilhelm WJ Jr (2003) IPO pricing in the dot-com bubble. J Financ 58(2):723–752
Lundberg A (1996) Psychiatric aspects of air pollution. Otolaryngol Head Neck Surg 114(2):227–231
Mayer JD, Gaschke YN, Braverman DL, Evans TW (1992) Mood-congruent judgment is a general effect. J Pers Soc Psychol 63(1):119–132
Mittal V, Ross WT (1998) The impact of positive and negative affect and issue interpretation and risk taking. Organ Behav Hum Decis Process 76(3):298–324
Rosenblitt JC, Soler H, Johnson SE, Quadagno DM (2001) Sensation seeking and hormones in men and women: exploring the link. Horm Behav 40(3):396–402
Sagar A, Bhattacharya M, Joon V (2007) A comparative study of air pollution-related morbidity among exposed population of Delhi. Indian J Community Med 32(4):268–271
Saunders EM (1993) Stock prices and wall street weather. Am Econ Rev 83(5):1337–1345
Schiffman SS, Miller EAS, Suggs MS, Graham BG (1995) The effect of environmental odors emanating from commercial swine operations on the mood of nearby residents. Brain Res Bull 37(4):369–375
Schwarz N, Clore GL (1983) Mood, misattribution, and judgments of well-being: informative and directive functions of affective states. J Pers Soc Psychol 45(3):513–523
Tan L, Chiang TC, Mason JR, Nelling E (2008) Herding behavior in Chinese stock markets: an examination of a and B shares. Pac Basin Financ J 16(1–2):61–77
Tauni MZ, Fang H, Mirza SS, Memon ZA, Jebran K (2017) Do investor's big five personality traits influence the association between information acquisition and stock trading behavior? China Financ Rev Int 7(4):450–477

Tomei F, Rosati MV, Ciarrocca M, Baccolo TP, Gaballo M, Caciri T, Tomao E (2003) Plasma cortisol levels and workers exposed to urban pollutants. Ind Health 41(4):320–326

World Bank (2016) The cost of air pollution: strengthening the economic case for action. World Bank, Washington, DC

Wright WF, Bower GH, Wu Q, Hao Y, Lu J (1992) Mood effects on subjective probability assessment. Organ Behav Hum Decis Process 52(2):276–291

Wu Q, Hao Y, Lu J (2018) Air pollution, stock returns, and trading activities in China. Pac-Basin Financ J 51:342–365

Yuan K, Zheng L, Zhu Q (2006) Are investors moonstruck? Lunar phases and stock returns. J Empir Financ 13(1):1–23

Zhang X, Chen X, Zhang X (2018) The impact of exposure to air pollution on cognitive performance. Proc Natl Acad Sci U S A 115(37):9193–9197

Chapter 4
A Breath of Fresh Capital? Air Pollution and the IPO Market

Abstract Since the initiation of economic reforms and opening-up policies in China, the nation has witnessed rapid economic growth. However, alongside this economic development and modernization process, China has also grappled with an increasingly severe air pollution problem. As air pollution gradually worsened, the stock market began to react to this environmental concern. This study conducts empirical analysis using all IPO stocks listed on China's A-share market from 2014 to 2019. The results indicate that air pollution has garnered investors' attention and significantly negatively impacted the IPO market performance. The impact of air pollution on the IPO performance of environmental stocks is notably more pronounced than its impact on non-environmental stocks, suggesting that air pollution's influence through fundamental channels is substantial. Rational expectations can thus steer investors towards a preference for investing in IPOs of environmental stocks. This research enriches the field of studies related to the relationship between air pollution and the stock market, addressing the gap in understanding the impact of air pollution on IPO markets.

Keywords Air pollution · IPO · Investor sentiment · Investor attention

4.1 Introduction

Air pollution, as a consequence of industrial development and the modernization process driven by fossil fuels, has become one of the pressing issues that urgently need to be addressed in this century. This issue initially emerged in countries and regions that were at the forefront of industrialization and modernization, with notable examples including the 1930 Meuse Valley fog, the 1943 Los Angeles smog event, the 1948 Donora smog event, and the 1952 London smog event. In China, since the inception of economic reforms and opening up, the rapid economic development has led to severe air pollution problems due to the substantial consumption of fossil fuels. According to monitoring data from the National Climate Center of the China Meteorological Administration, China's air quality started to significantly deteriorate

M. Guo et al., *Social-Economic Impacts of Air Pollution*, Climate Change and Energy Transition, https://doi.org/10.1007/978-981-96-7858-7_4

from 2000 onwards. The frequency, duration, and geographical extent of haze days have all increased. By 2011, large-scale haze events occurred frequently in the central and eastern regions of China, especially during the autumn and winter seasons, with numerous prolonged episodes lasting more than 20 days in some cases. As a result, air pollution issues in China became highly visible and drew widespread attention from the public, media, and the government. In the same year, the air pollution index "PM2.5" was included as a yearly keyword. To address air pollution challenges and win the battle for clear skies, the government introduced a series of planning outlines and legislation. Air pollution received significant attention not only at the governmental level but also in the media and among the general public. Starting from 2011, terms like "haze," "PM2.5," and related vocabulary became annual keywords, and Baidu search indexes related to "air pollution," "haze weather," and "atmospheric pollution" surged, indicating that media reports and public concern regarding air pollution have been steadily increasing alongside deteriorating air quality.

As air pollution increasingly garners widespread attention, its effects on the stock market are gradually becoming apparent. Existing psychological research has already confirmed that environmental factors like sunlight, cloudy skies, precipitation, temperature, and air quality can influence people's moods. Exposure to polluted air, for instance, leads to elevated cortisol levels in the human body, resulting in pessimistic emotions, negative biases in evaluating situations, and reduced desires for excitement and risk-taking. According to the theories of modern behavioral finance, investors' negative emotions can affect their rational judgment and trading behavior. Some scholars, such as Levy and Yagil (2011), have linked air quality to the stock market and found that the state and changes in air quality can impact investors' investment decisions and trading behavior in the stock market, thereby exerting further influence on the stock market. However, these studies have focused on the overall stock market or sectors, lacking an examination of the relationship between air pollution and individual stock performance, and they have not investigated the IPO market.

China's IPO market has undergone multiple reforms and continuous development. However, due to the relatively late start of China's capital market, the IPO market system has yet to be perfected, with persistent issues such as high premiums, excessive over-subscription funds, and first-day under-performance hindering the healthy development of China's capital market. Throughout the IPO market, the most notable characteristic is the short-term excess returns of newly listed stocks and the phenomenon of consecutive trading limit-ups. Scholars generally believe that this is highly related to the dynamics among IPO participants and investor sentiment. In previous research on the IPO market, scholars have explored investor sentiment from a market perspective without analyzing factors like weather and have not discussed the impact of air pollution on the IPO market. However, given that air pollution has been established as a factor capable of affecting investor sentiment and trading behavior, it should be incorporated into research on the influence of the IPO market.

Therefore, this study employs the Air Quality Index and Baidu search index for air pollution-related terms as proxy variables for air pollution and investor attention to air pollution. The aim is to investigate whether air pollution affects the IPO market performance and the underlying mechanisms. Furthermore, we explore whether the impact of air pollution differs between IPOs of environmentally friendly concept stocks and those in polluting industries (referred to as "environmental IPOs" and "pollution IPOs").

This paper makes two main contributions. Firstly, existing literature, both domestic and international, contains numerous studies on the impact of weather on the stock market, some of which delve into research on air quality. However, studies focusing on the effects of air pollution on the stock market are relatively scarce, with most concentration on market-wide or sector-specific impacts, lacking research on individual stock performance, and there are no articles examining the IPO market. Hence, this research enriches the field of studies on the relationship between air pollution and the stock market, bridging the research gap in understanding the effects of air pollution on the IPO market.

Secondly, from a practical perspective, this study provides valuable insights. By validating that air pollution harms the IPO market performance, it demonstrates the adverse negative effects of air pollution on stock market resource allocation, IPO firm financing, and investor returns, thereby substantiating the economic rationale for governments to maintain and strengthen air pollution control efforts.

The main structure of this paper is as follows: Sect 4.2 presents a literature review. Section 4.3 discusses the theoretical mechanisms and research hypotheses. Section 4.4 outlines the empirical design. Section 4.5 presents the empirical results and analysis. Finally, Sect. 4.6 offers the conclusion.

4.2 Literature Review

4.2.1 Air Pollution and the Stock Market

As previously discussed, air pollution, as an environmental factor, impacts the stock market through investor sentiment, much like factors such as sunlight, temperature, and precipitation. Psychological studies, exemplified by Evans et al. (1987), have demonstrated that exposure to severe air pollution can influence individuals' psychological and emotional states, exacerbating feelings of distress, stress, and anxiety. These emotions can manifest in the trading behavior of investors.

Current research on the relationship between air pollution and stock returns is relatively limited, primarily focusing on market-wide and sectoral analyses using market indices. Foreign scholars, such as Levy and Yagil (2011), utilized data on the Air Quality Index and stock return rates from the four major U.S. stock exchanges between 1997 and 2007. They found that stock returns on days with "unhealthy" air quality were significantly lower than those on days with "healthy" air quality, confirming a negative correlation between air quality and stock returns. They suggested that air pollution negatively affects investor sentiment, increasing investors' risk aversion and ultimately leading to lower stock returns. Li and Peng (2016) conducted research using data from the Chinese stock market and found that air pollution could induce depressive moods in investors, thus influencing the stock market.

In summary, existing research indicates that air pollution affects the stock market through two main channels: investor sentiment and rational fundamental analysis. The former approach considers air pollution as an environmental factor that leads to physiological and emotional changes in investors when exposed to polluted air. This, in turn, makes their trading expectations more pessimistic and their risk preferences more conservative. The latter perspective views air pollution as a source of information. Investors incorporate their experiences of air pollution, media coverage of air pollution, and government policies addressing air pollution as crucial pieces of information when making investment decisions.

4.2.2 Factors Affecting the Performance of IPO Listings

Regarding the abnormal first-day and subsequent excess returns in Initial Public Offerings (IPOs), scholars primarily attribute them to the underpricing in the primary market issuance price and the overvaluation in secondary market trading prices. Concerning the perspective of underpricing in the primary market, researchers mainly investigate it from the angle of a three-way game involving underwriters, the issuing companies, and investors. Welch (1989) and Carter and Manaster (1990) both put forward the underwriter reputation theory, suggesting that underwriters, motivated by concerns about their reputation and brand image, reduce the risks associated with the IPO by opting for a lower offering price. In practice, many more scholars have focused on the overvaluation of secondary market prices, arguing that the soaring investor sentiment creates IPO price bubbles (Shiller 1990). Ritter (1986) and Dorn and Sengmueller (2009) attribute first-day excess returns to the presence of irrational investors in the market, contending that it is the investors' enthusiastic emotions and optimistic expectations that lead to high underpricing. Clarke et al. (2016) further dissect underpricing into two components: IPO underpricing before the issuance and first-day premiums after the IPO. They used IPO data from the Indian market to validate the significant influence of investor sentiment theory on IPO underpricing. Neupane et al. (2014) also argues that when investor sentiment is more optimistic, the first-day returns in IPOs tend to be higher, and the risk of trading below the offer price (breaking issue price) is lower.

Some scholars go even further to suggest that the overvaluation in the secondary market affects the pricing in the primary market, implying that underwriters use the trend of overvalued secondary market prices to set higher offering prices to maximize their profits. Combining underwriters' profit motives, Ljungqvist et al. (2006) and Derrien (2005) propose that underwriters often exploit the excessively optimistic sentiment of noise traders to lead the new shares to be issued at an intermediate price higher than the intrinsic value but lower than the noise traders' expected price.

This allows underwriters to earn more revenue while maintaining their reputation. Ruud (1993) views underwriters as market makers who use investors' heightened optimism to boost the offering price, thereby driving up the secondary market price of the stock. However, this behavior increases the probability of the stock trading below the offer price, so underwriters, to safeguard their reputation, will to some extent restrain this behavior. Just as in Carter and Manaster's (1990) study, underwriters lower IPO underpricing levels to maintain their reputation, suggesting that underwriter reputation has a positive impact on the pricing of new stock issues. In addition to the factors mentioned above, investor attention to the listed companies also influences the IPO performance. Grullon et al. (2004) and Chemmanur and Yan (2019) found that listed companies utilize advertising and other forms to attract investors' attention. Companies with higher advertising expenses attract both retail and institutional investors, leading to larger excess returns in the current year and smaller excess returns in the following year.

4.2.3 Investor Sentiment and Investor Attention

Analyzing the existing research on air pollution and the IPO market, it becomes evident that investor sentiment and investor attention play significant roles. Air pollution affects the stock market by influencing investor sentiment and attracting investor attention, and the IPO market, as an integral component of the stock market, is profoundly influenced by investor sentiment.

4.2.3.1 Investor Sentiment, Investor Attention, and Stock Markets

Research on investor sentiment has a long history. As early as 1936, Keynes observed that individuals with high levels of sentiment tend to make overly optimistic judgments, while those with low sentiment tend to be overly pessimistic. Driven by this "animal spirits", market prices can exhibit significant fluctuations unrelated to fundamentals. Long (1990) formally established the role of investor sentiment in financial markets, leading to more noise trading, greater mispricing, and excessive volatility.

The application of investor sentiment in the stock market primarily focuses on understanding how investor sentiment influences stock performance. This includes its impact on stock returns and return volatility. The analysis of the impact on stock returns encompasses its effects on the overall market, short-term and long-term horizons, and different types of stocks. For instance, Brown and Cliff (2005) discovered a correlation between investor sentiment and short-term as well as long-term returns, revealing a negative relationship between current investor sentiment and future returns over 1–3 years. Baker and Wurgler (2006) studied various types of stocks and found that fluctuations in investor sentiment significantly affect the returns of stocks that are highly subjective and difficult to arbitrage, such as small-cap stocks, high-volatility stocks, unprofitable companies, dividendless stocks, and extremely growth-oriented stocks. Research on the influence of investor sentiment on market volatility, as observed by Lee et al. (2002) and Kumari and Mahakud (2015), indicates that changes in investor sentiment have a notable impact on return volatility.

4.2.3.2 Investor Sentiment and Investor Attention Proxies

Investor sentiment is a challenging concept to measure directly, and in research, it is typically constructed through four main approaches. The first method involves survey-based data construction. Surveys and questionnaires are distributed to collect responses reflecting investors' bullish or bearish expectations of future stock prices. Examples of sentiment indicators created this way include the Consumer Sentiment Index (CSI) from the University of Michigan. In China, similar sentiment indicators include the CCTV Stock Index (BSI) and the Investor Confidence Index (ICI). The second approach involves extracting keywords from internet platforms and media reports to construct sentiment indicators. For instance, Tetlock (2007) quantitatively characterized pessimistic sentiment indices from media reports and used them to predict stock price movements. The third approach directly utilizes market trading data to construct sentiment indicators. Commonly used data points for this purpose include discounts on closed-end funds, trading volumes on the first day of IPOs, IPO first-day returns, and the number of new account openings. Prominent examples of this approach can be found in studies by Lee et al. (1991) and Baker and Stein (2004). More recently, many scholars prefer to combine the above-mentioned indicators into composite sentiment indices to create more comprehensive proxies for investor sentiment, as demonstrated by Baker and Wurgler (2006).

The final method involves building sentiment indicators using weather-related elements, which are also relevant to the subject of this study. Researchers often use weather factors such as sunshine duration, temperature, wind speed, and others as proxies for investor sentiment influenced by weather conditions. For example, Saunders (1993) utilized cloud cover in New York as a proxy variable to study the relationship between weather and stock market returns. The study found a strong correlation between stock returns on the New York Stock Exchange and local cloud cover, with this relationship being mediated by the sentiments of traders within the exchange. Among various weather indicators, air quality or air pollution can serve as a measure of good or bad weather. Unlike other climate indicators, air quality is more objective and not influenced by individual preferences. Different people may have opposing evaluations of the same weather conditions based on their personal preferences. However, poor air quality can lead to discomfort and is uniformly disliked. Therefore, using air quality as a proxy for sentiment has its rationale and advantages.

Investor attention, a concept that has gained prominence in recent years, is an important proxy variable used to explain rational investment behavior. The concept of investor attention is rooted in the psychology of limited attention theory, which posits that attention is a scarce cognitive resource, and focusing on one thing inevitably comes at the cost of neglecting another (Kahneman 1973). Due to constraints of time and mental resources, investors, particularly individual investors, often struggle to timely access and fully comprehend market information. Consequently, they typically rely on the information they are attentive to for analysis and decision-making when it comes to investments. As Rosa and Durand (2008) observed, investors subject to constraints on their attention may exhibit decision biases influenced by the information they focus on. This suggests that investor attention to a particular set of information can reflect the impact of that information on the market from a fundamental perspective. Therefore, employing investor attention as a proxy variable is a means to reflect the rational decisions made by investors based on information.

4.3 Analysis of Theoretical Mechanisms and Research Hypotheses

4.3.1 Theoretical Foundations

Traditional financial theories, rooted in the assumptions of rationality and the efficient market hypothesis, form the foundation for the study of asset pricing. These theories propose that investors make decisions in a fully rational manner, seeking to maximize expected utility by promptly and adequately processing all available market information. However, in the late twentieth century, numerous anomalies in the stock market, such as the "January effect," "Monday effect," "equity premium puzzle," and more, could not be explained by classical financial theory. This prompted scholars to relax the foundational assumptions of entirely rational investors and efficient markets, leading to the incorporation of disciplines like psychology, behavioral science, and sociology into the research of stock market investment behavior and pricing mechanisms. Behavioral finance emerged as a result.

The body of research in behavioral finance challenges the traditional assumptions of finance. Concerning the rationality assumption, behavioral finance contends that investors' decision-making is not solely based on rational beliefs. Human cognition is subject to limitations and decision biases, leading to phenomena such as overconfidence, ambiguity aversion, and prospect theory. Regarding the efficient market hypothesis, behavioral finance argues that not all participants are completely rational. Even rational investors are influenced by factors like time, capital, risk, and the availability of alternatives, which means they cannot always exploit arbitrage opportunities resulting from noise trading. Consequently, stock markets cannot rapidly eliminate mispricing, and stock prices may not fully reflect all available information.

Given that this study focuses on air pollution and the IPO market, the former has been validated by numerous studies to affect emotions, while the latter exhibits anomalies such as excess returns in reality and is believed by many researchers to be influenced by investor sentiment. Therefore, this study incorporates relevant theories from behavioral finance as its foundational framework.

4.3.1.1 Limited Rationality

In 1938, the founder of the social systems school, Chester Barnard, offered a revision of the classical economists' concept of the "completely rational economic man" in his work "The Functions of the Executive." He contended that humans are not the "appendages of a machine" or "passive production tools" as suggested by scientific management theory. Instead, he argued that people possess the capability to make choices and decisions, and exercise free will, even though these decision-making and choice abilities are limited by various biological, physical, and social forces from the past and the present. This concept is often referred to as "bounded rationality."

Renowned American sociologist and representative of the decision theory school, Herbert Simon, inherited and expanded upon this notion. He posited that no one can have a complete understanding of every factor that influences a decision, estimate every possible outcome and its associated probability, and rank these outcomes according to preferences. This is because people usually cannot access all the information relevant to their decisions. Human cognitive abilities are limited, and decisions are influenced by factors like learning, memory, habits, and psychology. Consequently, people are typically boundedly rational.

Under this fundamental assumption of bounded rationality, scholars, when studying the optimization of economic decisions, incorporate the constraint of the limited processing capacity of the human brain. They argue that due to cognitive limitations, individuals can only make suboptimal decisions under constraints and cannot achieve the optimal outcomes that would be possible under complete rationality.

4.3.1.2 Limited Attention

Attention, in psychological concepts, refers to the pointing and focusing that people show towards something, and is part of the cognitive process, accompanied by perception, memory, thinking, imagination and other mental processes. Since attention is directional and focused, i.e., people will selectively reflect part of the phenomenon and discard another part of the phenomenon, and stay on the phenomenon of the reaction and inhibit other external interferences when carrying out mental activities, the attention usually referred to is selective attention. Selective attention is limited attention, because at the same time people can only perceive a part or a certain thing so as to obtain a clear and complete reflection of things, it is impossible to perceive all things.

Behavioral finance absorbs the relevant research results of psychology, and believes that one of the important reasons for the "limited attention of economic man" is that there are cognitive limitations, that is, the human brain's ability to analyze and process information is limited, so at any given moment, people can not deal with all the information, but selectively respond to part of it, such as the most significant and important information. Important information. The limited attention theory proposed by Kahneman in 1973 views attention as a scarce resource from the perspective of cognitive resources, arguing that a person pays attention to one object at the expense of his or her attention to another object. The premise of this theory is that people are cognitively limited in the processes of perception, memory, thinking, and imagination. At the same time, the theory also suggests that allocable attention resources are affected by an individual's level of arousal, and that the higher the level of arousal, the higher the utilization of resources, and the more attention can be devoted to doing more and more difficult things. The level of arousal is stimulated by mental activity, emotional changes and various external factors according to one's needs.

For an investor, the attention required to learn, analyze and process the many pieces of information available in the market is a necessary information cost. Individuals have limited attention, so the attention behavior that an investor generates for a particular event at the expense of attention to other information increases the importance of that particular event in decision making, because investors can only rely on the information obtained from limited attention behavior for their investment decisions.

4.3.1.3 Limited Arbitrage

Traditional finance theory posits that even if investors engage in irrational trading behaviors leading to mispricing, rational investors will invariably arbitrage these mispricing, thus efficiently eliminating them in a timely manner. However, this assertion contradicts the many discrepancies found in real market situations and has been challenged, especially with the introduction of the concept of limited arbitrage in the 1990s. Limited arbitrage points out that when mispricing occur, rational investors who aim to profit from them and restore market equilibrium face three obstacles: constraints involving perfect substitutes, risks associated with noise traders, and implementation costs.

The key to effective arbitrage lies in whether suitable substitute securities can be found for the arbitrage operation. However, in most cases, markets cannot provide appropriate substitutes for arbitrageurs to engage in riskless hedge trades. Even if fully substitutable security products exist in the market, arbitrageurs' actions are still constrained by limitations on time and capital. As the period for asset prices to revert to their fundamental value is relatively long, it is only when arbitrageurs have sufficient capital to hold securities and possess a holding period longer than the duration of the mispricing that security prices will gradually approach their fundamental values. Due to constraints related to capital and time, arbitrageurs cannot engage in securities trading or may have to sell or purchase relevant assets before the price correction takes place, limiting the effectiveness of arbitrage. Furthermore, when irrational investors cause price discrepancies in securities, the arbitrageurs' actions aimed at correcting these discrepancies may, in turn, exacerbate the deviations due to the noise trading of irrational investors, necessitating the allocation of additional capital and time to rectify these distortions.

For various reasons, such as market imperfections, irrational investors, and inadequate incentive mechanisms, arbitrageurs' actions are restricted, and market prices that are mispriced either remain partially uncorrected or persist for extended periods in the market.

4.3.2 *Theoretical Foundations of Psychology*

Medical research indicates that air pollution can have physiological effects on human health, with severe air pollution capable of triggering respiratory issues, cardiovascular problems, and more. Physiological discomfort can translate into psychological and emotional responses. Psychological studies have shown that exposure to air pollution can lead to elevated levels of cortisol in the human body, causing metabolic disruptions and resulting in emotional changes, leading to feelings of anxiety and depression (Evans et al. 1987).

Psychological and emotional states can influence human behavior. Therefore, the impact of air pollution on an individual's emotions further extends to their actions. Research by Morris (2000) found that individuals in positive or negative emotional states tend to make more optimistic or pessimistic decisions. Emotional changes can affect an individual's activities. Studies by Szyszkowicz (2010) have confirmed an association between air pollution and suicide attempts. Research by Levy and Yagil (2011) has established a link between air pollution and investors' negative investment behavior.

Hence, air pollution has negative effects on an individual's physical health and physiological experiences, ultimately leading to negative emotions such as distress, anxiety, stress, and sadness. As emotions influence behavior, air pollution ultimately has an adverse impact on human actions, resulting in aggressive, negative, and self-destructive behaviors.

4.3.3 *Mechanisms of Action and Research Hypotheses*

Drawing upon existing literature and research, this paper asserts that air pollution affects the IPO performance of publicly-listed companies through two distinct channels: the emotional channel and the fundamental channel.

4.3.3.1 Emotional Channels of Action

When air pollution, as an environmental factor, directly affects investors, it results in an increase in the cortisol levels in their bodies. Cortisol, as a stress hormone, can lead to metabolic disruptions in the human body, exacerbating negative emotions like depression, anxiety, tension, helplessness, and anger. Consequently, investors exhibit a negative bias in their assessments of things, giving rise to pessimistic sentiments (Evans et al. 1987). Studies by Levy and Yagil (2011) and Li and Peng (2016) have both found that air pollution influences the stock market through investor sentiment. Air pollution leads to pessimism and an increased aversion to risk, reducing investors' expectations and their willingness to trade, thus impacting the stock market. Extending this to the IPO market, air pollution-induced pessimism not only results in more negative expectations for IPO stocks but also diminishes investors' desire for excitement and risky behaviors in the IPO market, implying that investors' risk preferences tend to become more conservative during the process of trading new stocks. From both the perspective of future expectations and risk preferences, investors' willingness and enthusiasm to participate in IPO investments and to continue chasing IPO stocks decrease. Consequently, this leads to a reduction in the IPO's price fluctuations, turnover rates, and the number of consecutive days hitting the daily price limit. Therefore, when air pollution is considered an environmental factor, it affects the IPO performance through the emotional channel. This influence is predominantly negative; that is, the more severe (mild) the air pollution, the lower (higher) the IPO's price fluctuations and turnover rates after listing, and the shorter (longer) the consecutive days with the daily price limit. Based on these observations, we propose Hypothesis 1:

H1: Air pollution is significantly negatively correlated with IPO price fluctuations, turnover rates, and the number of consecutive days with a daily price limit.

4.3.3.2 Fundamental Role Channels

When air pollution is recognized as information by investors, its influence on the IPO stock's performance operates through the fundamental channel. Air pollution not only captures the attention of investors but also garners attention from the government and media. Reports by news media on air pollution, environmental policies enacted by government agencies, and measures for pollution control implementation all serve as information that investors capture, further stimulating their interest in air pollution.

Investor attention to air pollution-related information implies that investors make investment decisions based on air pollution. By gaining access to air pollution information, investors form judgments and predictions about IPO companies' policy environment, financial performance, future prospects, social reputation, etc., which subsequently influences their trading and investment strategies concerning IPO stocks. Particularly for IPO stocks in industries and businesses related to atmospheric pollution, investors pay special attention to the consequences of air pollution, such as environmental regulations, and their impact on the future development and operating profits of the companies. Based on this premise, we propose Hypothesis 2:

H2: Investor attention to air pollution is significantly related to IPO price fluctuations, turnover rates, and the number of consecutive days with a daily price limit.

In particular, worsening air pollution triggers and escalates public, media, and government attention toward air pollution. It is anticipated that relevant government departments will enact policies and regulations to regulate and control air pollution. For instance, the government may establish stricter pollution emission standards and harsher penalties for pollution violations, which would restrain high-pollution and high-emission behaviors of companies. Stringent environmental policies could impose greater pollution cost burdens and environmental pressures on industries such as coal, steel, and heating, which are characterized by high investments, pollution, and energy consumption in their production processes. Consequently, these policies could negatively impact their operational performance and future prospects. For example, during periods of severe air pollution, the government may supervise and manage high-pollution and high-emission companies' production activities through administrative orders, and even enforce production stoppages. Given the significant constraints that air quality imposes on a company's operations, air pollution can adversely affect a company's profitability. For IPO companies in highly-polluting industries, deteriorating policy environments due to air pollution may restrict and impair their operational performance and growth potential. Investors who take note of this issue would consequently lower their future expectations and investment intentions for such IPO stocks, resulting in poorer IPO performance.

Furthermore, it is also expected that government agencies will adjust relevant industrial policies to provide more favorable and supportive measures for environmental protection, pollution control, and related industries. For instance, companies engaged in environmentally friendly businesses like atmospheric pollution control, desulfurization, air purification, and air filtration receive support from environmental policies and industry policies. They may benefit from lower interest rates and more lenient borrowing standards for corporate loans. In terms of business operations, they enjoy government tax reductions and production subsidies, which significantly reduce their production and operation costs. This, in turn, has a positive impact on their profitability and future development. Moreover, in the context of air pollution, environmentally friendly businesses that contribute to monitoring, improving, and controlling air pollution garner favor with the public, media, and government. This helps them build a positive corporate image, which also plays a positive role in the future development of IPO companies. Therefore, for IPO companies in environmental protection, such as those involved in atmospheric pollution control, the optimized policy environment resulting from air pollution will have a positive impact on their operational performance and growth potential. Investors who notice this trend would raise their future expectations and investment intentions for such IPO stocks, leading to better IPO performance. Based on these considerations, we propose Hypothesis 3:

H3: Compared to non-pollution stocks, air pollution has a stronger negative impact on the IPO performance of pollution stocks. Compared to non-pollution stocks, air pollution has a weaker negative impact on the IPO performance of environmentally friendly stocks.

4.4 Empirical Design

4.4.1 Sample Selection and Data Sources

This study focuses on all A-share IPOs that successfully listed on the Shanghai and Shenzhen stock markets in China from January 1, 2014, to December 31, 2019, as its research sample. The research dataset comprises air quality index data, Baidu search index data related to air pollution, daily returns of the CSI 300 Index, IPO price change percentages, turnover rates, the number of days an IPO stock hit the daily price limit, as well as various company characteristics and issuance features. After filtering out samples with missing data, the sample size for this study consists of 1279 IPO stocks.

Data sources for this study include the following: the air quality index data is publicly released by the Ministry of Ecology and Environment of the People's Republic of China, providing hourly air quality data for key cities across the country. Daily Baidu search index data related to air pollution was collected through web scraping using Python. Daily returns of the CSI 300 Index, IPO performance data, basic company information such as location, and issuance details like the issue size, as well as corporate financial data including total assets, were sourced from the Wind and CSMAR databases. Underwriting rankings were obtained from the annual disclosure reports of the Securities Industry Association. The list of environmentally-focused concept stocks was obtained from the Ruixin database, and the catalog of heavily-polluting industries is based on the "Guidelines for Environmental Information Disclosure of Listed Companies" published by the Ministry of Environmental Protection in 2010.

4.4.2 Variable Setting and Indicator Definition

4.4.2.1 Main Explained Variables

The primary focus of this study pertains to the post-listing performance of IPOs. To gauge the level of investor activity and optimism regarding IPO stocks, three trading metrics are employed: IPO stock price change percentages since their initial public offering (IPO), trading turnover rates, and the number of days these stocks hit the daily price limit.

1. Stock Price Change Percentages (Underp). Data for IPO stock price changes on the first, third, and fifth trading days following their IPO are computed using information from the Wind and CSMAR databases. The calculation method is as follows: (closing price on the current day—closing price on the previous day)/ closing price on the previous day, with the option to use either a compound interest calculation or (closing price on the end date—closing price on the day before

the start date)/closing price on the day before the start date for multi-day price changes. Notably, when calculating the price change percentage on the first day of IPO, the IPO's primary market issuance price is used in place of the previous day's closing price, rendering the IPO's first-day price change equivalent to the IPO premium level. Higher price increases in IPO stocks signify greater optimism among investors, stronger buying intentions, and a more favorable performance upon listing.

It is worth noting that, with the exception of the Science and Technology Innovation Board, Chinese stock exchanges impose restrictions on the first-day price change percentages for all A-share IPOs: the maximum increase is capped at 44%, while the maximum decrease is capped at 64%. New stocks often experience consecutive daily limit-up scenarios within one to several trading days following their listing. Consequently, a significant portion of first-day price changes in the research sample approaches the 44% limit, limiting the effectiveness of reflecting IPO performance when evaluating results. Therefore, in the empirical testing process, this study additionally includes stock price change percentages for the first 3 and 5 days after listing, as well as the number of days when these IPO stocks hit the daily price limit to provide a more comprehensive assessment of IPO performance.

2. Stock Turnover (Turnover). Also known as "stock turnover ratio," it refers to the frequency of stock transactions in the market within a specific period. It is one of the indicators reflecting the liquidity of a stock. The calculation method is as follows: the trading volume during a certain period divided by the total number of issued shares, multiplied by 100%. A higher stock turnover rate indicates greater liquidity of the stock, more active trading and investment, and a higher willingness among people to purchase that particular stock. This corresponds to stocks in high demand. Similar to other metrics, data for the first, third, and fifth days following the IPO are computed using information from the Wind and CSMAR databases.
3. Consecutive Limit-Up Days (Limit). The term "consecutive limit-up days" refers to a specific candlestick pattern where a stock opens at the daily price limit and continues to trade at that limit until the closing. A stock experiences a consecutive limit-up day when there are a substantial number of buy orders at the opening price that quickly reach the daily price limit, while the number of sell orders is much lower. This pattern indicates strong investor confidence in the stock. The longer the duration of consecutive limit-up days, the stronger and more persistent the positive sentiment towards the stock. In this study, "consecutive limit-up days" refers to the number of consecutive days from the IPO listing date when a stock continuously reaches the daily price limit. Data for this metric are sourced from the Wind database.

4.4.2.2 Main Explanatory Variables

The main focus of this study is air pollution. Therefore, the Air Quality Index (AQI), which is a widely recognized and comprehensive measure of air pollution, has been selected as the proxy indicator for how air pollution affects investor sentiment. Additionally, the Baidu search index data, using air pollution-related search terms, has been chosen to represent the level of investor attention to air pollution.

1. Air Quality Index (AQI): The AQI is a national air quality assessment standard introduced in March 2012 and officially implemented in January 2014. It monitors six pollutants: sulfur dioxide, nitrogen dioxide, particulate matter less than 10 μm in diameter (PM10), fine particulate matter less than 2.5 μm in diameter (PM2.5), carbon monoxide, and ozone. Data is updated hourly, and the AQI presents these six pollutants using a unified evaluation standard. The AQI is divided into six levels: Level 1 is "Excellent," Level 2 is "Good," Level 3 indicates "Mild Pollution," Level 4 is "Moderate Pollution," Level 5 signifies "Heavy Pollution," and Level 6 represents "Severe Pollution."

   To use AQI data for this study, daily data for each city is first averaged from the 24-h AQI data provided by the Ministry of Ecology and Environment. Then, the national daily AQI data is derived by taking a weighted average of these regional daily data, where the weight is determined by the proportion of A-share trading volume for each region to the total A-share trading volume nationwide.

   The rationale for using a weighted average based on the proportion of A-share trading volume in each city is as follows: Cities with higher A-share trading volumes have more active investors, indicating a larger number of A-share investors and more funds invested in the A-share market in those areas. Therefore, it is expected that the number of investors participating in IPO market transactions and the capital invested in the IPO market in those regions will also be higher, resulting in a more significant impact on the IPO market. For this reason, the study employs the proportion of A-share trading volume in each city as a weight to calculate the weighted average AQI. This approach aims to ensure that the air pollution level in regions with the most active IPO trading is more prominently reflected in the overall air quality index.
2. Baidu Search Index for Air Pollution: The data used in this study includes daily Baidu search index values for keywords related to air pollution. These keywords consist of "air pollution," "air quality," "haze weather," "atmospheric pollution," "smog," and "PM2.5." The daily search index values for these keywords are averaged to obtain a single representative value. Given the substantial numerical difference between search index values and the values of the primary dependent variable, this dataset is subject to logarithmic transformation in this study. The Baidu search index is based on the search volume of Internet users on both desktop and mobile Baidu platforms, focusing on specific keywords. It calculates the weighted sum of the frequency of searches for these keywords on the Baidu web search engine. Just as Google search data is widely used for similar purposes in international studies, Baidu, as the largest domestic search engine in China,

provides a reliable source for estimating Chinese investors' level of concern about air pollution. Therefore, the Baidu search index for these keywords can effectively serve as a proxy variable to gauge investor attention to air pollution in China, reflecting the degree of concern among investors regarding air pollution.

4.4.2.3 Main Control Variables

The control variables used in this study are as follows, and the relevant data are all obtained from the Wind database and relevant official sources:

1. Company Characteristics Variables: Company Size (Scale): Measured as the logarithm of total assets before listing. Company Age (Age): The number of years since the company's establishment. Ownership Type (Soe): A binary variable indicating whether the company is state-owned (1 for state-owned, 0 for non-state-owned). Industry of the Listed Company (Industry): Categorized based on the company's registered scope of operations and the "Guidelines for Industry Classification of Listed Companies."
2. IPO Characteristics Variables: Underwriter Reputation (Underwriter): A binary variable indicating whether the lead underwriter is among the top ten underwriters, based on the annual ranking of stock underwriting amounts published by the China Securities Association (1 for top ten, 0 for not in the top ten). Offering Size (Liscale): The size of the IPO. Time to Listing (Liday): The number of days it takes for a company to go public. Price-to-Earnings Ratio at Listing (Liperatio): The price-to-earnings ratio when the company goes public. Offering Fee Rate (Issuerate): The fee rate for the IPO.
3. Stock Market Performance Variables: Market Return (Rmkt): The daily return of the China Securities Index (CSI) 300 Index, reflecting the overall market performance.
4. Environmental Stocks (envir) and Polluting Stocks (pollute): These are binary variables used for heterogeneity analysis. The list of environmental concept stocks is obtained from the Ruixi database and includes second-level environmental concept stocks, such as PM2.5 concept stocks and tailings control concept stocks. The list of polluting industries is sourced from the "Guidelines for Environmental Information Disclosure of Listed Companies" published by the Ministry of Ecology and Environment in 2010. These variables are introduced into the model for heterogeneity analysis to examine whether there are differences in the impact of air pollution on the performance of environmental and polluting stocks during IPO, providing supporting evidence for the influence of air pollution through the fundamental channel.

4.4.3 Model Construction

To analyze the impact of air pollution on investor behavior and IPO performance, this study employs air quality index and Baidu search index related to air pollution as explanatory variables. The dependent variables include IPO post-listing price changes, turnover rates, and the number of days with limit-up (one-character increase). The study controls for various factors, including company characteristics, offering features, market performance, as well as year, quarter, region, industry, and sector fixed effects. Multiple regression models are used to investigate the influence of air pollution on IPO performance based on the hypotheses and variable selection outlined above.

Given the hypotheses and variable selection, the model is constructed as follows:

Model 4.1: Testing the Impact of Air Pollution on IPO Performance:

$$\begin{aligned}\text{Performance}_{it} &= \alpha + \beta_1 AQI_{it} + \beta_2\text{Scale}_{it} + \beta_3\text{Age}_{it} + \beta_4\text{Soe}_{it}\\ &+ \beta_5\text{Liscale}_{it} + \beta_6\text{Liday}_{it} + \beta_7\text{Board}_{it} + \beta_8\text{Liperatio}_{it}\\ &+ \beta_9\text{Issuerate}_{it} + \beta_{10}\text{Rmkt}_{i,t-1} + \epsilon_{it}\end{aligned} \tag{4.1}$$

Model 4.2: Testing the Impact of Investor Attention to Air Pollution on IPO Performance:

$$\begin{aligned}\text{Performance}_{it} &= \alpha + \beta_1\text{Index}_{it} + \beta_2\text{Scale}_{it} + \beta_3\text{Age}_{it} + \beta_4\text{Soe}_{it}\\ &+ \beta_5\text{Liscale}_{it} + \beta_6\text{Liday}_{it} + \beta_7\text{Board}_{it} + \beta_8\text{Liperatio}_{it}\\ &+ \beta_9\text{Issuerate}_{it} + \beta_{10}\text{Rmkt}_{i,t-1} + \epsilon_{it}\end{aligned} \tag{4.2}$$

Here, "Performance" represents IPO stock performance, including price changes, turnover rates, and the number of days with limit-up. "AQI" denotes the average air quality index during the listing period, while "Index" represents the average Baidu search index during the listing period. Further details are presented in the following Table 4.1.

4.5 Analysis of Empirical Results

4.5.1 Descriptive Statistics

Before examining the relationship between air pollution and IPO performance, this section provides a descriptive statistical analysis of the key variables. Utilizing a mixed cross-sectional dataset, the table below illustrates that the average values of IPO first-day price changes and the number of days with limit-up are positive, yet they exhibit considerable standard deviations. Additionally, there is a significant range between the minimum and maximum values. This variation is due to the inclusion of

Table 4.1 Details of the variables performance, AQI and index

Variable		Definition
Performance	$Underp_1$	First day of trading up or down
	$Underp_3$	Listed 3 days up or down
	$Underp_5$	Listed 5 days up or down
	$Turnover_1$	Turnover rate on the first day of listing
	$Turnover_3$	Changing hands ratio in 3 days of listing
	$Turnover_5$	5-day turnover rate
	Limit	Number of days to limit up
AQI	AQI_0	Average AQI for 1–2 weeks prior to listing
	AQI_1	Average AQI for 1 week to 1 day prior to listing
	AQI_3	Average AQI from 1 week to 3 days before listing
	AQI_5	Average AQI from 1 week to 5 days prior to listing
	AQI	Average AQI from 1 week prior to listing to the halt
Index	$Index_0$	Average Baidu search index in the first 1–2 weeks before listing
	$Index_1$	Average Baidu search index from 1 week to 1 day before listing
	$Index_3$	Average Baidu search index from 1 week to 3 days before listing
	$Index_5$	Average Baidu search index from 1 week to 5 days before listing

IPOs from the Sci-Tech Innovation Board (STAR Market) in the sample, which often have substantial price fluctuations and are not subject to limit-up restrictions. Given that the A-share market in China imposes price limit rules, a large proportion of IPOs experience a 44% price change on their first day of trading. To mitigate this effect, the study also incorporates price changes over the first 3 and 5 days post-listing. The study comprises a total of 1279 IPO stocks, among which 129 are environmentally friendly (environmental stocks), 418 are pollution-related (pollution stocks), and 1199 stocks encountered limit-up periods of varying durations.

Both proxy variables for air pollution, AQI and PM2.5, exhibit substantial standard deviations and substantial differences between their minimum and maximum values. The averages for these variables are typically within the "good" to "slight pollution" range. It is noteworthy that the air pollution proxy variables, AQI and PM2.5, demonstrate a similar trend to the air pollution attention proxy variable, Index. However, the standard deviations of AQI and PM2.5 are smaller than that of Index, suggesting that investors may be particularly sensitive to fluctuations in air pollution, indicating a strong response to such changes (Table 4.2).

Table 4.2 Descriptive statistics

Variable	Observations	Mean	Std. Dev.	Min	Max
Limit	1207	9.8020	50.0460	0	29
Underp1	1278	48.0332	26.3025	−8.3794	400.1531
Turnover1	1279	4.8332	17.8000	0.0048	86.1931
AQI1	1258	78.8935	32.7657	0	226.5760
Index	2191	27.6302	33.6197	2.3567	612.4100
AQI5	1258	80.4970	24.4726	26.3403	173.7868
AQI	1187	81.0798	21.1624	27.4901	154.4141
Scale	1274	4.9898	0.4280	4.2216	7.5679
Liperatio	1279	32.2190	39.6901	8.5808	1270.9270
Age	1279	14.8006	5.7031	3.2603	61.0986
Liscale	1272	3.5300	0.3066	3	5.7033
Issuerate	1272	11.2618	4.5025	1.4663	29.5678
Rmkt	1279	0.0054	1.2532	−7.3902	5.5219

4.5.2 Correlation and Causal Analysis

Before investigating the impact of air pollution on IPO performance, this section initiates a Granger causality test to establish the statistical causation between proxy variables for air pollution and proxy variables for investor attention to air pollution. This aims to demonstrate that changes in air pollution lead to increased investor attention to air pollution, rather than merely being attributed to heightened environmental awareness. To assess the causal relationship between proxy variables for air pollution and proxy variables for investor attention to air pollution, the test for time series data stationarity is conducted, and the unit root test confirms that the time series data are stationary. The Granger causality test results are displayed in Table 4.3.

At a 1% significance level, it is revealed that air pollution is a Granger cause for investor attention to air pollution, while investor attention is not a Granger cause for air pollution. This is consistent with theoretical logic, implying that changes in air pollution induce increased investor attention to air pollution. The reverse causation is not supported. Thus, it is substantiated that heightened investor attention to air pollution is one of the consequences of air pollution.

Subsequently, this section also conducts a preliminary correlation analysis between proxy variables for air pollution, proxy variables for investor attention to

Table 4.3 Granger causality test

Null hypothesis	P-value	Results
AQI is not the Granger reason for index	0.000	Rejection of the null hypothesis
Index is not the Granger reason for AQI	0.324	Null hypothesis cannot be rejected

air pollution, and IPO performance indicators (price changes, turnover rate, and the number of days with limit-up). The results are presented in table below (Tables 4.4 and 4.5):

The data indicates that there exists a negative correlation between air pollution and IPO performance, while the relationship between investor attention to air pollution and IPO performance appears to be inconclusive. These initial findings align with our research hypotheses. In the subsequent analysis, we will introduce the necessary control variables and employ regression models for a more in-depth investigation.

Table 4.4 Correlation between air pollution and IPO listing performance

	aqi0	aqi1	aqi3	aqi5	aqi
underp1	−0.1809***	−0.1719***			
underp3	−0.2068***	−0.1925***	−0.1879***		
underp5	−0.1602***	−0.1631***		−0.1770***	
turnover1	−0.1605***	−0.1424***			
turnover3	−0.0593**	−0.0504*	−0.0333		
turnover5	−0.0551*	−0.0455		−0.0128	
limit					−0.119*

Note Due to space constraints, the above table contains multiple regression model variables and correlations between different model variables have been removed. *, **, and *** denote statistical significance at the 10%, 5% and 1% level, respectively

Table 4.5 Correlation between investors' air pollution concerns and IPO listing performance

	index0	index1	index3	index5	index
underp1	−0.0842***	−0.0845***			
underp3	−0.0575**	−0.0556**	−0.0535***		
underp5	−0.0966***	−0.1031***		0.1085***	
turnover1	−0.1061***	−0.1071***			
turnover3	−0.1063***	−0.1089***	−0.1099***		
turnover5	−0.1048***	−0.1110***	−0.1159***	−0.1190***	
limit					0.0053*

Note Due to space constraints, the above table contains multiple regression model variables and correlations between different model variables have been removed. *, **, and *** denote statistical significance at the 10%, 5% and 1% level, respectively

4.5.3 Direct Impact of Air Pollution on IPO Listing Performance

In this section, we investigate how air pollution directly affects the initial public offering (IPO) performance of stocks. We examine the impact of the air quality index on stock price fluctuations, turnover rates, and the occurrence of daily limit-up situations. Considering the prevailing high optimism on the first day of A-share IPOs in China, along with the existence of limits on daily price fluctuations, and drawing insights from existing literature that air pollution's influence on the stock market is primarily short-term, our research incorporates the analysis of price fluctuations and turnover rates not only on the first day but also during the first 3 and 5 days following IPO.

During the research process, we discover that the effect of air pollution gradually diminishes. Stock market performance is not solely influenced by the air quality on the same day but is also impacted by the prior air pollution conditions. Furthermore, the air pollution status continuously changes during the IPO process and can affect the current stock trading.

Taking these factors into consideration, our study evaluates the impact of air pollution on IPO stock performance in different timeframes: (1) The average air pollution levels in the 2 weeks preceding the IPO to the week before the IPO, and how they influence the stock's performance on the first day, over 3 days, and 5 days following the IPO; (2) The average air pollution levels from the week before the IPO to the IPO day itself and their effect on the stock's performance on the first day, over 3 days, and 5 days following the IPO; (3) The average air pollution levels from the week before the IPO to the third day after IPO and their influence on the stock's performance during the first 3 days, and from the week before the IPO to the fifth day after IPO for the stock's performance over 5 days, and from the week before the IPO to the end of the lock-up period to assess the effect on the number of consecutive limit-up days for the IPO stock.

The results of our multiple regression model for the investigation mentioned in point (1) are presented below (Table 4.6):

The table above examines the impact of average air pollution levels during the 2 weeks preceding the IPO to the week just before the IPO on the IPO stock's

Table 4.6 Impact of air pollution 1–2 weeks before listing on IPO listing performance

	underp1	turnover1	underp3	underp5
AQI0	−0.0628***	−0.0592***	−0.0830***	−0.0619***
	(−2.82)	(−3.81)	(−4.03)	(−3.16)
N	1249	1249	1249	1249
Adj.R^2	0.5403	0.5168	0.4704	0.5481

Notes SRobust t values are in parentheses. The regressions include all control variables, year FE, season FE, city FE, industry FE, and sector FE. *, **, and *** denote statistical significance at the 10%, 5% and 1% level, respectively performance on the first day, over 3 days, and 5 days. The results indicate that at a 99% confidence level, the average air pollution levels during the 2 weeks prior to the IPO exhibit a significant negative impact on the IPO stock's price fluctuations on the first day, over 3 days, and 5 days. However, the average air pollution levels during the 2 weeks prior to the IPO only have a significant negative impact on the stock's turnover rate on the first day. This suggests that air pollution before the IPO has a significant adverse influence on the stock's short-term performance, with the primary impact being on the price fluctuations.

We also conducted multiple regression models for the investigation mentioned in point (2), and the regression results are presented below (Table 4.7):

The table above investigates the impact of the average air pollution levels during the week leading up to the IPO until the day of the IPO on the IPO stock's performance on the first day, over 3 days, and 5 days. The results indicate that at a 95% confidence level, the average air pollution levels during the week leading up to the IPO until the day of the IPO have a significant negative impact on the IPO stock's price fluctuations on the first day, over 3 days, and 5 days. However, the average air pollution levels during the week leading up to the IPO until the day of the IPO only have a significant negative impact on the stock's turnover rate on the first day. This also suggests that air pollution before the IPO significantly affects the stock's short-term performance, with the primary impact being on the price.

We also conduct multiple regression models for the investigation mentioned in point (3), and the regression results are presented below (Table 4.8):

The table above examines the impact of average air pollution levels in the week leading up to the IPO until 3 days after the IPO on the IPO stock's performance over 3 days, and the impact of the average air pollution levels in the week leading up to the IPO until 5 days after the IPO on the IPO stock's performance over 5 days, as well as the impact of the average air pollution levels in the week leading up to the IPO until the end of the lock-up period on the IPO stock's continuous days with limit-up. The results show that at a 99% confidence level, the average air pollution levels in the week leading up to the IPO until 3 days after the IPO have a significant negative impact on the IPO stock's price fluctuations over 3 days. Similarly, at a 99% confidence level, the average air pollution levels in the week leading up to the IPO until 5 days after the IPO have a significant negative impact on the IPO stock's price

Table 4.7 Impact of air pollution on IPO listing performance from 1 week to the day before listing

	underp1	turnover1	underp3	underp5
AQI1	−0.0537**	−0.0461***	−0.0484**	−0.0773***
	(−2.13)	(−2.62)	(−2.33)	(−3.62)
N	1249	1249	1249	1249
Adj.R^2	0.5394	0.5147	0.4667	0.5494

Notes Robust t values are in parentheses. The regressions include all control variables, year FE, season FE, city FE, industry FE, and sector FE. *, **, and *** denote statistical significance at the 10%, 5% and 1% level, respectively

Table 4.8 Impact of air pollution during listing on IPO listing performance

	underp3	underp5	limit
AQI3	−0.0583***		
	(−2.62)		
AQI5		−0.1168***	
		(−4.75)	
AQI			−0.0126*
			(−1.93)
N	1249	1249	1184
Adj.R^2	0.4671	0.5527	0.5018

Notes Robust t values are in parentheses. The regressions include all control variables, year FE, season FE, city FE, industry FE, and sector FE. **, **, and *** denote statistical significance at the 10%, 5% and 1% level, respectively

fluctuations over 5 days. Additionally, at a 90% confidence level, the average air pollution levels in the week leading up to the IPO until the end of the lock-up period have a significant negative impact on the IPO stock's continuous days with limit-up. Continuous limit-up performance reflects the ability to maintain consistently high price increases, indicating that air pollution during the IPO period significantly affects short-term performance, with the primary impact being on price fluctuations.

From the empirical results mentioned above, it is evident that air pollution has a significant negative impact on the IPO stock's performance. This impact is primarily observed in the price fluctuations and continuous limit-up days of IPO stocks. The coefficients of the air pollution proxy variables are negative, aligning with research hypothesis 1. This indicates that as air pollution worsens, IPO stocks have lower price increases, lower turnover rates, and shorter continuous limit-up periods. Since the negative impact of air pollution is indiscriminate and does not target stocks of any particular nature, this paper argues that at this stage, it can be confirmed that air pollution operates through the channel of investor sentiment by influencing investor physical health. This influence prompts pessimistic sentiment, reduces risk appetite, lowers trading intent, and trading expectations, ultimately leading to poorer IPO stock performance when air quality is good.

4.5.4 Impact of Investors' Air Pollution Concerns on IPO Listing Performance

In this section, we examine the impact of investor attention to air pollution on the IPO stock's performance. We investigate the effects of the Baidu search index for air pollution on stock price fluctuations, turnover rates, and the number of days with limit-up performance. Similar to the previous section, we also consider the stock's price fluctuations and turnover rates over 3 and 5 days after the IPO.

Considering that the impact of investor attention to air pollution persists for some time, a stock's market performance is influenced not only by the attention to air pollution during the IPO period but also by the preceding attention to air pollution. Therefore, we examine the impact of air pollution attention on the IPO stock's performance both before the IPO (short-term) and during the IPO period.

Specifically, in this section, we examine: (1) The impact of the average air pollution attention in the 2 weeks leading up to the IPO until 1 week before the IPO on the IPO stock's performance on the first day, over 3 days, and over 5 days after the IPO. (2) The impact of the average air pollution attention in the week leading up to the IPO until the IPO day itself on the IPO stock's performance on the first day, over 3 days, and over 5 days after the IPO. (3) The impact of the average air pollution attention in the week leading up to the IPO until 3 days after the IPO on the IPO stock's performance over 3 days, and the impact of the average air pollution attention in the week leading up to the IPO until 5 days after the IPO on the IPO stock's performance over 5 days, as well as the impact of the average air pollution attention in the week leading up to the IPO until the end of the lock-up period on the IPO stock's continuous limit-up days.

The regression results for examination (1) using a multiple regression model are presented below (Table 4.9):

The table above examines the impact of the average air pollution attention during the 2 weeks leading up to 1 week before the IPO on the IPO stock's performance on the first day, over 3 days, and over 5 days after the IPO. The results indicate that at a 95% confidence level, the average air pollution attention during the 2 weeks leading up to 1 week before the IPO has a significant effect on the stock price fluctuations and turnover rates of the IPO stock on the first day, over 3 days, and over 5 days. This suggests that the attention of investors to air pollution prior to the IPO affects the short-term performance of the IPO stock. However, the direction of this impact is uncertain because the process of investors forming value judgments between their concern for air pollution and their investment decisions for IPO stocks, as discussed earlier, may lead to different outcomes for companies with varying environmental characteristics.

Table 4.9 Impact of air pollution concerns 1–2 weeks prior to listing on IPO listing performance

	underp1	turnover1	underp3	turnover3	underp5	turnover5
Index0	0.0018**	−0.0027***	0.0040***	−0.0054***	0.0035***	−0.0089***
	(2.11)	(−3.44)	(3.93)	(−5.44)	(3.47)	(−3.34)
N	1271	1271	1271	1271	1271	1271
Adj.R^2	0.5276	0.4652	0.5036	0.8239	0.5673	0.7354

Notes Robust t values are in parentheses. The regressions include all control variables, year FE, season FE, city FE, industry FE, and sector FE. *, **, and *** denote statistical significance at the 10%, 5% and 1% level, respectively

The regression results for examination (2), using a multiple regression model, are presented below (Table 4.10):

The results examined in the table above similarly demonstrate, with a 95% confidence level, that the average air pollution attention during the 1 week leading up to the day of the IPO significantly affects the IPO stock's performance on the first day, over 3 days, and over 5 days in terms of both price fluctuations and turnover rates. Furthermore, the direction of this impact remains uncertain.

The regression results for examination (3), employing a multiple regression model, are presented below (Table 4.11):

The results examined in the table above indicate, at a 99% confidence level, that the average air pollution attention during the week leading up to the first 3 days of trading after the IPO significantly affects both the price fluctuations and turnover rates. Furthermore, the average air pollution attention during the week leading up to the first 5 days of trading following the IPO significantly impacts both the price fluctuations and turnover rates with an uncertain direction. Additionally, the influence of air

Table 4.10 Impact of air pollution concerns on IPO listing performance 1 week to the day before listing

	underp1	turnover1	underp3	turnover3	underp5	turnover5
$Index_1$	0.0020**	−0.0027***	0.0043***	−0.0058***	0.0038***	−0.0099***
	(2.26)	(−3.38)	(4.17)	(−5.71)	(3.76)	(−3.82)
N	1271	1271	1271	1271	1271	1271
Adj.R^2	0.5277	0.4652	0.4987	0.8241	0.5678	0.7355

Notes Robust t values are in parentheses. The regressions include all control variables, year FE, season FE, city FE, industry FE, and sector FE. *, **, and *** denote statistical significance at the 10%, 5% and 1% level, respectively

Table 4.11 Impact of air pollution concerns during IPO on IPO listing performance

	underp3	turnover3	underp5	turnover5	limit
index3	0.0051***	−0.0071***			
	(4.42)	(−5.88)			
index5			0.0051***	−0.0138***	
			(4.21)	(−4.67)	
index					−0.0014*
					(−1.67)
N	1271	1271	1271	1271	1197
Adj.R^2	0.6784	0.8244	0.5685	0.7363	0.5031

Notes Robust t values are in parentheses. The regressions include all control variables, year FE, season FE, city FE, industry FE, and sector FE. *, **, and *** denote statistical significance at the 10%, 5% and 1% level, respectively

pollution attention during the week leading up to the expiration of the continuous trading limit (halted trading due to price limits) has also passed a significance test.

In summary, taking into account the control of key variables and fixed effects, it is evident that investor attention to air pollution significantly affects the IPO stock's market performance. This suggests that air pollution, from the perspective of fundamental analysis and value judgment, impacts investors' expectations regarding the future development of the stock. Consequently, it influences investors' decisions and behavior in participating in the IPO market.

4.5.5 Impact of Air Pollution on the IPO Performance of Environmental and Pollution Stock IPOs

Among the 1279 samples studied in this paper, there were 129 environmentally friendly stocks and 418 polluted stocks. As mentioned earlier, empirical tests used Baidu search index data related to air pollution as a proxy for investor attention to air pollution, confirming that air pollution can impact investor expectations and trading willingness through fundamental channels for IPO stocks.

Given this, it is natural to assume that air pollution would have varying effects on stocks with different levels of environmental friendliness. To investigate whether air pollution has different effects on environmental and polluted stocks, the stocks are first categorized for comparison. The average IPO returns, turnover rates, and days of trading limit-up were examined for different categories of stocks. It was found that there were significant differences in IPO returns, turnover rates, and days of trading limit-up between environmental and non-environmental stocks, as well as between polluted and non-polluted stocks.

To test whether air pollution has different impacts on the market performance of different types of IPO stocks, i.e., to verify if air pollution affects environmental concept stocks' IPO differently from non-environmental concept stocks' IPO, and if it affects pollution industry stocks' IPO differently from non-pollution industry stocks' IPO, this section introduces interaction terms AQI*envir and AQI*pollute into the model. The regression results are as follows (Table 4.12):

The results indicate, at a 90% confidence level, that concerning stock returns, the impact of air pollution during the 2 weeks leading up to 1 week before the IPO is significantly more favorable for environmental concept stock IPOs compared to non-environmental concept stock IPOs. It also significantly differs for polluted industry stock IPOs compared to non-polluted industry stock IPOs. At a 95% confidence level, for stock returns, the effect of air pollution during the week leading up to the IPO day is significantly more favorable for environmental concept stock IPOs than for non-environmental concept stock IPOs. Furthermore, at a 95% confidence level, regarding the consecutive days of trading limit-up, the impact of air pollution from the week leading up to the limit-up period is significantly more favorable for environmental concept stock IPOs compared to non-environmental concept stock

Table 4.12 Impact of air pollution on IPO listing performance

	underp5	underp5	underp5	underp5	Limit
AQI_0	−0.0548***	−0.0659***			
	(−2.87)	(−3.36)			
AQI_0 *pollute	−0.0190*				
	(−1.66)				
AQI_0 *envir		0.0399**			
		(2.35)			
AQI_1			−0.0794***		
			(−3.68)		
AQI_1 *envir			0.0374**		
			(2.22)		
AQI_5				−0.1192***	
				(−4.80)	
AQI_5 *envir				0.0370**	
				(2.19)	
AQI					−0.0143*
					(−1.85)
AQI*envir					0.0208***
					(2.72)
N	1249	1249	1249	1249	1185
Adj.R^2	0.5428	0.4897	0.5252	0.4976	0.5032

Notes Robust t values are in parentheses. The regressions include all control variables, year FE, season FE, city FE, industry FE, and sector FE. The regressions include all control variables, year FE, season FE, city FE, industry FE, and sector FE. *, **, and *** denote statistical significance at the 10%, 5% and 1% level, respectively

IPOs. This suggests that the influence of air pollution leads to significantly higher stock returns for environmental stock IPOs in the first 5 days of trading compared to non-environmental stock IPOs. Conversely, it leads to significantly lower stock returns for polluted stock IPOs in the first 5 days of trading compared to non-polluted stock IPOs. Additionally, the duration of trading limit-up for environmental stock IPOs is significantly longer than for non-environmental stocks.

Overall, the hypothesis that "air pollution significantly improves the performance of environmental stock IPOs compared to non-environmental stocks, while it significantly worsens the performance of polluted stock IPOs compared to non-polluted stocks" has been confirmed, though the latter's impact is relatively less pronounced. Significant differences in impact occur during the first 5 days of IPO trading, affecting stock returns and trading limit-up times. Considering the conclusions drawn earlier about the relationship between air pollution and investor attention to air pollution, it is reasonable to believe that there is a certain lag between when investors are exposed to air pollution information and when they begin to pay attention to it. Therefore, air pollution, through fundamental channels, takes a slightly longer time to influence investors' decisions regarding IPO stock investments. Furthermore, these effects pertain to investor expectations about stocks rather than their enthusiasm for participating in IPO trading.

4.6 Conclusion

This paper aims to investigate the presence and mechanisms of the impact of air pollution on the performance of IPO stocks. By reviewing relevant domestic and international literature, this study summarizes the theoretical mechanisms and channels through which air pollution affects the performance of IPO stocks. Subsequently, using the Air Quality Index and Baidu search index for keywords related to air pollution as proxies for air pollution and investor attention to air pollution, this study empirically examines whether air pollution has an impact on IPO performance, how air pollution influences IPO performance, and whether air pollution's effects differ for IPOs of environmental concept stocks vs. non-environmental concept stocks and for IPOs of polluted industry stocks vs. non-polluted industry stocks.

The empirical findings reveal the following: (1) Multiple linear regression models using the Air Quality Index as the focus demonstrate that air pollution has a significantly negative correlation with the post-IPO stock returns, turnover rates, and consecutive limit-up days. This suggests that air pollution significantly negatively affects IPO performance, primarily influencing stock returns and consecutive limit-up days. (2) Multiple linear regression models using the Baidu search index for air pollution as the focus reveal that investor attention to air pollution has a significant relationship with post-IPO stock returns, turnover rates, and consecutive limit-up days, indicating that investor attention to air pollution significantly impacts IPO performance. (3) The introduction of dummy variables for environmental concept stocks and polluted industry stocks into multiple linear regression models shows that the effect of air pollution on the stock returns and consecutive limit-up days of environmental concept stock IPOs is significantly more favorable compared to its effect on non-environmental concept stock IPOs. However, the impact of air pollution on the stock returns and consecutive limit-up days of polluted industry stock IPOs is significantly worse than its effect on non-polluted industry stock IPOs, although the supporting evidence for the latter is comparatively less. This implies that the influence of air pollution through fundamental channels is significant and can lead investors to prefer investing in IPOs of environmental concept stocks.

To examine the robustness of the empirical findings in this study, the proxy variables for air pollution were replaced. The Air Quality Index was replaced with the corresponding Air Pollution Level, and the regression analysis was conducted once again. Air Pollution Level categorizes the Air Quality Index based on numerical values, providing a more intuitive reflection of the air pollution conditions. The results of this empirical test were consistent with the results obtained from the original regression models constructed in this study. It reaffirms that air pollution significantly negatively affects IPO performance, that investor attention to air pollution significantly impacts IPO performance, and that air pollution's impact differs for IPOs of environmental concept stocks vs. non-environmental concept stocks and for IPOs of polluted industry stocks vs. non-polluted industry stocks.

In summary, through a combination of literature review and empirical research, this study concludes that air pollution does indeed influence the performance of IPOs. This influence is transmitted through both investor sentiment and rational fundamental analysis. Through the channel of sentiment, air pollution can dampen investor expectations and enthusiasm for participating in IPOs, leading to a significant reduction in IPO market performance. Through the fundamental analysis channel, air pollution captures investor attention, and this attention affects the valuation of IPOs, subsequently influencing their market performance. Specifically, for IPOs of environmental concept stocks and those in polluted industries, the policy and profitability effects of air pollution evidently influence investors' judgments of stock value and future returns, leading investors to favor environmental concept stock IPOs over polluted industry stock IPOs.

References

Baker M, Stein JC (2004) Market liquidity as a sentiment indicator. J Financ Mark 7(3):271–299

Baker M, Wurgler J (2006) Investor sentiment and the cross-section of stock returns. J Financ 61(4):1645–1680

Beatty RP, Ritter JR (1986) Investment banking, reputation, and the underpricing of initial public offerings. J Financ Econ 15(1):213–232

Brown GW, Cliff MT (2005) Investor sentiment and asset valuation. J Bus 78(2):405–440

Carter R, Manaster S (1990) Initial public offerings and underwriter reputation. J Financ 45(4):1045–1067

Chemmanur TJ, Yan A (2019) Advertising, attention, and stock returns. Q J Financ 9(3):1950009

Clarke J, Khurshed A, Pande A, Singh A (2016) Sentiment traders & IPO initial returns: the Indian evidence. J Corporate Financ 37:24–37

Derrien F (2005) IPO pricing in "hot" market conditions: who leaves money on the table? J Financ 60(1):487–521

Dorn D, Sengmueller P (2009) Trading as entertainment? Manag Sci 55(4):591–603

Evans GW, Jacobs SV, Dooley D, Catalano R (1987) The interaction of stressful life events and chronic strains on community mental health. Am J Community Psychol 15(1):23–34

Grullon G, Kanatas G, Weston JP (2004) Advertising, breadth of ownership, and liquidity. Rev Financ Stud 17(2):439–461

Kahneman D (1973) Attention and effort, vol 1063. Prentice-Hall

Kumari J, Mahakud J (2015) Does investor sentiment predict the asset volatility? Evidence from emerging stock market India. J Behav Exp Financ 8:25–39

Lee CMC, Shleifer A, Thaler RH (1991) Investor sentiment and the closed-end fund puzzle. J Financ 46(1):75–109

Lee WY, Jiang CX, Indro DC (2002) Stock market volatility, excess returns, and the role of investor sentiment. J Bank Financ 26(12):2277–2299

Levy T, Yagil J (2011) Air pollution and stock returns in the US. J Econ Psychol 32(3):374–383

Li Q, Peng CH (2016) The stock market effect of air pollution: evidence from China. Appl Econ 48(36):3442–3461
Ljungqvist A, Nanda V, Singh R (2006) Hot markets, investor sentiment, and IPO pricing. J Bus 79(4):1667–1702
Long JB (1990) Noise trader risk in financial markets. J Polit Econ 98(4):703–738
Morris WN (2000) Some thoughts about mood and its regulation. Psychol Inq 11(3):200–202
Neupane S, Paudyal K, Thapa C (2014) Firm quality or market sentiment: what matters more for IPO investors? J Bank Financ 44:207–218
Rosa SR, Durand RB (2008) The role of salience in portfolio formation. Pac Basin Financ J 16(1–2):78–94
Ruud JS (1993) Underwriter price support and the IPO underpricing puzzle. J Financ Econ 34(2):135–151
Saunders EM (1993) Stock prices and wall street weather. Am Econ Rev 83(5):1337–1345
Shiller RJ (1990) Speculative prices and popular models. J Econ Perspect 4(2):55–65
Szyszkowicz M, Willey JB, Grafstein E, Rowe BH, Colman I (2010) Air pollution and emergency department visits for suicide attempts in vancouver, Canada. Environ Health Insights 4:79–86
Tetlock PC (2007) Giving content to investor sentiment: the role of media in the stock market. J Financ 62(3):1139–1168
Welch I (1989) Seasoned offerings, imitation costs, and the underpricing of initial public offerings. J Financ 44(2):421–449

Chapter 5
Hazy Perceptions: How Air Pollution Colors Customer Ratings

Abstract Our study examines the negative impact of air pollution on consumer reviews. Using a unique dataset, we find that higher air pollution, measured by the Air Quality Index (AQI), leads to lower restaurant ratings while featuring a significant nonlinear pattern for more severe pollution (AQI > 200). Moreover, air pollution can exert both immediate and cumulative effects on consumer reviews. A 25-day average AQI increase of one standard deviation will result in a 0.011-point reduction in ratings. Sentiment analysis can also support our findings, which helps us identify consumer sentiments as a pivotal mechanism through which air pollution adversely affects consumers' dining experience. Our paper provides the first precise estimation of air pollution's negative impact on consumer reviews, emphasizing the importance of improving air quality to enhance consumer experiences.

Keywords Air pollution · Emotions · Consumer reviews · Sentiment analysis

5.1 Introduction

A substantial body of extant research has demonstrated the detrimental effects of air pollution on people's physical well-being (Dockery and Pope III 1994; Pope III 2000; Pope III and Dockery 2006). Air pollution significantly harms the human respiratory and cardiovascular systems, giving rise to respiratory infections, heart disease, chronic obstructive pulmonary disease, stroke, lung cancer, and other diseases. It is estimated that in 2012, approximately seven million deaths were attributed to air pollution, constituting one-eighth of the total global mortality count.[1] The economic ramifications caused by reduced productivity and diminished quality of life due to air pollution are translated into an annual loss of $5 trillion for the world economy.[2]

[1] This is the estimation sourced from the World Health Organization. (https://www.who.int/mediacentre/news/releases/2014/air-pollution/en/).

[2] More comprehensive information can be found in https://www.commondreams.org/news/2016/09/08/making-case-clean-air-world-bank-says-pollution-cost-global-economy-5-trillion.

M. Guo et al., *Social-Economic Impacts of Air Pollution*, Climate Change and Energy Transition, https://doi.org/10.1007/978-981-96-7858-7_5

Air pollution also poses risks to individuals' mental health. Previous research shows that elevated concentrations of fine particulate matter (PM2.5), a component of air pollution, not only damage individuals' physical health but also undermine their psychological well-being (Evans et al. 1988; Zijlema 2016). Tallon (2017) demonstrate that prolonged exposure to high concentrations of fine particulate matter, nitrogen dioxide, and other air pollutants induces emotional disturbances, ultimately resulting in impairments in cognitive function. Yin (2018) surveyed 1709 participants in Beijing to assess the welfare losses attributed to air pollution. They find that the welfare losses in terms of health and emotional impacts caused by fine particulate matter pollution are equivalent to 1388.4 yuan/person-year and 897.7 yuan/person-year, respectively. On the one hand, this reveals the adverse effects of air pollution on people's health status. On the other hand, it underscores the heightened emphasis the public places on their emotional well-being and happiness. Hence, the negative impact of air pollution on individuals' emotions ought not to be underestimated.

Air pollution can impact individuals' emotions, and these sentiments can influence their decision-making process in turn (Forgas 1991). Despite the considerable studies assessing the impact of emotions (triggered by air pollution, weather, seasons, etc.) on economic behaviors (Levy and Yagil 2011; Hirshleifer and Shumway 2003; Kamstra et al. 2003), to the best of our knowledge, there has been no in-depth study conducting the causal inference between air pollution and consumer evaluations through the emotional channel. Thus, this paper can help fill the gap.

Currently, numerous websites have amassed substantial online consumer review data that reflects consumers' appraisals of their personal consumption experiences. Prior research has demonstrated that online comments written by previous consumers can aid potential consumers in understanding the quality of products, thus mitigating issues of information asymmetry (Reinstein and Snyder 2005; Duflo and Saez 2002). Furthermore, the ratings assigned by consumers can significantly impact restaurant sales volumes and revenues (Anderson and Magruder 2012; Luca 2016). The consumer online review data we collected originates from Dianping, a platform established in 2003 which primarily provides information about businesses in various sectors, including dining, shopping, leisure, and lifestyle services, across massive cities in China. Over years of development, it has accumulated a rich repository of consumer review data. Consequently, this research has procured all restaurant information and related review data from Dianping for the year 2015 in Beijing, aiming to investigate the causal relationship between air pollution and consumer evaluations.

In terms of theoretical significance, previous research has indicated that air pollution can affect various aspects of individuals such as labor supply, labor productivity, and cognitive abilities (Hanna and Oliva 2015; Zivin and Neidell 2012; Ebenstein et al. 2016). This suggests that the harmful effects of air pollution on individuals are exerted through both physiological and psychological pathways. Our study explores how air pollution impacts individuals' assessments, thus offering new evidence regarding the adverse effects of air pollution on human beings. On another note, we also seek to demonstrate whether air pollution, as an exogenous shock, influences consumers' consumption experiences, subsequently changing their ratings.

This study can thus provide a valuable complement to the field of consumer evaluations. With regard to real-world significance, the focus of this paper pertains to the following questions: Does air pollution affect consumer evaluations? If it does, what is the magnitude of this impact, and does heterogeneity exist? Apart from its immediate influence, does air pollution also entail cumulative effects, and do the effects vary with different lengths of exposure duration to air pollution? Answering these questions is instrumental in comprehending the causal link between air pollution and consumer assessments. Moreover, we estimate the impact of consumer ratings on overall restaurant ratings and the effect of overall restaurant ratings on their rankings and customer visibility. This indicates the potential negative effect air pollution inflicts on restaurant revenues, hence underlining the necessity for restaurants to employ corresponding strategies to counterbalance the systemic bias caused by severe air pollution.

To accurately dissect the relationship between air pollution and consumer evaluations, we have implemented the following strategies. Initially, we collected data encompassing over five million reviews and restaurant details from Dianping, a popular online platform, for all establishments in Beijing during the year 2015. This extensive and unskewed dataset can elevate the reliability of our findings. Subsequently, we generated a unique panel dataset by precisely identifying consumer IDs and restaurant IDs so that consumer and restaurant fixed effects can be controlled to address the omitted variable concerns due to unobservable characteristics and potential estimation biases. Furthermore, we meticulously calculated air pollution levels across various administrative districts in Beijing to match consumer reviews with corresponding pollution data, thereby refining the precision of regression estimates. Air pollution not only undermines people's physical health but also jeopardizes psychological and emotional well-being, and emotions could further influence individuals' decision-making processes. Based on this mechanism, we analyze the "air pollution-emotion-evaluations" mechanism which we resort to sentiment analysis techniques on text to validate. We also thoroughly analyzed potential sample selection problems in the model specification section, and we find it unlikely that individuals would respond to air pollution preemptively by changing their dining plan. Therefore, we could substantially contend that our study accurately identifies the effect of air pollution on consumer assessments.

The main contribution of this paper is threefold. First, it fills the gap in the relationship between air pollution and consumer evaluations. According to our findings, with each standard deviation increase in the Air Quality Index (AQI), consumer ratings decrease by 0.002 points on average. This indicates a 20% higher probability of decreasing the overall restaurant rating and a decline of 34 positions in the restaurant's overall ranking. Moreover, we discover that the air pollution's impact on consumer evaluations is nonlinear, with the negative effect primarily driven by moderate to high levels of air pollution, namely when AQI is higher than 200. The effect of air pollution on consumer sentiments also amasses over time, with the cumulative effect reaching its maximum at an average AQI over 25 days, where one standard deviation increase brings about a consumer rating reduction of 0.011 points. A battery of robustness checks further confirms the credibility of our conclusions. Second, this paper comprehensively reviews the relevant literature linking air pollution, emotions, and evaluative judgments, providing support for the "air pollution-emotions-evaluative judgments" mechanism which is rationalized by discerning consumers' underlying emotional tendencies by virtue of sentiment analysis techniques on textual comments. A strong positive correlation between consumers' emotional tendencies and their ratings is then identified, while air pollution is significantly and negatively correlated to consumers' emotional tendencies. As a result, this study substantiates the plausibility of the mechanism by offering evidence that air pollution negatively impacts consumers' emotions. The innovative application of textual sentiment analysis to quantify consumer emotions also presents a novel method for investigating emotion-related matters in future research. Third, the identification of air pollution's effect on individuals' evaluations presents air pollution as one vital influencing factor in the evaluation process. Hence, the conclusions drawn in this research could also provide valuable implications for restaurant managers when severe air pollution occurs.

The rest of this paper is organized as follows. Section 5.2 reviews the existing literature on air pollution and som. Section 5.3 describes the data and variables while laying out hypotheses of the adverse effects of air pollution and discusses several endogenous concerns. Section 5.4 reports the baseline results, robustness checks, and mechanism results. Section 5.5 concludes.

5.2 Literature Review

This paper is related to several strands of literature, with the first pertaining to the impact of consumer reviews. From the perspective of consumers, people increasingly rely on relevant online rating platforms to make their consumption decisions. A survey carried out by Cone Communications Inc. in 2011 revealed that 64% of consumers search for online reviews about a particular service before purchasing it, and 85% of consumers are more likely to buy a service when there are online recommendations endorsing it. The same study found that 87% of consumers believe that positive consumer reviews would bolster their purchasing decisions, while 80% think that negative consumer evaluations could cause them to reconsider.

Specifically, customer assessments primarily assist customers in addressing the challenge of information asymmetry through expert recommendations and social learning. On the one hand, consumers can consult consumer reports and critiques authored by experts before buying the products or the service. Reinstein and Snyder (2005) document that favorable evaluations from professional movie critics would enhance movie box office revenues, and a more pronounced impact is expected on comedies and small-scale films. Additionally, Hilger et al. (2011) show that expert ratings on wine labels could impact consumers' demand for wine. On the other hand, consumers can interact with other consumers who have already bought the goods or dined at the restaurant to obtain information about the quality of their intended purchase. While these consumer evaluations may not feature the same level of professionalism as expert reports, their preferences should be more consistent with potential consumers. Studies by Duflo and Saez (2002) and Sorensen (2006) respectively suggest that the retirement and health plan choices of an employee influence that of other employees in the same department. Moretti (2011) discovers that individuals modify their judgments of movie quality according to feedback from other audiences. Cai et al. (2009) find that after acquiring information about the most popular dishes of a restaurant, customers' demand for these specific dishes increases by 13–20%. However, when it comes to the influence on service providers, relevant literature is limited due to the inaccessibility of restaurants' financial data. Anderson and Magruder (2012) utilize the regression discontinuity approach to analyze the effect of product reputation on reservation levels on Yelp and find that every half-star increase in restaurant rating results in a corresponding 19% increase in reservation rates. Similarly, Luca (2016) also adopts a regression discontinuity design to investigate the impact of Yelp ratings on restaurant revenues in the Seattle area, eventually revealing a significantly positive correlation between them.

Another strand this paper contributes to relates to the influence of air pollution. On account of the fact that suspended particulate matter is the predominant component causing air pollution, we would particularly focus on suspended particulate matter as a hazardous determinant. Initially, numerous early epidemiology studies have long quantified the exposure effect exerted by various air pollutants on physiological health (Dockery and Pope III 1994; Seaton 1995; Pope III 2000; Pope III and Dockery 2006). When it is limited to a specific group, Chay and Greenstone (2003a, 2003b) use the exogenous changes from the amendments to the U.S. Clean Air Act in 1970 and 1977 to estimate the impact of air pollution on infant mortality. Their findings suggest that each reduction of 1 $\mu m/m^3$ in suspended particulate matter is correlated to a decrease of 5–8 infant deaths per 100,000 newborns. Currie (2009) also find that high concentrations of carbon monoxide could lead to significantly increased absenteeism in students. In the context of China, previous research also links higher air pollution to shorter expected lifespans and higher cardiovascular mortality as the ramification of China's Huai River heating policy. On top of that, a range of extant literature also examines the repercussions of air pollution on labor forces. Aragon et al. (2016) find that every 10 $\mu m/m^3$ increase in PM2.5 results in a reduction in workers' weekly working hours by nearly 2 h, while Hanna and Oliva (2015) leverage the closure of a large petroleum refinery in Mexico City as a natural experiment and document that a 19.7% decrease in sulfur dioxide concentration leads to an increase of 1.3 h in residents' labor supply. Apart from that, prior research has also explored the negative effect that air pollution inflicts on labor productivity. Adhvaryu et al. (2014) reveal that with every 10 $\mu m/m^3$ rise in suspended particulate matter concentration, worker output is reduced by at least 0.3%/h based on a garment factory located in Bangalore. Chang (2016) utilize the production data from a pear packaging plant in northern California and discern that each 10 $\mu m/m^3$ increase in PM2.5 causes workers' productivity to decrease by $0.41. In the field of sports, Guo and Fu (2019) analyze a sample of more than 300,000 marathon runners from 56 marathon events held in 2014 and 2015 across numerous Chinese cities to obtain an elasticity of 0.041 for the influence of air pollution on these runners' finishing times. Finally, a series of preceding research has identified people's diminished cognitive abilities as the consequence of air pollution. In theory, given that the brain consumes a large portion of the inhaled oxygen, any deterioration in oxygen quality could have potential impacts on human cognitive abilities (Clark and Sokoloff 1999; Calderon-Garciduenas 2008). Moreover, ultrafine particles are minuscule substances that can be absorbed into the bloodstream and ultimately embedded into the brainstem (Oberdörster 2004). Disturbances in the central nervous system, cortical stress, and damage to cerebral blood vessels could then arise (Peters et al. 2006). Considerable medical studies have demonstrated the link between enhanced exposure to fine particles and deteriorated intelligence and cognitive abilities (Suglia 2008; Power 2011; Weuve 2012; Ailshire and Clarke 2015; Wilker 2015). Numerous empirical studies also lend support to this causation. Ebenstein et al. (2016) reveal that students tend to perform more poorly on days with higher concentrations of particulate matter based on the exam scores of the Israeli Bagrut (high school matriculation) exams between 2000 and 2002. Roth (2016) finds that every unit increase in PM10 could decrease students' exam scores by 0.06 points. Zhang et al. (2018) test the conclusion based on a broader population and assert that both long-term and short-term exposure to air pollution could significantly impede individuals' cognitive abilities according to their language and math test results.

Air pollution not only impairs physical health but also affects cognitive function, suggesting the broad impact air pollution exerts on the human body. Hence, we can hypothesize consumer emotions as an essential mechanism through which air pollution influences consumer evaluations. The effect caused by air pollution on individual emotions has been well-documented by preceding scholars. Specifically, aggressiveness, negative sentiments, and depression are all correlated with exposure to air pollutants. Herrnstadt (2016) present the first evidence of the causal link between short-term environmental pollution changes and violent crime: air pollution leads to a heightened daily incidence of violent crimes in Chicago and Los Angeles. Furthermore, it is found that the physical discomfort arising from air pollution would incur negative sentiments in individuals, such as anxiety and irascibility (Adgate et al. 2014). Zhang et al. (2017a, b) find that long-term air pollution could lead to dwindled happiness while increasing the occurrence of depressive symptoms. These emotional changes could then in return affect decision processes and economic behaviors. Existing research primarily approaches it from the perspectives of intertemporal choice, risk preferences, and social preferences (Tiedens and Linton 2001; Lerner and Keltner 2001; Sanfey 2003). Another string of literature also focuses on the influence of emotions on individuals' evaluative judgments. An individual's emotional status has been demonstrated to affect a multitude of evaluative judgments, including satisfaction with consumer goods (Isen 1978), assessments of others (Clore et al. 1988), assessments of past experiences (Clark and Teasdale 1985), and perceptions of overall life happiness (Schwarz and Clore 1983). In the field of consumer reviews, Bakhshi et al. (2014) document that consumers give higher ratings on days with milder weather conditions, and rainy or snowy weather also contributes to lower consumption ratings.

5.3 Data and Identification

5.3.1 Data

The consumer review data employed in this research are collected from Dianping.com, a major Chinese online consumer review platform. When submitting a review, consumers are required to provide ratings for three specific aspects in addition to the overall rating: taste, environment, and service ranging from 1 to 5. Moreover, consumers are encouraged to offer textual comments about their dining experience and exhibit relevant images. The relatively rich aspects involved in the evaluative process enable us to gain insights into consumers' dining experiences from diverse perspectives. Specifically, these four variables can be compared and cross-checked to consolidate our understanding of the adverse effects of air pollution. Furthermore, apart from investigating the impact of air pollution on consumer ratings, we also need to validate the mechanisms underneath, which can be achieved by utilizing text sentiment analysis techniques to identify consumer emotions in their textual comments. Therefore, gathering relevant information from the online platform is vital to conduct our research. We collected all the restaurant information and review data in Beijing from Dianping.com during a 1-year period (2015) and constructed three categories of variables based on that.

To mitigate the issue of omitted variables, we also include weather-related variables (temperature, precipitation, wind speed, air pressure, humidity, visibility) in our specification to account for the effect of other ambient factors that contribute to the variations in consumer evaluations. Hence, we collected daily weather data for Beijing in 2015 from Bloomberg's Global Weather Database. Particularly, we constructed a dummy variable to denote whether there was precipitation on a certain day. It is noteworthy that this data is collected from meteorological stations in Beijing, which merely captures city-level longitudinal variations. While the ideal situation would be to have access to daily weather data for each administrative district in Beijing, weather conditions do not showcase substantial variations among districts as air pollution does. Thus, we can confidently stick to our current variable setting.

Eventually, our air pollution data is obtained from the Beijing Municipal Environmental Monitoring Center. Numerous air quality monitoring stations are distributed across the various administrative districts in Beijing, which allows us to use hourly air pollution data from these stations in 2015. In addition to the Air Quality Index (AQI), we also have data for six specific air pollutants: fine particulate matter, inhalable particulate matter, carbon monoxide, nitrogen dioxide, ozone, and sulfur dioxide. The AQI is computed according to these six air pollutants to provide an all-sided reflection of daily air pollution conditions and is thus selected as the primary indicator of air pollution in our study. We also use PM2.5 as the robustness check for air pollution in the later analysis. Furthermore, we calculated the 24-h averages for each district's air pollution level. While we have street-level information for each restaurant and ideally could match the air pollution to every street, the unevenly distributed air quality monitoring stations across streets make it more feasible to calculate the 24-h average pollution level for each administrative district. The descriptions of all the variables referred to above are presented in Table 5.1.

Table 5.1 Variable description of consumer review data

Category	Variable	Definition
User-level variables	Overall	The overall rating scored on a range from 1 to 5
	Taste	The taste rating scored on a range from 1 to 5
	Environment	The environment rating scored on a range from 1 to 5
	Service	The service rating, which is scored on a range from 1 to 5
	User_ID	The unique ID for each user
	Price	The price of consumption
	Review	Textual reviews written by users
	Review_Num	The word count of textual reviews
Restaurant-level variables	Shop_ID	The unique ID for each restaurant
	Cuisine	The restaurant's main cuisine or specialty
	District	The specific administrative district
	Street	The specific administrative street
	Spending	The average spending per person
Time-level variables	Holiday	Dummy that equals 1 on the holiday and 0 otherwise
	Date	The date when the review is made
Weather variables	Average_Tem	Average temperature
	Rain	Dummy that equals 1 if it rains and 0 otherwise
	Wind_Speed	Wind speed (km/h)
	Humidity	Relative humidity (%)
	Air_Pressure	Air pressure (hPa)
	Visibility	Visibility (km)
Air pollution variables	AQI	Air quality index
	PM2.5	All measured in $\mu m/m^3$
	PM10	All measured in $\mu m/m^3$
	CO	All measured in $\mu m/m^3$
	NO_2	All measured in $\mu m/m^3$
	O_3	All measured in $\mu m/m^3$
	SO_2	All measured in $\mu m/m^3$

5.3.2 *Descriptive Statistics*

Our unique dataset is comprised of 16 districts, 27 cuisines, 58,621 restaurants, 1,507,566 reviewers, and 5,030,834 reviews, whose descriptive statistics are provided descriptive statistics in Table 5.2. It is observed that Chaoyang District, Haidian District, Dongcheng District, and Xicheng District have more restaurants, resulting in a larger number of reviews. Chaoyang District, the most prosperous district in Beijing, has the most restaurants and the largest number of reviews. By comparison, Pinggu District has the fewest reviews among its counterparts in Beijing. The average AQI in all districts throughout the year 2015 exceeded 85, and the average annual Air Quality Index (AQI) in certain districts was greater than 100, which indicates the rather severe air pollution issue Beijing confronted in that year. Additionally, the significant difference between maximum and minimum AQI values complements the existence of great standard deviations, thus suggesting nonnegligible variations in air pollution levels in Beijing in 2015. Therefore, it is essential to dig out the heterogeneous effects of air pollution in our research.

Table 5.2 Descriptive statistics

District	Number of restaurants	Number of reviews	AQI			
			Mean	Std.Dev	Min	Max
Chaoyang	18,686	1,924,104	118.6	81.9	492.2	14.9
Haidian	10,730	990,648	110.9	74.0	445.0	16.9
Dongcheng	5800	674,691	118.1	82.1	491.5	16.5
Xicheng	4546	458,131	123.0	86.3	489.3	15.2
Fengtai	5464	293,170	121.2	82.7	478.5	13.6
Daxing	2597	191,600	128.6	90.0	482.9	19.3
Changping	3313	153,348	96.3	67.6	459.2	17.5
Tongzhou	2336	120,079	130.3	87.7	455.1	22.2
Shijingshan	1079	104,772	117.5	78.5	484.2	16.1
Shunyi	907	45,436	111.7	81.0	441.9	13.5
Fangshan	659	30,624	135.1	95.2	496.9	21.3
Mentougou	461	14,140	99.7	69.4	488.2	15.0
Miyun	758	8808	89.0	66.3	463.1	13.8
Huairou	280	7762	100.0	72.5	438.5	15.0
Yanqing	543	7659	87.5	58.1	455.7	16.0
Pinggu	462	5862	107.7	73.0	481.1	18.1
Overall	58,621	5,030,834	112.2	79.6	471.5	16.6

5.3.3 Research Hypotheses

Based on the research evidence and mechanism analysis in the previous sections, our research posits three hypotheses as follows:

Hypothesis 1 Air pollution will negatively affect consumer reviews during the evaluative process. We expect an immediate negative effect of air pollution inflicted on consumers' emotions, thus affecting their evaluations of the dining experience.

Hypothesis 2 The effect of air pollution on consumer reviews is heterogeneous and features nonlinearity. According to the classification criteria of the Air Quality Index, the influence of air pollution on healthy individuals and susceptible individuals differs at different levels, and people might demonstrate adaptability to air pollution.

Hypothesis 3 The negative effect of air pollution on consumer emotions is cumulative. Thus, constant exposure to air pollution ought to result in more pronounced negative effects on consumer evaluations. He et al. (2019) find that workers' productivity exhibits no significant prompt response to air pollution, but exposure to fine particulate matter for over 25 days can reduce productivity by 1%. Moreover, Zhang et al. (2018) document that a higher 7-day average Air Pollution Index could reduce individuals' cognitive abilities. These studies suggest that the long-term cumulative effects of air pollution on human behaviors should be considered. Thus, we hypothesize that as the duration of air pollution exposure broadens, a more substantial cumulative effect should be observed.

5.3.4 Endogeneity

This paper aims to figure out the impact of air pollution on consumer reviews, with AQI serving as our key independent variable. Despite controlling for weather conditions in our specification, several endogenous problems can still preclude precise causal estimates, which are discussed as follows.

Our first concern is omitted variables. Various consumer-related factors such as physical tolerance, food preferences, gender, education level, income, etc. are likely to be associated with air pollution and could be involved in their evaluative processes. Our estimates might thus be biased. Similarly, various restaurant-specific characteristics such as geographical location, cuisine classification, operating situation, average spending per person, etc., might also bias our estimates. To alleviate such concerns, given that individual and restaurant characteristics do not change in the short term (e.g., in a year), we resort to user and restaurant fixed effects to address the omitted variable problem by controlling for individual heterogeneity of both users and restaurants. We also employ a multiple fixed-effects model for estimation, which allows us to control for both consumer and restaurant fixed effects in the model estimation.

Second, there is a sample selection issue. Individuals' exposure to air pollution levels is often unevenly distributed. Chay and Greenstone (2005) already show that individuals tend to purchase houses in areas with better air quality. Furthermore, even if air pollution is exogenous, individuals can respond by reducing their time outdoors, thus making their exposure to air pollution endogenous. However, we assume that air pollution has little effect on the dining experience. The main reasons are the following. With an annual average AQI exceeding 100, the air pollution issue in Beijing is relatively severe. Consequently, residents might have adapted to moderate air pollution levels and their daily activities are thus unlikely to be affected. Air pollution also mainly affects outdoor activities while dining mostly occurs indoors and does not require substantial physical activity. Therefore, it can be inferred that air pollution has a minimal impact on dining itself. Moreover, in 2015, public awareness of air pollution was relatively low. The inattention to air pollution conditions and inaccessibility of relevant information make it less possible for them to respond to air pollution in advance. Furthermore, people are unlikely to leave Beijing due to air pollution because purchasing a house elsewhere is expensive and people need more time for preparation. Eventually, most air pollutants are colorless and odorless, making it difficult to detect them. People might attribute their discomfort to other factors such as work-related stress, as previous research suggests (Hirshleifer and Shumway 2003). In conclusion, we can confidently assert that air pollution is exogenous to dining out. People are unlikely to alter their dining out plans when exposed to air pollution.

The third concern is the inconsistent timing between dining and reviewing. Due to data limitations, we could only gather the date on which the review was submitted, and it is not viable to determine whether the consumer review time aligns with the precise dining time. However, our major focus in this paper is on the immediate influence of air pollution on consumer reviews, specifically the impact of air pollution at the time of review writing. Therefore, the time difference between dining and evaluative times has a negligible impact on our study.

Finally, there is a concern for date effects that can bias our estimation. For instance, increased traffic congestion on holidays due to heightened visitor flows can affect consumers' emotions and assessments. Moreover, increased traffic can also result in higher emissions from cars, which may aggravate the air pollution problem. To address this issue, we include date dummy variables in the model to control for date effects. One benefit of this approach is that it can simultaneously control for other omitted variables associated with dates, thus allaying bias in our estimation. Particularly, introducing date variables can also control weather-related information, making it unnecessary to separately add weather-related controls to the model, which contributes to the parsimony of the model.

5.4 Empirical Results

5.4.1 Baseline Results

We examine the effect of air pollution on consumer reviews using the following model:

$$Rating_{ijt} = \beta_0 + \beta_1 AQI_{dt} + \alpha_i + \delta_j + \lambda_t + \varepsilon_{ijt}$$

where i, j, t, and d represent individual consumers, individual restaurants, the date, and the administrative district in Beijing respectively. Rating denotes the ratings given by consumers, including the overall rating, taste, environment, and service ratings. AQI stands for the Air Quality Index. α, δ, and λ index consumer fixed effects, restaurant fixed effects, and date effects respectively. Since the date effects already contain information related to weather, there is no need to include weather variables as controls in the model. We then utilize this multiple fixed-effects model for estimation.

Table 5.3 presents the regression results for the baseline model. It is observed from Panel A that AQI has a statistically significant negative impact on overall ratings, taste, environment, and service ratings. However, despite the strong statistical significance, the coefficient estimates are relatively small. Therefore, we proceed to estimate the effects of standardized AQI on consumer ratings, and the results are demonstrated in Panel B. The statistical significance remains after the variable standardization using the same model. It is noteworthy that the effect of AQI on overall ratings is the smallest, while its effect on environment ratings is the largest, which is consistent with our intuition. In terms of economic significance, a one standard deviation increase in AQI leads to a decrease of 0.0027 points in environment ratings. On average, for each increase of one standard deviation in AQI, consumer ratings will decrease by 0.002 points, which implies a 20% increase in the probability of decreasing the overall restaurant rating by 0.01 points. Our estimates can thus confirm Hypothesis 1 that air pollution has an immediate negative impact on consumer ratings.

The decrease in ratings is usually accompanied by a decline in restaurant rankings. Therefore, it is expected that a decrease of 0.01 points would lead to a significant change in restaurant rankings. In this study, we use the restaurant information from 2015 to make a rough estimate. First, we calculate the average ratings for each restaurant's four categories and their rankings based on these ratings. Then, we perform a regression analysis using the model below:

$$Rank_i = \beta_0 + \beta_1 Rating\_Mean_i + \varepsilon_i$$

The results are shown in Table 5.4, suggesting a statistically significant negative impact of restaurant overall ratings on restaurant overall rankings. On average, a one-point decrease in restaurant ratings could result in an average decrease of 16,870 positions in its overall rankings. Therefore, a one standard deviation increase in air

Table 5.3 Effect of exposure to air pollution on restaurant rankings

Dep. Var.	Overall	Taste	Environment	Service
	(1)	(2)	(3)	(4)
Panel A				
AQI	−1.30e − 05**	−1.98e − 05***	−3.12e − 05***	−2.23e − 05***
	(6.40e − 06)	(6.40e − 06)	(5.99e − 06)	(6.72e − 06)
Consumer F.E.	Yes	Yes	Yes	Yes
Restaurant F.E.	Yes	Yes	Yes	Yes
Date F.E.	Yes	Yes	Yes	Yes
Observations	4,171,237	4,159,028	4,161,471	4,162,273
R^2	0.468	0.460	0.508	0.473
Panel B				
AQI_std	−0.00114** (0.000563)	−0.00174*** (0.000563)	−0.00274*** (0.000527)	−0.00197*** (0.000592)
Consumer F.E.	Yes	Yes	Yes	Yes
Restaurant F.E.	Yes	Yes	Yes	Yes
Date F.E.	Yes	Yes	Yes	Yes
Observations	4,171,237	4,159,028	4,161,471	4,162,273
R^2	0.468	0.460	0.508	0.473

Notes Robust standard errors are in parentheses. The regressions include consumer FE, restaurant FE, and date FE. *10%, **5%, ***1%

pollution would lead to a decrease of 0.002 points in restaurant overall ratings and end up with a decrease of 34 positions in restaurant overall rankings.

Table 5.4 The effect of restaurant overall ratings on rankings

Dep. Var.	Overall	Taste	Environment	Service
	(1)	(2)	(3)	(4)
Overall_Mean	16,604*** (30.58)			
Taste_Mean		16,949*** (32.55)		
Environment_Mean			17,257 (29.12)	
Service_Mean				16,671*** (28.02)
Observations	58,620	58,420	58,496	58,546
R^2	0.834	0.823	0.857	0.858

Notes Robust standard errors are in parentheses. *10%, **5%, ***1%

In reality, certain consumers might be more sensitive to the rankings of restaurants from a specific district and street in Beijing, or within a particular cuisine type. Thus, the real-world influence of air pollution on restaurant rankings would possibly be smaller in such contexts. Our analysis above is merely intended to highlight the adverse effects of ratings on rankings.

Our results reveal that air pollution can influence restaurant ratings and subsequently their rankings. One ramification of the changes in rankings is the reduction of the restaurant's display position on the web pages, which could mainly generate two effects. The first effect is the contrast effect. When restaurants move to lower positions on the webpage, consumers would then possess negative presuppositions and evaluations of those restaurants. The exposure effect is the second potential consequence. Lower rankings on webpages are usually followed by reduced consumer attention since it usually signals a lower quality of the food and service. Moreover, decreased exposure could lessen the likelihood for consumers to discover relevant information about the restaurants and eventually lead to declined revenues for those food service providers. Particularly, if a restaurant depends heavily on its presence on platforms like Dianping, the effects referred to above could be more significant.

5.4.2 Linear Probability Model

In this section, we further investigate the effect of air pollution on the likelihood of consumers giving a full score. Nearly 60% of the consumers in our sample have given the highest rating (5 stars). We conjecture that if a consumer's dining experience in a restaurant can fulfill their expectations, they tend to award a 5-star rating as suggested by the platform. In other words, a perfect score is usually the default score offered by most consumers. Hence, we create a dummy variable for consumer ratings, which equals 1 when representing a rating of 5 stars and 0 otherwise. The baseline model is also employed in this section and the results are showcased in Table 5.5. Still, we also conduct regression after standardizing our key independent variable and present the results in Panel B.

On average, for each one standard deviation increase in AQI, the probability of consumers giving a 5-star rating will significantly decrease by 0.12%. This suggests a relatively small influence on the likelihood of consumers giving a full score, with only a small proportion of users giving lower ratings in response to heightened air pollution. Our calculation suggests that each one standard deviation increase in air pollution will shift on average 1809 individuals from giving a five-star rating to a lower rating.

Table 5.5 The results of the linear probability model

Dep. Var. (dummy)	Overall	Taste	Environment	Service
	(1)	(2)	(3)	(4)
Panel A				
AQI	−1.29e − 05*** (3.14e − 06)	−1.24e − 05*** (3.21e − 06)	−1.62e − 05*** (3.09e − 06)	−1.58e − 05*** (3.15e − 06)
Consumer F.E.	Yes	Yes	Yes	Yes
Restaurant F.E.	Yes	Yes	Yes	Yes
Date F.E.	Yes	Yes	Yes	Yes
Observations	4,171,237	4,159,028	4,161,471	4,162,273
R^2	0.507	0.487	0.524	0.507
Panel B				
AQI_std	−0.00113***	−0.00109***	−0.00143***	−0.00139***
	(0.000276)	(0.000282)	(0.000272)	(0.000277)
Consumer F.E.	Yes	Yes	Yes	Yes
Restaurant F.E.	Yes	Yes	Yes	Yes
Date F.E.	Yes	Yes	Yes	Yes
Observations	4,171,237	4,159,028	4,161,471	4,162,273
R^2	0.507	0.487	0.524	0.507

Notes Robust standard errors are in parentheses. The regressions include consumer FE, restaurant FE, and date FE. *10%, **5%, ***1%

5.4.3 Heterogeneous Effects

Given that different levels of AQI could have heterogeneous effects on consumers, we convert the AQI into a categorized variable to test hypothesis 2 in this section. Figure 5.1 displays the frequency distribution of AQI in Beijing in 2015. It can be seen that the distribution of AQI levels is a typical right-skewed distribution, where the mode occurs at the AQI level near 100.

Thus, based on the AQI classification standards, we divide the AQI into four categories. The AQI is below 100 in the first category, signifying excellent or good air quality. In the second category, the AQI ranges from 100 to 200, indicating light to moderate pollution. In the third category, the AQI falls between 200 and 300, denoting heavy pollution. In the fourth category, the AQI exceeds 300, which indicates severe pollution.

Table 5.6 demonstrates the estimated results of consumer ratings on categorized AQI variables. It is observed that the second category of air pollution does not show a significant negative impact on consumer ratings, which could be derived from the fact that Beijing has long faced the air pollution problem throughout the year, and the public has gradually acclimated to such conditions. In contrast, the third and fourth categories of air pollution display significant negative effects on consumer assessments. This implies that more severe air pollution would have substantial adverse

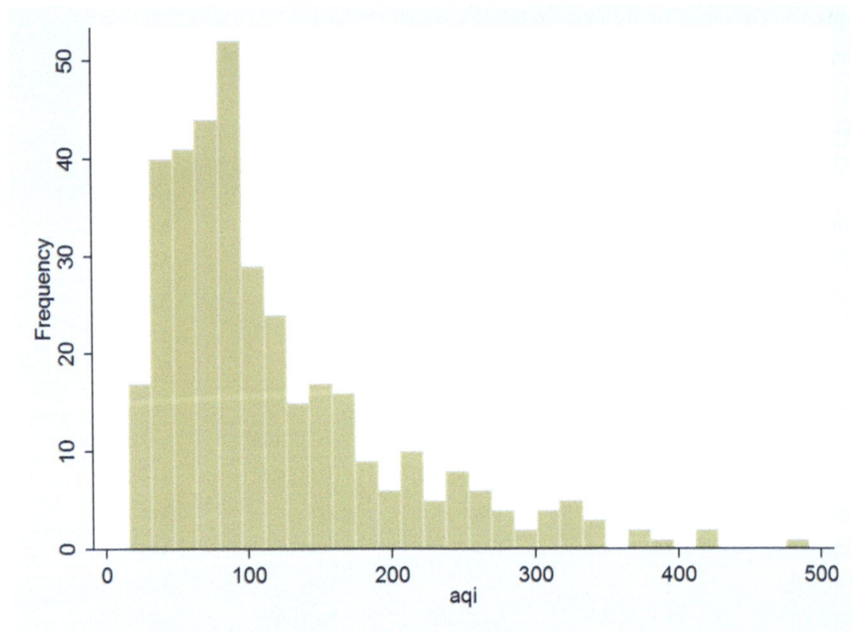

Fig. 5.1 The frequency distribution of AQI in 2015

effects on consumers' sentiments, affecting their rating processes thereafter. Furthermore, it is shown that as air pollution worsens, its negative influence on consumer ratings will intensify. For instance, during times of relatively extreme air pollution (AQI > 300), it could lead to a 0.01-point decline in consumer ratings of the restaurant environment and service. To encapsulate the main points, our results reveal that air pollution has a nonlinear impact on consumer evaluations, which is characterized by the absence of significant effects for the second AQI category, while the third and fourth categories exhibit sizable negative impacts on ratings. This also implies that the negative influence of air pollution primarily stems from more harsh air pollution (AQI > 200), which is also consistent with our Hypothesis 2.

5.4.4 Cumulative Effects

To examine whether air pollution has a cumulative effect on consumer ratings, we also obtain the average AQI for the past 3 days, 7 days, 15 days, 20 days, 25 days, 30 days, 35 days, and 40 days to measure the extent of constant exposure to air pollution over different time windows. Table 5.7 presents the results for the cumulative effects of air pollution. For ease of comparison, we have combined the estimated results for different exposure windows into one table.

Table 5.6 Categorized 24-h average AQI results

Dep. Var.	Overall	Taste	Environment	Service
	(1)	(2)	(3)	(4)
AQI_2	0.000425 (0.00115)	−0.000144 (0.00115)	−0.00174 (0.00108)	0.00104 (0.00121)
AQI_3	−0.00419** (0.00177)	−0.00613*** (0.00177)	−0.00723*** (0.00166)	−0.00536*** (0.00186)
AQI_4	−0.00736*** (0.00207)	−0.00798*** (0.00207)	−0.0101*** (0.00194)	−0.0102*** (0.00218)
Consumer F.E.	Yes	Yes	Yes	Yes
Restaurant F.E.	Yes	Yes	Yes	Yes
Date F.E.	Yes	Yes	Yes	Yes
Observations	4,210,095	4,197,722	4,200,176	4,200,993
R^2	0.468	0.459	0.507	0.472

Notes Robust standard errors are in parentheses. The regressions include consumer FE, restaurant FE, and date FE. *10%, **5%, ***1%

Our results shows a clear pattern that as the duration of exposure to air pollution broadens, the adverse effects on consumer ratings will then intensify. Table 5.7 shows that the negative influence of air pollution steadily escalates as time accumulates and reaches the maximum at 25 days, after which the impact will gradually diminish. As a result, the coefficients would exhibit an inverted U-shape. To put it into numerical terms, a one standard deviation increase in the 25-day average AQI accumulation would result in a decrease of 0.011 points in consumer ratings. This also confirms our Hypothesis 3: air pollution inflicts a cumulative effect on consumer reviews, and sustained exposure to air pollution exerts a more significant influence.

5.4.5 Robustness Checks

5.4.5.1 12-h Average AQI

Our previous analysis uses the 24-h average AQI as the key independent variable. Considering that dining out overall takes place between 10 AM and 10 PM, we decided to construct the 12-h average AQI during this time slot for robustness checks. After standardizing the 12-h average AQI, the results are documented in Table 5.8. Compared to the results of the 24-h average AQI results, the coefficients of the 12-h average AQI appear relatively larger, suggesting that air pollution in the daytime poses a more intense impact on consumers due to increased exposure during this time.

Similarly, we create a categorized 12-h average AQI variable to explore the heterogeneous effects, of which the results are presented in Table 5.9. A nonlinear impact on

Table 5.7 Cumulative effect results

Dep. Var.	Overall	Taste	Environment	Service
	(1)	(2)	(3)	(4)
AQI_std	−0.00114** (0.000563)	−0.00174*** (0.000563)	−0.00274*** (0.000527)	−0.00197*** (0.000592)
AQI_3_std	−0.00132** (0.000597)	−0.00209*** (0.000597)	−0.00291*** (0.000559)	−0.00221*** (0.000627)
AQI_7_std	−0.00392*** (0.000725)	−0.00428*** (0.000724)	−0.00519*** (0.000678)	−0.00513*** (0.000761)
AQI_15_std	−0.00642*** (0.000952)	−0.00706*** (0.000952)	−0.00678*** (0.000891)	−0.00770*** (0.00100)
AQI_20_std	−0.00746*** (0.00110)	−0.00856*** (0.00110)	−0.00871*** (0.00103)	−0.00869*** (0.00115)
AQI_25_std	−0.00970*** (0.00128)	−0.0112*** (0.00128)	−0.0116*** (0.00120)	−0.0113*** (0.00134)
AQI_30_std	−0.00826*** (0.00130)	−0.00966*** (0.00130)	−0.0104*** (0.00122)	−0.00948*** (0.00137)
AQI_35_std	−0.00884*** (0.00139)	−0.00919*** (0.00139)	−0.00993*** (0.00130)	−0.00912*** (0.00146)
AQI_40_std	−0.00658*** (0.00142)	−0.00704*** (0.00142)	−0.00683*** (0.00133)	−0.00437*** (0.00150)
Consumer F.E.	Yes	Yes	Yes	Yes
Restaurant F.E.	Yes	Yes	Yes	Yes
Date F.E.	Yes	Yes	Yes	Yes
Observations	4,171,237	4,159,028	4,161,471	4,162,273
R^2	0.468	0.460	0.508	0.473

Notes Robust standard errors are in parentheses. The regressions include consumer FE, restaurant FE, and date FE. *10%, **5%, ***1%

Table 5.8 Effect of 12-h average AQI on consumer reviews

Dep. Var.	Overall	Taste	Environment	Service
	(1)	(2)	(3)	(4)
AQI_std	−0.00123** (0.000557)	−0.00187*** (0.000557)	−0.00290*** (0.000521)	−0.00208*** (0.000585)
Consumer F.E.	Yes	Yes	Yes	Yes
Restaurant F.E.	Yes	Yes	Yes	Yes
Date F.E.	Yes	Yes	Yes	Yes
Observations	4,159,546	4,147,455	4,149,889	4,150,697
R^2	0.469	0.460	0.508	0.473

Notes Robust standard errors are in parentheses. The regressions include consumer FE, restaurant FE, and date FE. *10%, **5%, ***1%

Table 5.9 Categorized 12-h average AQI results

Dep. Var.	Overall	Taste	Environment	Service
	(1)	(2)	(3)	(4)
AQI_2	0.00161 (0.00112)	0.000266 (0.00112)	−0.000854 (0.00105)	0.000873 (0.00117)
AQI_3	−0.00278 (0.00175)	−0.00426** (0.00175)	−0.00658*** (0.00164)	−0.00530*** (0.00184)
AQI_4	−0.00605*** (0.00220)	−0.00745*** (0.00220)	−0.0102*** (0.00206)	−0.00868*** (0.00232)
Consumer F.E.	Yes	Yes	Yes	Yes
Restaurant F.E.	Yes	Yes	Yes	Yes
Date F.E.	Yes	Yes	Yes	Yes
Observations	4,174,826	4,162,601	4,165,043	4,165,861
R^2	0.469	0.460	0.508	0.473

Notes Robust standard errors are in parentheses. The regressions include consumer FE, restaurant FE, and date FE. *10%, **5%, ***1%

consumer ratings from air pollution is observed once again. Specifically, the negative effects are primarily attributed to the third-category and fourth-category AQI.

5.4.5.2 Alternate Pollutant: PM2.5

PM2.5 is the major determinant contributing to the well-known air pollution issue in Beijing and is mostly the dominant pollutant of the AQI index. Thus, in this section, we also conduct a robustness check by regressing consumer ratings on PM2.5, and a negative effect on consumer evaluations is expected. Table 5.10 presents the regression results after standardizing PM2.5. A significant negative impact on taste, environment, and service ratings is obtained except for the overall rating. Moreover, for each one standard deviation increase in PM2.5, the environment rating decreases by 0.0022 points. Comparing these results with our baseline results, we find that AQI exhibits higher statistical significance and greater negative effects. We conjecture that AQI, as a full-scale indicator of air pollution, includes information about other air pollutants that can also affect consumer behaviors. Consequently, adopting AQI as the air pollution measure is supposed to produce more precise estimates.

5.4.6 Mechanism

This section will test the mechanism proposed in the previous sections, namely the consumer sentiments. When consumers submit their assessments, they are required to not only assign ratings to their dining experiences but also write textual comments

Table 5.10 Effect of PM2.5 on consumer reviews

Dep. Var.	Overall	Taste	Environment	Service
	(1)	(2)	(3)	(4)
PM2.5_std	−0.000789 (0.000547)	−0.00142*** (0.000547)	−0.00225*** (0.000511)	−0.00143** (0.000574)
Consumer F.E.	Yes	Yes	Yes	Yes
Restaurant F.E.	Yes	Yes	Yes	Yes
Date F.E.	Yes	Yes	Yes	Yes
Observations	4,174,826	4,162,601	4,165,043	4,165,861
R^2	0.469	0.460	0.508	0.473

Notes Robust standard errors are in parentheses. The regressions include consumer FE, restaurant FE, and date FE. *10%, **5%, ***1%

Table 5.11 Effect of consumer sentiment on consumer reviews

Dep. Var.	Overall	Taste	Environment	Service
	(1)	(2)	(3)	(4)
Sentiment	0.547*** (0.000471)	0.529*** (0.000476)	0.408*** (0.000471)	0.517*** (0.000512)
Consumer F.E.	Yes	Yes	Yes	Yes
Restaurant F.E.	Yes	Yes	Yes	Yes
Date F.E.	Yes	Yes	Yes	Yes
Observations	4,210,089	4,197,716	4,200,170	4,200,987
R^2	0.617	0.601	0.595	0.593

Notes Robust standard errors are in parentheses. The regressions include consumer FE, restaurant FE, and date FE. *10%, **5%, ***1%

to exposit their feelings about the service and meal. This enables us to utilize text sentiment analysis techniques to identify the underlying consumer sentiments within these comments. To conduct the analysis, we have employed Baidu Artificial Intelligence's sentiment analysis technology to quantify the sentiment tendencies within Dianping users' comments. We then obtain the key variable Sentiment for this part, which takes the value of 1 when identifying positive emotions and 0 for negative ones.[3] Using this variable to measure sentimental tendency, we bring forward another model as follows:

$$Rating_{ijt} = \beta_0 + \beta_1 Sentiment_{ijt} + \alpha_i + \delta_j + \lambda_t + \varepsilon_{ijt}$$

Of which the estimated results are exhibited in Table 5.11. We find that consumers' sentiments are positively correlated with their ratings.

[3] Due to the limited number of neutral sentiment samples, we have excluded them from the dataset.

Table 5.12 Effect of air pollution on consumer sentiments

Dep. Var.	Sentiment	Sentiment	Sentiment_std
	(1)	(2)	(3)
AQI	−8.53e − 06*** (3.13e − 06)		
AQI_std		−0.000751*** (0.000276)	−0.00216*** (0.000685)
Confidence	0.258*** (0.000823)	0.258*** (0.000823)	
Consumer F.E.	Yes	Yes	Yes
Restaurant F.E.	Yes	Yes	Yes
Date F.E.	Yes	Yes	Yes
Observations	4,030,699	4,030,699	4,030,699
R^2	0.323	0.323	0.302

Notes Robust standard errors are in parentheses. The regressions include consumer FE, restaurant FE, and date FE. *10%, **5%, ***1%

Then, we also examine the effect of air pollution on consumers' sentiment inclination using an analogous model. The results presented in Table 5.12 suggest that AQI has a significant negative impact on consumers' sentiment inclination, which aligns with our expectation. Therefore, it empirically attests that air pollution, as an exogenous shock, does exert a negative impact on individuals' emotions, through which air pollution can further diminish consumers' dining experiences and instigate them to give negative dining reviews.

5.5 Conclusion

This research conducts a relatively thorough investigation of the causal relationship between air pollution and consumer evaluations. After reviewing existing literature on both air pollution and consumer evaluations, we highlight the significance of their potential relationship. Then we proceed to examine the mechanisms through which air pollution can impact consumer evaluations, drawing on previous studies that connect air pollution with sentiments and sentiments with evaluative processes. To empirically disentangle the intricate correlations, we construct a unique dataset by collecting consumer reviews from Dianping.com about restaurants in Beijing throughout the year 2015 and then matching them with air pollution data. We also adopt several robust statistical methods and robustness checks rigorously to obtain precise estimates of air pollution's adverse effects on consumer ratings. Our results suggest that AQI significantly and negatively influences consumer ratings, with both immediate and cumulative effects, meanwhile exhibiting a nonlinear pattern. Furthermore, our research validates the "air pollution-sentiment-evaluation" mechanism by identifying sentiment inclinations in users' textual comments. In summary, this research provides comprehensive empirical evidence of the negative impact of air pollution on consumer assessments, offering valuable insights into the field.

To the best of our knowledge, this paper provides the first evidence of air pollution's impact on consumer evaluations. It uncovers the adverse effects of air pollution on consumer ratings, demonstrating both immediate and cumulative effects while featuring a nonlinear pattern. This implies that air pollution could diminish individuals' life satisfaction and detrimentally affect consumers' dining experiences. Consequently, improving air quality emerges not only as a way to mitigate health risks and improve labor productivity but also to enhance consumers' dining experiences, which are all pivotal compositions of human welfare. Thus, our research underscores the pressing importance of air pollution control. Our findings also suggest that restaurant operators ought to consider improving their business strategies during times of severe air pollution. The negative effect of air pollution on restaurant ratings and rankings would ultimately result in reduced media exposure and decreased revenue. Hence, we suggest restaurants take measures such as ameliorating their service quality and providing discounts during periods of intense air pollution to counteract the adverse effects brought by air pollution.

References

Adgate JL, Goldstein BD, McKenzie LM (2014) Potential public health hazards, exposures and health effects from unconventional natural gas development. Environ Sci Technol 48(15):8307–8320

Adhvaryu A, Kala N, Nyshadham A (2014) Management and shocks to worker productivity: evidence from air pollution exposure in an Indian Garment Factory. Unpublished. University of Michigan

Ailshire JA, Clarke P (2015) Fine particulate matter air pollution and cognitive function among US older adults. J Gerontol Ser B Psychol Sci Soc Sci 70(2):322–328

Anderson M, Magruder J (2012) Learning from the crowd: regression discontinuity estimates of the effects of an online review database. Econ J 122(563):957–989

Aragon F, Miranda JJ, Oliva P (2016) Particulate matter and labor supply: evidence from Peru. Unpublished Working Paper, Simon Fraser University

Bakhshi S, Kanuparthy P, Gilbert E (2014) Demographics, weather and online reviews: a study of restaurant recommendations. Unpublished Working Paper, Proceedings of the 23rd International Conference on World Wide Web

Cai H, Chen Y, Fang H (2009) Observational learning: evidence from a randomized natural field experiment. Am Econ Rev 99(3):864–882

Calderon-Garciduenas L (2008) Air pollution, cognitive deficits and brain abnormalities: a pilot study with children and dogs. Brain Cogn 68(2):117–127

Chang T (2016) Particulate pollution and the productivity of pear packers. Am Econ J Econ Policy 8(3):141–169

Chay KY, Greenstone M (2003a) Air quality, infant mortality, and the clean air act of 1970. J Political Economy 111 (4): 716–772

Chay KY, Greenstone M (2003b) The impact of air pollution on infant mortality: evidence from geographic variation in pollution shocks induced by a recession. Q J Econ 118(3):1121–1167

Chay Y, Greenstone M (2005) Does air quality matter? Evidence from the housing market. J Polit Econ 113(2):376–424

Clark DM, Teasdale JD (1985) Constraints on the effects of mood on memory. J personality and social psychology 48(6): 1595

Clark D, Sokoloff L (1999) Circulation and energy metabolism of the brain. In: Basic neurochemistry: molecular, pp 637–670

Clore G, Schwartz N (1988) Affect Cognition and Social Behaviour. Hogrefe

Currie J (2009) Does pollution increase school absences? Rev Econ Stat 91(4):682–694

Dockery DW, Pope CA III (1994) Acute respiratory effects of particulate air pollution. Annu Rev Public Health 15(1):107–132

Duflo E, Saez E (2002) Participation and investment decisions in a retirement plan: the influence of colleagues' choices. J Public Econ 85(1):121–148

Ebenstein A, Lavy V, Roth S (2016) The long-run economic consequences of high-stakes examinations: evidence from transitory variation in pollution. Am Econ J Appl Econ 8(4):36–65

Evans GW, Colome S, Shearer F (1988) Psychological reactions to air pollution. Environ Res 45(1):1–15

Forgas JP (1991) Emotion and social judgments. Taylor & Francis

Guo M, Fu S (2019) Running with a mask? The effect of air pollution on marathon runners performance. J Sports Econ 20(7):903–928

Hanna R, Oliva P (2015) The effect of pollution on labor supply: evidence from a natural experiment in Mexico city. J Public Econ 122:68–79

He J, Liu H, Salvo H (2019) Severe air pollution and labor productivity: evidence from industrial towns in China. Am Econ J Appl Econ 11(1):173–201

Herrnstadt E (2016) Air pollution as a cause of violent crime: evidence from Los Angeles and Chicago. Manuscript in Preparation

Hilger J, Rafert G, Villas-Boas S (2011) Expert opinion and the demand for experience goods: an experimental approach in the retail wine market. Rev Econ Stat 93(4):1289–1296

Hirshleifer D, Shumway T (2003) Good day sunshine: stock returns and the weather. J Financ 58(3):1009–1032

Isen AM (1978) Affect, accessibility of material in memory, and behavior: a cognitive loop? J Pers Soc Psychol 36(1):1–12

Kamstra MJ, Kramer LA, Levi MD (2003) Winter blues: a SAD stock market cycle. Am Econ Rev 93(1):324–343

Lerner JS, Keltner D (2001) Fear, anger, and risk. J Pers Soc Psychol 81(1):146–159

Levy T, Yagil J (2011) Air pollution and stock returns in the US. J Econ Psychol 32(3):374–383

Luca M (2016) Reviews, reputation, and revenue: the case of yelp.com. Unpublished Working Paper, Harvard Business School

Moretti E (2011) Social learning and peer effects in consumption: evidence from movie sales. Rev Econ Stud 78(1):356–393

Oberdörster G (2004) Translocation of inhaled ultrafine particles to the brain. Inhal Toxicol 16(6–7):437–445

Peters A, Veronesi B, Calderón-Garcidueñas L, Gehr P, Chen LC, Geiser M, Reed W, Rothen-Rutishauser B, Schürch S, Schulz H (2006) Translocation and potential neurological effects of fine and ultrafine particles a critical update. Particle and Fibre Toxicology 3: 13

Pope CA III (2000) Epidemiology of fine particulate air pollution and human health: biologic mechanisms and who's at risk? Environ Health Perspect 108(suppl):713–723

Pope CA III, Dockery DW (2006) Health effects of fine particulate air pollution: lines that connect. J Air Waste Manag Assoc 56(6):709–742

Power MC (2011) Traffic-related air pollution and cognitive function in a cohort of older men. Environ Health Perspect 119(5):682–687

Reinstein DA, Snyder CM (2005) The influence of expert reviews on consumer demand for experience goods: a case study of movie critics. J Ind Econ 53(1):27–51

Roth S (2016) The contemporaneous effect of indoor air pollution on cognitive performance: evidence from the UK
Sanfey AG (2003) The neural basis of economic decision-making in the ultimatum game. Science 300(5626):1755–1758
Schwarz N, Clore GL (1983) Mood, misattribution, and judgments of well-being: informative and directive functions of affective states. J Pers Soc Psychol 45(3):513–523
Seaton A (1995) Particulate air pollution and acute health effects. Lancet 345(8943):176–178
Sorensen AT (2006) Social learning and health plan choice. RAND J Econ 37(4):929–945
Suglia SF (2008) Association of black carbon with cognition among children in a prospective birth cohort study. Am J Epidemiol 167(3):280–286
Tallon LA (2017) Cognitive impacts of ambient air pollution in the national social health and aging project (NSHAP) cohort. Environ Int 104:102–109
Tiedens LZ, Linton S (2001) Judgment under emotional certainty and uncertainty: the effects of specific emotions on information processing. J Pers Soc Psychol 81(6):973–988
Weuve J (2012) Exposure to particulate air pollution and cognitive decline in older women. Arch Intern Med 172(3):219–227
Wilker EH (2015) Long-term exposure to fine particulate matter, residential proximity to major roads and measures of brain structure. Stroke 46(5):1161–1166
Yin H (2018) Contingent valuation of health and mood impacts of PM2.5 in Beijing, China. Sci Total Environ 630:1269–1282
Zhang X, Zhang X, Chen X (2017a) Happiness in the air: how does a dirty sky affect mental health and subjective well-being? J Environ Econ Manag 85:81–94
Zhang X, Zhang X, Chen X (2017b) Valuing air quality using happiness data: the case of China. Ecol Econ 137:29–36
Zhang X, Chen X, Zhang X (2018) The impact of exposure to air pollution on cognitive performance. Proc Natl Acad Sci 115(37):9193–9197
Zijlema WL (2016) The association of air pollution and depressed mood in 70,928 individuals from four European cohorts. Int J Hyg Environ Health 219(2):212–219
Zivin JG, Neidell M (2012) The impact of pollution on worker productivity. Am Econ Rev 102(7):3652–3673

Chapter 6
The Unseen Cost of Travel: Air Pollution and the Tourism Industry

Abstract This paper explores the direct costs of air pollution within China's domestic tourism sector. We construct a unique data set spanning the years 2006–2016, comprising monthly data on domestic tourism revenue and the monthly count of domestic tourists at the city level. Our findings indicate that a one standard deviation increase in air pollution is associated with a substantial 9.1% decrease in domestic tourism revenue and a 3.8% reduction in the number of domestic tourists. It is also noteworthy that these effects demonstrate a significant nonlinear pattern. To gain further insights, we explore potential mechanisms by incorporating public perceptions of air pollution measured by the Baidu Index and observe that the adverse effects intensify as public concern about air pollution rises. A battery of heterogeneous analyses also lend support to the robustness of our main results. Importantly, our findings remain robust when employing alternative air pollution measures, considering numerous aspects of the tourism industry, and addressing endogeneity concerns.

Keywords Air pollution · Tourism industry · Avoidance behavior · Public perception

6.1 Introduction

As Chinese household income rises, travel has become a critical form of consumption for the average citizen, while tourism also serves as an essential driver of the nation's GDP. According to World Bank statistics, each dollar spent on tourism globally generates $3.2 in economic growth. China's tourism industry has witnessed significant growth over the recent decades, emerging as a significant contributor to the national economic expansion. Notably, over 80% of China's total tourism income is ascribed to domestic tourism, making China a dominant player in the global domestic tourism market. Figure 6.1 illustrates the growth rates and aggregate contributions to the GDP of the tourism industry from 2014 to 2017. In 2017 alone, Chinese tourists embarked on more than 5 billion domestic trips, resulting in a 13% increase in travel expenses relative to the previous year. The number of domestic tourists exceeded 5.01

M. Guo et al., *Social-Economic Impacts of Air Pollution*, Climate Change and Energy Transition, https://doi.org/10.1007/978-981-96-7858-7_6

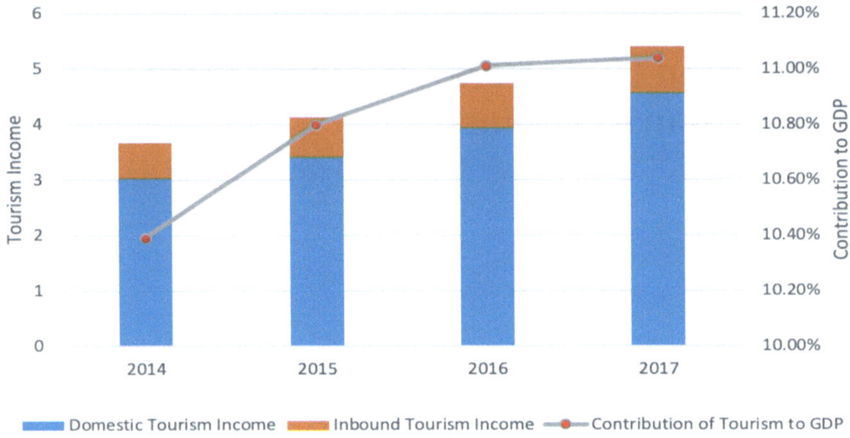

Fig. 6.1 China's tourism income and contribution to GDP from 2014 to 2017

billion, with revenues reaching 4.57 trillion yuan, displaying year-on-year growth rates of 12.8% and 15.9%, respectively. This highlights the tourism sector's ongoingly increasing contribution to GDP, underscoring its vital role in China's economic development.

In addition to factors like natural endowments and transportation accessibility, the tourism industry is substantively influenced by environmental factors. Choices of travel destinations are greatly influenced by various environmental conditions, including weather conditions, air quality, and climate change (Becken and Wilson 2013; Becken et al. 2016; Freitas 2003; Goh 2012). However, China's rapid economic growth over the past few decades has also posed a significant challenge—air pollution—to both the authorities and the public. Since 2013, considerable Chinese cities have been struggling with intense smog pollution. The consequences of air pollution also extend beyond health and productivity concerns since they also contribute to a pessimistic mental state and a higher level of risk avoidance. People are keen to seek out travel destinations with high air quality, propelling numerous Chinese travel agencies, such as Ctrip and Mafengwo, to launch specialized "clean lung" travel packages. These packages have gained substantial popularity among consumers, especially during China's peak periods of pollution. This trend of "avoidance" has emerged as a key theme in the tourism sector. Given that tourism activities predominantly occur outdoors, the environmental conditions of a destination should thus play a crucial role in their choice-making processes and the overall happiness generated. Consequently, air quality has become an integral factor in people's selection of travel destinations, underlining its importance within the tourism industry.

A considerable body of existing literature has provided strong evidence of the detrimental health effects caused by air pollution (Chay and Greenstone 2003; EPA 2004; Chen et al. 2013), its impact on labor productivity (Chang et al. 2016; Fu et al. 2021, and its influence on risk avoidance behaviors (Neidell 2009; Chen et al. 2022; Qin and Zhu 2018). Nonetheless, the repercussions of air pollution on various economic sectors, especially those firmly tied to human behavior and activities, continue to call for further investigations. In the context of the tourism industry, previous scholars have explored the ramifications of environmental factors, including air pollution, on both the inbound and outbound tourism sector (Bigano et al. 2007; Rosselló et al. 2011; Wang et al. 2018). Notably, despite the significant role of domestic tourism within the whole tourism landscape, research into the impact of air pollution on the domestic tourism industry, particularly in China where domestic tourism holds substantial importance, still presents conspicuous scarcity. This paper contributes to the existing literature by exploring the relationship between air pollution and the domestic tourism sector, thereby enhancing our understanding of this important economic area.

To assess the consequences of air pollution on the tourism sector, we adopt a dynamic panel data model, utilizing data covering monthly domestic tourism income and the monthly influx of domestic tourists across over 30 cities over the period of 2006–2016. This extensive dataset, characterized by its national representativeness and high-frequency feature, enables us to precisely comprehend how air pollution influences the tourism industry. Additionally, our analysis further investigates potential mechanisms by focusing on the public's perception of air pollution. These mechanisms include changes in air pollution levels and public attention to air pollution, as measured by the Baidu index. Our results indicate a significant negative impact of local air pollution on the tourism industry, manifested in lower tourism revenue and a decrease in tourist numbers. Specifically, a one standard deviation increase in air pollution levels, equivalent to 24.7 in our dataset, is associated with a 9.1% reduction in domestic tourism revenue and a 3.8% decline in the number of domestic tourists. Notably, these effects display even greater magnitude as public attention to air pollution becomes severe. To mitigate potential concerns related to endogeneity, such as reverse causality and omitted variables, we adopt a widely recognized instrumental variable (IV)—thermal inversion (Arceo et al. 2016; Fu et al. 2021)—to instrument air pollution. Importantly, our results remain robust even after addressing these endogeneity concerns. Furthermore, to ensure the credibility of the air pollution data, we employ two distinct measures for air quality: ground-based data from the MEPC and satellite-based data from NASA. Consequently, these two distinct measures produce consistent effects on domestic tourism income, reconfirming our main conclusions.

This paper makes several important contributions to the existing literature. First, we employ a high-frequency dataset to scrutinize a key subset of the tourism sector, namely the domestic tourism industry. Our dataset includes monthly records of domestic tourism revenue and the monthly count of domestic tourists from over 30 key tourism cities, enabling us to investigate the immediate or short-term effects of air pollution on the tourism industry. Furthermore, in contrast to annual data, our monthly dataset can alleviate potential sample selection biases. For instance, tourists may visit the same location in different months within the same year, and our monthly data can capture the corresponding seasonal nuances that annual data tend to overlook. Moreover, our dataset not only features national representativeness but also includes multiple essential cities well-known for their tourism appeal. Second, we establish a causal relationship between air pollution and its effects on the tourism industry. It is plausible that this causal relationship is subject to reverse causality and thus causes endogeneity concerns. To address this issue, our research uses an instrumental variable—thermal inversion—to instrument air pollution. By employing this methodology, we obtain a more accurate estimation of the impact of air pollution on the tourism industry. Third, we evaluate the effects of air pollution on decision-making processes within an environmentally connected industry—the tourism sector. Specifically, we identify the potential mechanisms underneath the tourism industry losses. Our investigation explores the influence of public perception of air pollution on the tourism sector. As a result, it can be concluded that not only does ambient air pollution affect decision-making, but the public's perception of air pollution also plays a crucial role in shaping these decisions.

6.2 Literature Review

The existing literature relevant to our paper can be divided into two main areas. The first area includes studies documenting the harmful effects of air pollution on human health, labor productivity, and risk avoidance behaviors. The second area comprises literature examining the relationship between environmental factors, such as air pollution, and the tourism sector. Clearly, the primary motivation behind our research is to understand the negative impact of air pollution on individuals.

First, regarding the negative effects of air pollution, a substantial body of literature has extensively documented its impact on various economic outcomes. Prolonged exposure to air pollution is associated with considerable types of health risks encompassing cardiopulmonary ailments, respiratory infections, lung malignancies, infant morbidity, asthma, and decreased life expectancy (Chay and Greenstone 2003; Neidell 2004; Chen et al. 2013). Short-term exposure to such pollution can result in reduced lung function, irregular heart rhythms, increased respiratory problems, nonfatal cardiac events, and angina (Graff Zivin and Neidell 2012; Schlenker and Walker 2015; Chen et al. 2018a; Lin and Liu 2019). Moreover, air pollution can inflict adverse psychological impacts, including heightened anxiety, reduced happiness, and other negative emotional consequences (Bullinger 1989; Zhang et al. 2017; Chen et al. 2023). It is also noteworthy that air pollution can lead to increased healthcare expenditures in both the short and medium term (Barwick et al. 2018). In addition to these health consequences, a significant body of literature has explored the adverse effects of air pollution on labor productivity, affecting both outdoor and indoor work environments (Graff Zivin and Neidell 2012; Adhvaryu et al. 2014; Chang et al. 2016, 2019). In the context of China, extensive evidence from a national-level longitudinal firm survey, covering 90% of the country's manufacturing output, indicates that air pollution reduces the labor productivity of manufacturing firms (Fu et al. 2021). Guo and Fu (2019) also demonstrate that air pollution can lower the productivity of athletes, influencing their marathon performance. Meanwhile, a body of research has examined risk avoidance behaviors and decision-making during severe air pollution events. Neidell (2009) finds that individuals are more likely to stay indoors under such conditions, while Zhang et al. (2017) investigate the impact of air pollution on national migration patterns in China, highlighting significant shifts in migration behavior. Qin and Zhu (2018) further observe that air pollution increases people's propensity to consider emigration. Moreover, in response to poor air quality, precautionary and defensive measures like obtaining air cleaners and facemasks are widely adopted (Ito and Zhang 2020; Zhang and Mu 2018). Given that tourism mainly occurs outdoors, we can hypothesize that tourists are not apt to select heavily polluted cities as their travel destinations due to concerns about health and trip satisfaction.

Another strand of literature pertains to identifying the considerable factors affecting the tourism sector and tourists' decision-making processes. Recently, increased attention has been drawn to weather and climate within tourism research, recognizing their crucial roles in driving people's tourist travel decisions (Alvarez-Díaz and Rosselló 2010; Goh 2012; Becken and Wilson 2013). It is also notable that environmental factors also exert a substantial influence on the overall tourism experience (Jeuring and Peters 2013). More importantly, climate change will reduce the demand for international tourism (Bigano et al. 2007), and an analysis of outbound tourist flows from the UK reveals that weather conditions are crucial in determining the travel destination (Rosselló et al. 2011). As air pollution has arisen as an urgent global concern, a growing body of research either constructs survey data or undertakes case studies to identify individuals' reactions to air pollution. For instance, Zhang et al. (2015) leverage a case study to unveil the significant impact of haze pollution on travel plans. Similarly, a survey of 600 US and Australian residents by Becken et al. (2016) suggests that air quality risks have significant deterrent effects on intentions to visit China. Chen et al. (2017), Peng and Xiao (2018), Choi et al. (2019), and Yoon (2019) corroborate these findings by providing further evidence. Some previous literature also depends on aggregated data and focuses on either inbound or outbound markets rather than the domestic tourism sector. For instance, Xu and Reed (2017) document that perceived air pollution reduces inbound tourism, while Wang et al. (2018) use transaction data from a major online travel agency in China to assess the impact of air quality on outbound tourism demand, revealing an increase in local outbound tourism demand as local air quality deteriorates. Moreover, Zhou et al. (2018) confirm air pollution's adverse effects on inbound tourism.

While the aforementioned studies shed light on air pollution's impact on macroeconomic sectors via avoidance behaviors, our research differentiates from them from several key aspects. First, we identify air pollution as a catalyst influencing the domestic tourism industry, which is the China's dominant tourism sector. Second, our study employs a panel data model incorporating monthly data from over 30 cities to capture a comprehensive and representative effect while mitigating seasonal fluctuations. Moreover, relative to prior literature, we rigorously address the endogeneity issue by introducing an innovative instrumental variable, assuring a relatively precise estimation of the causal effect of air pollution on the tourism sector.

6.3 Data

Our dataset covers the period from 2006 to 2016 with monthly frequency. The primary data sources include the Ministry of Environmental Protection of the People's Republic of China (MEPC), from which we obtain our key explanatory variable, the air quality index (AQI). Notably, it's vital to underscore that air pollution measurement standards underwent an important transformation in 2013. Prior to this change, the commonly used measure for assessing air pollution was the air pollution index (API), which included only three components: PM10, SO_2, and NO_2. In 2013, the Ministry of Environmental Protection of China (MEPC) introduced an updated and more comprehensive air pollution metric, the air quality index (AQI). The AQI includes six components: particulate matter with a diameter of 2.5 μm or less (PM2.5), particulate matter with a diameter of 10 μm or less (PM10), sulfur dioxide (SO_2), nitrogen dioxide (NO_2), carbon monoxide (CO), and ozone (O_3).

Figure 6.2 illustrates the distribution of monthly air pollution levels. Notably, the majority of monthly average AQI values fall below 100. However, approximately 12% of these values exceed 100. An AQI below 100 is classified as a "Blue Sky" day, indicating no significant health concerns. In contrast, when AQI is larger than 100, it begins to pose health risks to humans. Notably, the extent of air pollution varies significantly across cities. For example, in March 2013, Xi'an consistently recorded AQI values more than 100, whereas Sanya rarely experienced air pollution issues. Moreover, 9.53% of our sample comprises cities where AQI levels surpass 100 for at least half of every month, suggesting potential health risks endured by residents in these areas.

The data pertaining to variables related to tourism, specifically domestic tourism income and the number of domestic tourists for each city, are gathered from the WIND database. We procure data on domestic tourism income for 24 cities and the number of domestic tourists for 34 cities in total. We also introduce quarterly indicators such as hotel revenue per room per night and total revenue per room. Given the significant correlation between the hotel and tourism industries, these indicators emerge as appropriate proxies for the prosperity of the tourism sector. The characteristics of these cities comprise crucial factors influencing the local tourism landscape. Indicators such as the economic growth rate, gauged by GDP per capita, and ancillary support services like the number of all the star hotels, are gathered from the National Statistical Bureau of China (NBSC). Each city's tourism endowment is measured by the count of all the star scenic spots, which is manually compiled by us. Furthermore, information about transportation accessibility, measured by the presence of a high-speed train station in the city, is collected from NBSC.

To control for the impact of other weather-related factors, we have also collected weather data from the website of the China Meteorological Administration (CMA). Monthly averages for each weather measure are computed from daily records. Furthermore, to alleviate potential endogeneity concerns, we utilize thermal inversion data from NASA as an instrumental variable. Public attention to air pollution is measured by the Baidu index of air pollution. Baidu (www.baidu.com) stands as the

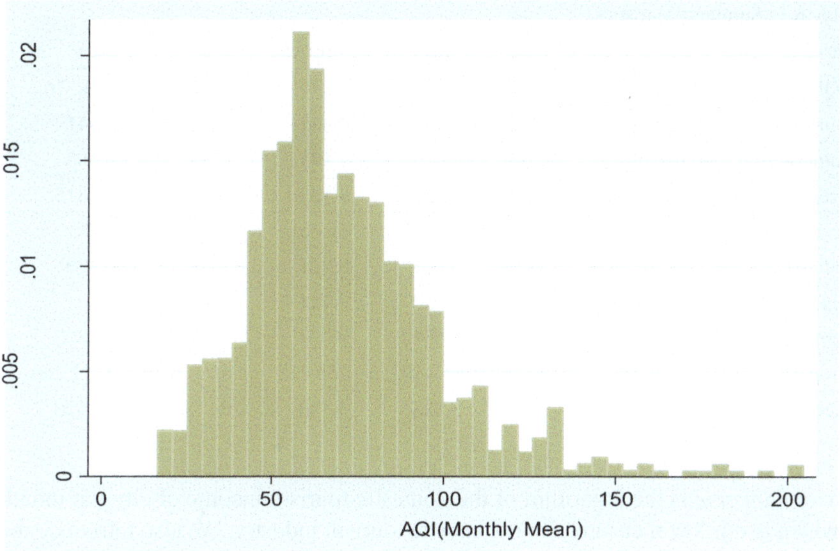

Fig. 6.2 Distribution of the monthly average AQI from 2006 to 2016

primary web search engine for Chinese Internet users, often deemed as the "Chinese version of Google." Thus, the Baidu index of air pollution can serve as a useful proxy for gauging public attention to air quality problems.

Eventually, our sample encompasses monthly data on domestic tourism income for 21 cities and monthly number of domestic tourists for 34 cities. Table 6.1 provides a summary of our key variable statistics. The average monthly AQI stands at 69.35, with the highest recorded monthly average AQI in our sample hitting 204.5, indicating the presence of prolonged heavy air pollution during the whole month, far surpassing the acceptable health standards.

6.4 Empirical Results

6.4.1 Model Specification

To investigate the effects of air pollution on the tourism industry, we propose the following baseline dynamic panel data model:

$$
\begin{aligned}
lnincome_{it} =& \alpha_i + \beta_1 AQI_{it} + \beta_2 lnincome_{it-1} \\
& + \beta_3 X_{it} + \beta_4 W_{it} + \lambda_t + \epsilon_{it}
\end{aligned}
$$

Table 6.1 Summary statistics

Variable	Obs	Mean	Std.Dev.	Min	Max
AQI	1355	69.350	24.703	16.667	204.516
Lnincome (10,000 CNY)	907	3.496	0.845	1.535	5.941
Lntourists (10,000 persons)	1146	5.676	1.195	2.960	9.005
Avegdp (10,000 CNY/person)	1318	6.297	3.122	1.889	14.815
Scenicspot	1318	58.695	66.861	0	250
Lnhotel	1253	4.581	0.924	2.708	6.729
Highspeed	1318	0.580	0.494	0	1
Temp (°C)	1318	17.540	9.028	−18.732	31.800
temp2	1318	389.102	258.215	0	1011.240
Prec (mm)	1318	3.828	3.750	0	46.520

where *lnincome* is the logarithm of the domestic tourism income of city i at month t, which is our key measure of the domestic tourism industry. We also introduce the logarithm of the number of domestic tourists as one of the robustness checks. *AQI* represents the air quality index. In our paper, air quality is measured in different ways. The initial measure is the monthly average AQI of each city; the second is the ratio of the number of days with an AQI exceeding 100, 200, or 300 over the entire month. This ratio is used to capture tourists' sensitivity to air pollution conditions and to assess the nonlinear effect of air pollution on the tourism sector. X serves as a vector of city characteristics that measure the attractiveness and convenience of the tourist destinations, which could contribute to the tourism income. More specifically, we control annual GDP per capita, the number of all-star scenic spots, whether there is a high-speed train station, and the total number of all-star hotels for each city. Furthermore, W represents the vector of weather controls, encompassing the monthly average temperature as well as its squared term and the amount of precipitation for each city. On one hand, weather conditions are important cofounders and can influence tourists' choice of travel destination. On the other hand, weather conditions are also correlated with air quality. Finally, we control for both year and month fixed effects to account for seasonal variations in air pollution and tourism, as well as to absorb the impact of national holidays. α is the city fixed effect, which can help eradicate other city-specific and time-invariant effects.

Our coefficient of interest is β_I, which captures the effect of air pollution on the domestic tourism industry. It is essential to acknowledge that high-frequency macro data often exhibit autocorrelation. Hence, we address this issue by adopting a dynamic panel data model. However, we employ a fixed effect estimation method rather than a dynamic panel data estimation method since if the sample period is long enough, the fixed effect estimation can still ensure the consistency of our estimator of interest (Hsiao 2003). Under the premise of an ever-expanding time period T, even with the introduction of lag terms for the dependent variable, potential violations of the strict exogeneity assumption can be alleviated, while satisfying the assumption of weak exogeneity, thus ensuring the consistency of the OLS estimator.

We hypothesize that cities with different characteristics may experience varying impacts of air pollution on the development of their tourism industry. Additionally, varying levels of air pollution may produce different consequences for the tourism sector. Consequently, this study integrates a battery of heterogeneity analyses based on city attributes and varying air pollution levels. Furthermore, to unravel the potential mechanisms underlying air pollution's role in tourists' decision-making processes, we resort to two plausible mechanisms. The first pertains to the adoption of the new air pollution measure introduced by the authorities in 2013, known as AQI, which covers more pollutant information and cities. The second mechanism centers on the increased public awareness of air pollution, measured by the search index for air pollution.

We then introduce a second specification to examine the effect of public attention to air pollution, as indicated by the Baidu index of air pollution, on the domestic tourism industry. A higher Baidu index of air pollution reflects greater public attention to air pollution. The model is presented as follows:

$$\begin{aligned} lnincome_{it} = &\alpha_i + \beta_1 AQI_{it} \beta_2 lnincome_{it-1} + \gamma_1 AQI_{i,t} \times SearchIndex_{i,t} \\ &+ \gamma_2 SearchIndex_{i,t} + \beta_3 X_{it} + \beta_4 W_{it} + \lambda_t + \varepsilon_{it} \end{aligned}$$

6.4.2 Baseline Results

In this section, we empirically examine the effects of air pollution on the local tourism industry. Table 6.2 presents the results for the baseline model, with all columns controlling for both city and time fixed effects. Notably, we observe a significant positive autocorrelation in tourism income. Furthermore, in Column (1), which excludes weather conditions and city characteristics, the estimated effect of air pollution on tourism income is significantly negative and economically meaningful. Specifically, a one-unit increase in the monthly average AQI is associated with a 0.37% decrease in domestic tourism income. Specifically, if the monthly average AQI rises by one standard deviation, equivalent to 24.7, domestic tourism income will experience a significant 9.1% decline, which is a substantial loss in tourism revenue that can further convert to more far-reaching economic impacts including GDP. In Column (2), we further introduce weather variables, and the coefficient of AQI remains robust. The coefficients for the weather variables also display an interesting pattern: temperature's effect on domestic tourism income yields an inverted U-shaped trajectory, while precipitation exerts a negative influence, in line with extant literature on the impact of weather conditions on tourism choices (Bigano et al. 2006; Goh 2012). In Column (3), which includes both weather conditions and city-level characteristics, the pollution effect does not fade away. Moreover, given our adoption

Table 6.2 The effect of air pollution on analyst ratings

	FE	FE	FE	FE-IV
	(1)	(2)	(3)	(4)
L.lnincome	0.2986*** (0.0346)	0.2680*** (0.0357)	0.2672*** (0.0369)	0.2913*** (0.0536)
AQI	−0.0037*** (0.0008)	−0.0038*** (0.0009)	−0.0039*** (0.0009)	−0.0288** (0.0128)
Temp		0.0459*** (0.0113)	0.0456*** (0.0118)	−0.0043 (0.0305)
Temp2		−0.0012*** (0.0003)	−0.0012*** (0.0003)	−0.0008 (0.0005)
Prec		−0.0063* (0.0035)	−0.0064* (0.0036)	−0.0226** (0.0097)
Avegdp			−0.0196 (0.0341)	0.0065 (0.0501)
Scenicspot			0.0050** (0.0023)	0.0062* (0.0033)
Restaurant			−0.1349 (0.2252)	−0.2173 (0.3216)
Highspeedrail			−0.0379 (0.0611)	−0.0172 (0.0871)
Year F.E.	Yes	Yes	Yes	Yes
Month F.E.	Yes	Yes	Yes	Yes
City F.E.	Yes	Yes	Yes	Yes
Observations	862	829	791	791
Adj. R^2	0.675	0.689	0.661	

Robust standard errors in parentheses. *** $p < 0.01$, ** $p < 0.05$, * $p < 0.1$

of high-frequency monthly data and controls for the lagged tourism income, only the count of scenic spots exerts a positive influence on domestic tourism income. Column (4) presents the results of the instrumental variable (IV) regression. The negative impact of air pollution on tourism income remains consistent, and it is noteworthy that the magnitude of this effect is more pronounced compared to the results from the ordinary least squares (OLS) regression model. Additionally, the F-statistic for the weak identification test in the first stage is 26.09, which confirms the reliability of thermal inversion as an appropriate instrumental variable.

6.4.3 *Heterogeneity Effects and Mechanism Tests*

In this section, we first conduct a series of heterogeneity analyses based on city characteristics and different AQI categories. Tourists often have distinct preferences, especially when confronted with highly polluted environments or cities. Next, we explore potential mechanisms to better understand the adverse effects of air pollution on the tourism sector.

6.4.3.1 Nonlinear Impact of Air Pollution on Domestic Tourism Income

Given the well-established negative effects of air pollution on health and emotional well-being, it is reasonable to assume that tourists are less likely to choose destinations with an AQI exceeding 100 or higher. Particularly, days with an AQI exceeding 100 are categorized as polluted, while those exceeding 200 are considered heavily polluted, with conditions worsening considerably when AQI is valued beyond 300. Consequently, different levels of air pollution severity are expected to produce divergent impacts on tourism income, reflecting a nonlinear relationship presented in Table 6.3. Column (1) replaces the AQI level in the baseline model with the proportion of days exceeding an AQI of 100 over the total monthly days. Column (2) reveals the results where the key variable is the ratio of days surpassing an AQI of 200 over the total monthly days, while Column (3) delves into outcomes utilizing the ratio of days exceeding an AQI of 300 over the total monthly days to estimate pollution intensity. The coefficient estimates are −0.36, −3.39, and − 4.32, respectively, all of which are statistically significant at the 1% level. Notably, the economic significance of these coefficients is also substantial. For example, an increase of 1 day featuring an AQI surpassing 100 results in a 1.2% (0.3620/30) reduction in domestic tourism income. In contrast, a single additional day with an AQI exceeding 200 or 300 leads to considerably more substantial negative ramifications, wielding an 11.3% and 14.4% decline in domestic tourism income, separately.

6.4.3.2 Heterogeneity Analysis of City Characteristics

Furthermore, tourists may display distinct preferences concerning cities characterized by varying degrees of air pollution, influenced by the tourism resources of these cities. In general, heavily polluted urban centers suffer from more significant air quality challenges. To shed light on this phenomenon, we divide our dataset into two categories: heavily polluted cities and lightly polluted cities, demarcated by the median AQI value. Columns (1) and (2) in Table 6.4 present evidence related to these distinct subgroups. Specifically, our results indicate that air pollution has a detrimental effect on tourism income only in cities with high levels of pollution. Here, the coefficient obtained is −0.0063, exceeding the magnitude observed in the baseline model. This aligns with our intuition that air pollution can significantly impact a destination's attractiveness to tourists. On the contrary, for less polluted cities, where the AQI typically falls below the median value of approximately 68, the effect is not statistically significant.

Furthermore, it is essential to admit that cities vary in terms of their popularity, especially when travelers consider air pollution in their decision-making processes.

Table 6.3 Nonlinear effect of air pollution on domestic tourism

	FE	FE	FE
	(1)	(2)	(3)
L. lnincome	0.2687*** (0.0370)	0.2585*** (0.0358)	0.2630*** (0.0371)
AQI100	−0.3620*** (0.0953)		
AQI200		−3.3902*** (0.4220)	
AQI300			−4.3272*** (1.4654)
Controls	Yes	Yes	Yes
Year F.E.	Yes	Yes	Yes
Month F.E.	Yes	Yes	Yes
City F.E.	Yes	Yes	Yes
Observations	791	791	791
Adj. R^2	0.636	0.659	0.633

Robust standard errors in parentheses. *** $p < 0.01$, ** $p < 0.05$, * $p < 0.1$

Table 6.4 Heterogeneity analysis of city characteristics

	High polluted cities	Low polluted cities	"Hot" tourist cities	Non-"Hot" cities
	(1)	(2)	(3)	(4)
L. lnincome	0.2627*** (0.0548)	0.2877*** (0.0506)	0.1060* (0.0575)	0.2165*** (0.0546)
AQI	−0.0063*** (0.0014)	0.0011 (0.0013)	−0.0076*** (0.0015)	−0.0018* (0.0011)
Controls	Yes	Yes	Yes	Yes
Year F.E.	Yes	Yes	Yes	Yes
Month F.E.	Yes	Yes	Yes	Yes
City F.E.	Yes	Yes	Yes	Yes
Observations	371	420	334	457
Adj. R^2	0.514	0.766	0.745	0.586

Robust standard errors in parentheses. *** $p < 0.01$, ** $p < 0.05$, * $p < 0.1$

These choices tend to entail a subtle trade-off between air quality and city attractiveness. We presume that more popular cities might experience more significant adverse effects from air pollution compared to their less popular counterparts. To elaborate on this distinction, we turn to the 2018 annual report ranking the top 50 most popular cities and then select the top 20 cities as our "hot" cities. We classify 9 cities as "hot" and categorize the remainder as non-"hot" cities. The results are showcased in columns (3) and (4) of Table 6.4. Notably, the impact of air pollution on the tourism industry is particularly significant in the "hot" cities, with a coefficient of −0.0076, demonstrating statistical significance at the 1% level. This magnitude is twice as large as the effect observed in the baseline model. Conversely, for the less popular cities, the effect reaches statistical significance only at the 10% level. These insights are valuable, particularly for policymakers who seek to design effective strategies.

6.4.3.3 Mechanism Analysis

In this section, we endeavor to identify potential mechanisms through which this observed effect is achieved. Initially, as discussed earlier, a crucial shift occurred in 2013 when the air pollution metrics expanded from measuring 3 pollutants to encompassing 6 pollutants, which provides a more robust assessment of air quality. Figure 6.3 visually generalizes the nation-level pattern of daily AQIs exceeding 100. Evidently, the frequency of AQIs surpassing 100 substantially intensified post-2013. Notably, the newly employed measure effectively captures a greater number of days marked by heightened pollution levels.

Furthermore, since 2013, the issue of air pollution has obtained increasing public attention. In their decision-making processes, people have begun to put greater reliance on the new air quality standard as opposed to the older one. Therefore, we divide our dataset into two distinct subgroups: one encompassing data from before 2013 and another from 2013 to 2016. The results are presented in Table 6.5. Column (1) shows the results based on the dataset from 2006 to 2012, indicating that the effect

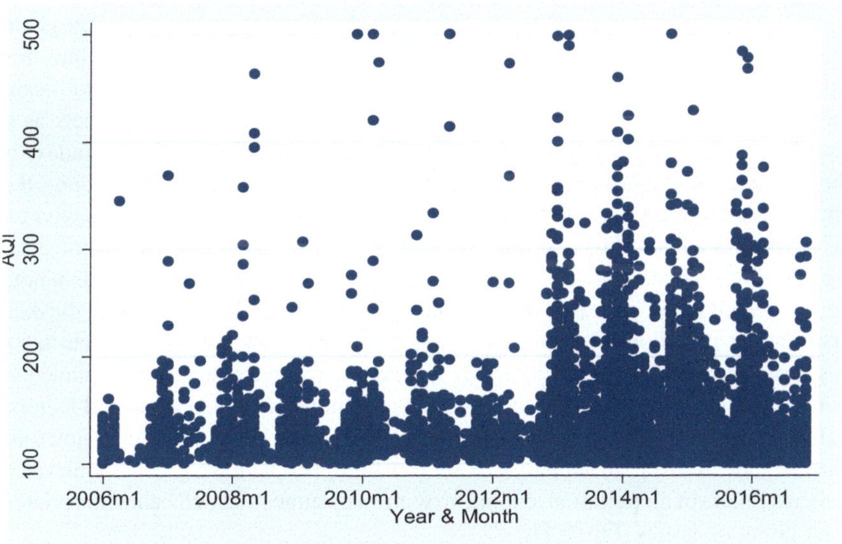

Fig. 6.3 The scatterplot of the number of cities with daily AQIs > 100

Table 6.5 Robustness checks for alternative AQI

	2006–2012	2013–2016
	(1)	(2)
L. lnincome	0.0956* (0.0579)	0.3316*** (0.0484)
AQI	−0.0019 (0.0016)	−0.0042*** (0.0012)
Controls	Yes	Yes
Year F.E.	Yes	Yes
Month F.E.	Yes	Yes
City F.E.	Yes	Yes
Observations	317	474
Adj. R^2	0.766	0.310

Robust standard errors in parentheses. *** $p < 0.01$, ** $p < 0.05$, * $p < 0.1$

of the API on domestic tourism income is not statistically significant. In contrast, Column (2), which pertains to the dataset from 2013 to 2016, reveals that the effect of the AQI is statistically significant at the 1% level, with its magnitude surpassing that of the baseline result. Specifically, a one standard deviation increase in the monthly average AQI leads to a significant 10.3% decrease in domestic tourism income. This effect can be ascribed to the mechanism where individuals, when recognizing the severity of air pollution, adjust their decisions correspondingly, leading to significant ramifications for the destination city's tourism sector.

The second potential mechanism relates to the level of public attention given to air pollution. Our analysis in the preceding table offers some insights into this aspect of public perception. Given that the effect becomes statistically significant only after 2013, we explore whether public awareness of air pollution acts as a plausible mechanism. The Baidu index, analogous to the Google search index, is a widely accepted measure for assessing public attention, effectively reflecting the perceived level of air pollution. Our dataset encompasses complete information on the Baidu index from 2011, in line with the period of 2011 to 2016 in our data. Fig. 6.4 shows monthly air pollution search index from 2011 to 2016. One can note that the search index increased dramatically after 2013, which concurs with the date when the air pollution measure was changed. Before 2013, the daily search index was approximately 300, while after 2013, the daily average search index doubled to more than 600. The increase in the Baidu index can be attributed to several factors, including the onset of haze and severe air pollution that began affecting numerous Chinese cities starting in January 2013. Over time, people have gradually elevated their awareness of air pollution, ending up with an upsurge in search behaviors related to air pollution issues (Fig. 6.4).

To assess the impact of public-perceived air pollution on the tourism industry, we examine the interaction term between actual air pollution and perceived air pollution, as outlined in the second specification. Both real and perceived air pollution are

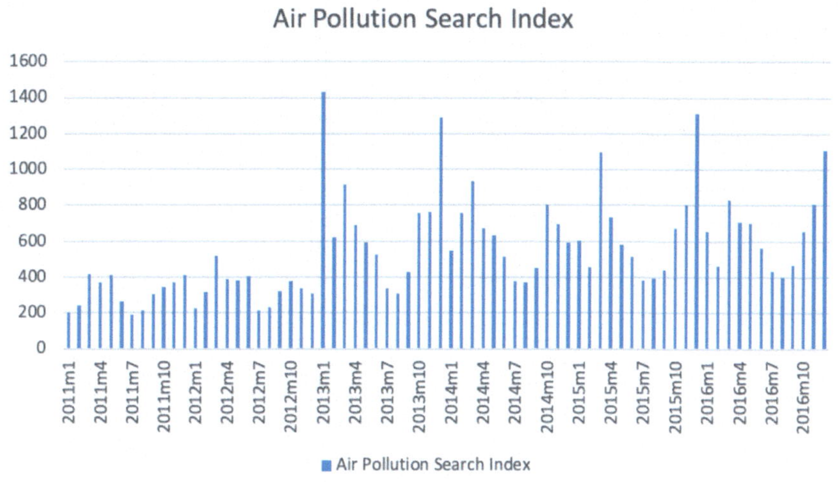

Fig. 6.4 Monthly air pollution search index from 2011 to 2016

decentralized for analysis. The results are presented in Table 6.6. In Column (1), where only time fixed effects are controlled for, it is evident that the effect of actual air pollution on the tourism industry remains statistically significant, with a magnitude similar to that observed in the baseline model. However, our primary focus is on the interaction term, which is significantly negative at the 5% level. In Column (2), where we add controls for city characteristics, weather conditions, and time fixed effects, the results remain consistent with those in Column (1). Notably, increased public awareness of air pollution amplifies the negative impact of air pollution on the tourism sector. Our results offer compelling evidence confirming the significant role played by public attention in the people's decision-making processes.

6.4.4 *Robustness Checks*

6.4.4.1 Alternative Measures of the Tourism Industry

In addition to domestic tourism income, the count of domestic tourists serves as a reasonable measure for estimating the appeal and prosperity of tourist destinations. Furthermore, we consider two additional alternative indicators within the tourism sector, both closely pertaining to the hotel industry. Given its crucial role in offering support services for the tourism sector, the hotel industry exerts substantial influence in this domain. During periods of increased tourism activity, the demand for accommodations heightens, ultimately achieving increased hotel revenue. According to the statistics from the World Tourism Organization, the hotel industry depends on

Table 6.6 Results of the effect of the search index on the tourism sector

	FE	FE
	(1)	(2)
L. lnincome	0.3260*** (0.0394)	0.2995*** (0.0417)
AQI	−0.0029*** (0.0011)	−0.0028** (0.0012)
AQI × SearchIndex	−0.0033** (0.0013)	−0.0031** (0.0015)
SearchIndex	0.1484* (0.0759)	0.1527* (0.0779)
Controls	Yes	Yes
Year F.E.	Yes	Yes
Month F.E.	Yes	Yes
City F.E.	Yes	Yes
Observations	638	612
Adj. R^2	0.441	0.427

Robust standard errors in parentheses. *** $p < 0.01$, ** $p < 0.05$, * $p < 0.1$

tourism for over 85% of its business, accentuating the rationale for adopting measures from the hotel sector as proper proxies for gauging the broader tourism industry.

Specifically, two alternative measures are introduced—the revenue per available room per night (and the quarterly total operating income of each hotel room for all star hotels. We obtained the hotel revenue data for 50 cities from 2010 to 2016 at a quarterly frequency. It is without doubt that the number of tourists and tourism income are highly correlated with these two indicators. Our robustness checks are designed to test the consistency of the results regarding the effects of air pollution on hotel prices and income. Since the quarterly average AQI may not immediately capture tourists' choice of destination city, we also introduce the ratio of the number of days with an AQI above 100 to the total number of days in each quarter as our primary explanatory variable.

The estimation results are presented in Table 6.7. Column (1) reports the effect of air pollution on the number of domestic tourists. The impact is not only statistically significant but also economically meaningful. A one-unit increase in the AQI leads to a 0.15% decrease in the number of domestic tourists. Additionally, the effects of air pollution on hotel revenue align with our expectations, being both statistically and economically significant. Specifically, a 1-day increase in the number of days with an AQI above 100 results in a 0.2% decrease in hotel revenue per room per night and a 0.08% decrease in seasonal hotel revenue per room. Furthermore, all of our results indicate an indirect effect of air pollution on tourist avoidance behavior.

Table 6.7 Results of alternative measures of the tourism sector

	lntourists	lnrevenue_perroom	lntotalincome
	FE	FE	FE
L. Y	0.3494*** (0.0320)	0.2877*** (0.0506)	0.1060* (0.0575)
AQI	−0.0015** (0.0006)		
AQI100		−0.1915*** (0.0665)	−0.0816* (0.0478)
Controls	Yes	Yes	Yes
Year F.E.	Yes	Yes	Yes
Month F.E.	Yes	Yes	Yes
City F.E.	Yes	Yes	Yes
Observations	1024	1048	1048
Adj. R^2	0.562	0.123	0.233

Robust standard errors in parentheses. *** $p < 0.01$, ** $p < 0.05$, * $p < 0.1$

6.4.4.2 Alternative Air Pollution Measures

In addition to relying exclusively on ground-based air pollution data sourced from the MEPC, we further utilize supplementary data related to two significant air pollutants, namely PM2.5 and SO_2. These data are obtained using satellite-based aerosol optical depth (AOD) retrieval techniques, which are carefully maintained by the National Aeronautics and Space Administration (NASA). It is notable that satellite-derived data are less susceptible to manipulation when compared to ground-based air pollution data sources, as asserted by Ghanem and Zhang (2014). The results are detailed in Table 6.8, with Columns (1) and (2) displaying the effects of PM2.5 on tourism income, while Columns (3) and (4) showcase the effects of SO_2 on domestic tourism income. In all columns, the coefficients produce statistically significant negative values. Specifically, a one-unit increase in PM2.5 is associated with a 0.3% decrease in domestic tourism income. Notably, the effect is even more pronounced for SO_2. In conclusion, various measures of air pollution consistently reinforce the negative impact of air pollution on the domestic tourism sector.

Table 6.8 Results of alternative measures of the tourism sector

	FE	FE	FE	FE
	(1)	(2)	(3)	(4)
L. lnincome	0.2644*** (0.0359)	0.2631*** (0.0371)	0.2678*** (0.0360)	0.2673*** (0.0372)
PM2.5	−0.0027** (0.0011)	−0.0030*** (0.0011)		
SO_2			−0.0057** (0.0028)	−0.0063** (0.0029)
Controls	Yes	Yes	Yes	Yes
Year F.E.	Yes	Yes	Yes	Yes
Month F.E.	Yes	Yes	Yes	Yes
City F.E.	Yes	Yes	Yes	Yes
Observations	829	791	829	791
Adj. R^2	0.666	0.632	0.665	0.631

Robust standard errors in parentheses. *** $p < 0.01$, ** $p < 0.05$, * $p < 0.1$

6.5 Conclusion

This paper explores the impact of air pollution on the domestic tourism sector by analyzing monthly domestic tourism income, the monthly number of domestic tourists, and quarterly hotel revenue across more than 30 cities from 2006 to 2016. Our findings accentuate the existence of a notably negative correlation between air pollution and the domestic tourism sector. Specifically, Poor air quality hazards tourism income and the count of tourists through the mechanism of driving tourists away from polluted cities. Furthermore, this adverse impact is amplified in cities featuring heavy pollution, especially during periods of elevated pollution levels, and amid a surge in public awareness of air quality issues.

Our findings make a significant contribution to the growing body of research that examines the impact of air pollution on the tourism sector. They offer valuable insights to the authorities and travel agencies. First, it is imperative for policymakers, particularly those who govern cities suffering from harsh air pollution, to rigorously assess the trade-off between promoting industry development and building an environmentally friendly city. This consideration holds significance, especially for cities with more abundant tourism resources. In contrast, cities endowed with good air quality conditions should seize the opportunity to prepare for potential visitors, particularly during periods susceptible to poor air quality. Second, to achieve potential profits, travel agencies are supposed to provide different plans with regard to air pollution severity to satisfy tourists' demand for clean air.

References

Adhvaryu A, Kala N, Nyshadham A (2014) Management and shocks to worker productivity: evidence from air pollution exposure in an Indian garment factory. Unpublished working paper, University of Michigan

Alvarez-Díaz M, Rosselló J (2010) Forecasting British tourist arrivals in the Balearic Islands using meteorological variables. Tour Econ 16(1):153–168

Arceo E, Hanna R, Oliva P (2016) Does the effect of pollution on infant mortality differ between developing and developed countries? Evidence from Mexico city. Econ J 126(591):257–280

Barwick PJ, Li S, Rao D, Zahur NB (2018) The morbidity cost of air pollution: evidence from consumer spending in China. NBER Working Paper, (24688)

Becken S, Wilson J (2013) The impacts of weather on tourist travel. Tourism 15:620–639

Becken S, Miller G, Banhalmi-Zakar Z (2016) Making an impact: practices and views of tourism academics. Griffith Institute for Tourism, Griffith University

Bigano A, Hamilton JM, Tol RS (2006) The impact of climate on holiday destination choice. Clim Chang 76(3–4):389–406

Bigano A, Hamilton JM, Lau M, Tol RS, Zhou Y (2007) A global database of domestic and international tourist numbers at national and subnational level. Int J Tour Res 9(3):147–174

Bullinger M (1989) Psychological effects of air pollution on healthy residents—a time-series approach. J Environ Psychol 9(2):103–118

Chang T, Graff Zivin J, Gross T, Neidell M (2016) Particulate pollution and the productivity of pear packers. Am Econ J Econ Policy 8(3):141–169

Chang T, Graff Zivin J, Gross T, Neidell M (2019) The effect of pollution on worker productivity: evidence from call-center workers in China. Am Econ J Appl Econ 11(1):151–172

Chay KY, Greenstone M (2003) The impact of air pollution on infant mortality: evidence from geographic variation in pollution shocks induced by a recession. Q J Econ 118(3):1121–1167

Chen Y, Ebenstein A, Greenstone M, Li H (2013) Evidence on the impact of sustained exposure to air pollution on life expectancy from China's Huai River policy. Proc Natl Acad Sci 110(32):12936–12941

Chen CM, Lin YL, Hsu CL (2017) Does air pollution drive away tourists? A case study of the sun moon lake national scenic area, Taiwan. Transp Res Part D: Transp Environ 53:398–402

Chen S, Li Y, Yao Q (2018a) The health costs of the industrial leap forward in China: evidence from the sulfur dioxide emissions of coal-fired power stations. China Econ Rev 49:68–83

Chen S, Oliva P, Zhang P (2022) The effect of air pollution on migration: evidence from China. J Development Economics 156: 102833

Chen F, Zhang X, Chen Z (2023) Air pollution and mental health: Evidence from China Health and Nutrition Survey. J Asian Economics 86: 101611

Choi Y, Yoon H, Kim D (2019) Where do people spend their leisure time on dusty days? Application of spatiotemporal behavioral responses to particulate matter pollution. In: Annals of regional science, pp 1–23

EPA (2004) Air quality criteria for particulate matter. https://cfpub.epa.gov/ncea/risk/recordisplay.cfm?deid=87903

Freitas CR (2003) Tourism climatology: evaluating environmental information for decision making and business planning in the recreation and tourism sector. Int J Biometeorol 48(1):45–54

Fu S, Viard VB, Zhang P (2021) Air pollution and manufacturing firm productivity: nationwide estimates for China. The Economic Journal 131(640): 3241–3273

Ghanem D, Zhang J (2014) 'Effortless perfection:' do Chinese cities manipulate air pollution data? J Environ Econ Manag 68(2):203–225

Goh C (2012) Exploring impact of climate on tourism demand. Ann Tour Res 39(4):1859–1883

Graff Zivin J, Neidell M (2012) The impact of pollution on worker productivity. Am Econ Rev 102(7):3652–3673

Guo M, Fu S (2019) Running with a mask? The effect of air pollution on marathon runners' performance. J Sports Econ 20:903–928. https://doi.org/10.1177/1527002518822701

Hsiao C (2003) Analysis of panel data, 2nd edn. Cambridge University Press
Ito K, Zhang S (2020) Willingness to pay for clean air: evidence from air purifier markets in China. J Political Economy 128(5): 1627–1672
Jeuring JH, Peters KB (2013) The influence of the weather on tourist experiences: analysing travel blog narratives. J Vacat Mark 19(3):209–219
Lin Y, Liu F (2019) Indoor air quality and health: empirical evidence from fluoride pollution in China. China Econ Rev 63:101282. https://doi.org/10.1016/j.chieco.2019.03.001
Neidell MJ (2004) Air pollution, health, and socio-economic status: the effect of outdoor air quality on childhood asthma. J Health Econ 23(6):1209–1236
Neidell M (2009) Information, avoidance behavior, and health the effect of ozone on asthma hospitalizations. J Hum Resour 44(2):450–478
Peng J, Xiao H (2018) How does smog influence domestic tourism in China? A case study of Beijing. Asia Pac J Tour Res 23(12):1115–1128
Qin Y, Zhu H (2018) Run away? Air pollution and emigration interests in China. J Popul Econ 31(1):235–266
Rosselló J, Riera-Font A, Cárdenas V (2011) The impact of weather variability on British outbound flows. Clim Chang 105(1–2):281–292
Schlenker W, Walker WR (2015) Airports, air pollution, and contemporaneous health. Rev Econ Stud 83(2):768–809
Wang L, Fang B, Law R (2018) Effect of air quality in the place of origin on outbound tourism demand: disposable income as a moderator. Tour Manag 68:152–161
Xu X, Reed M (2017) Perceived pollution and inbound tourism in China. Tour Manag Perspect 21:109–112
Yoon H (2019) Effects of particulate matter (PM10) on tourism sales revenue: a generalized additive modeling approach. Tour Manag 74:358–369
Zhang J, Mu Q (2018) Air pollution and defensive expenditures: evidence from particulate-filtering facemasks. J Environ Econ Manag 92:517–536
Zhang A, Zhong L, Xu Y, Wang H, Dang L (2015) Tourists' perception of haze pollution and the potential impacts on travel: reshaping the features of tourism seasonality in Beijing, China. Sustain For 7(3):2397–2414
Zhang X, Zhang X, Chen X (2017) Happiness in the air: how does a dirty sky affect mental health and subjective well-being? J Environ Econ Manag 85:81–94
Zhou B, Qu H, Du X, Yang B, Liu F (2018) Air quality and inbound tourism in China. Tour Anal 23(1):159–164

Chapter 7
Breathing Easier? Air Pollution and the Health Insurance Sector

Abstract Air pollution has emerged as a persistent concern in Chinese society, affecting both individual health and economic development. This study employs behavioral finance principles and utilizes city-level panel data to investigate the relationship between air pollution and the demand for Chinese commercial health insurance, specifically examining the impact of annual PM2.5 concentration on premium income. Empirical analysis demonstrates a significant positive correlation between increasing PM2.5 levels and heightened demand for commercial health insurance. Moreover, the research reveals that a rise in the number of days with an AQI exceeding 150 in a given area and an increased societal emphasis on PM2.5 also contribute substantially to the demand for health insurance. These findings are robustly substantiated through comprehensive tests, underscoring the intricate interplay between air quality, health insurance, and broader economic implications in China.

Keywords Air pollution · Demand for commercial health insurance · PM2.5 · AQI · Baidu Index

7.1 Introduction

Air pollution's enduring significance in the realms of environmental conservation and economic progress has remained a longstanding concern in China. Extensive research attests to its substantial influence across various aspects of society. Air pollution impacts not only economic development but also individual welfare, which cannot be overlooked. Especially for individuals, the health risks stemming from air pollution cannot be completely mitigated through pension schemes and mandatory social health insurance. Commercial health insurance, serving as a risk management tool within personal financial planning, holds the potential to effectively shield individuals from such risks. Surprisingly, there is a scarcity of literature directly investigating the relationship between the demand for commercial health insurance and air pollution. Furthermore, adopting a behavioral finance framework in this research requires us to explore the intricate mechanisms beneath individual financial behaviors under

M. Guo et al., *Social-Economic Impacts of Air Pollution*, Climate Change and Energy Transition, https://doi.org/10.1007/978-981-96-7858-7_7

the pressure of air pollution. Consequently, it is of great necessity to examine the air pollution effect and the mechanism through which the impact is transferred to people's portfolios.

In this paper, we aim to examine the promoting role of air pollution on individuals' demand for commercial health insurance. Previous related studies have mainly relied on transaction-level samples or province-level panels to conduct analyses due to the inaccessibility of relevant data, which might introduce biases to their results. By comparison, our research employs a prefecture-level panel dataset which encompasses richer information to capture variations, while endowing our conclusions with more credibility and alignment with the prevailing real-world circumstances. Moreover, we build a theoretical framework from the perspective of behavioral finance and empirically demonstrate its presence in the public's confrontation with air pollution. More importantly, we find that individuals' risk perception could generate a variety of cognitive biases, such as differentiation, ambiguity, and time lag, during the process of information acquisition. Therefore, these cognitive biases are identified as a vital mechanism between air pollution and individuals' financial behaviors, and proper signals are needed to mitigate them.

Our paper mainly pertains to two strands of literature, with the first related to the impact of air pollution. In China, extensive research and discourse have been conducted to explore the various dimensions of the notorious air pollution issue. Existing works have delved into the adverse consequences of air pollution from various facets, ranging from physical and mental well-being to economic costs. From the perspective of individual health, the significant physical harm inflicted by air pollution on human bodies is intuitive. Notably, several groups including children and the elderly are particularly susceptible to air pollution by experiencing enhanced discomfort in polluted air. In the long term, chronic heart and lung diseases, respiratory infections, and a greatly elevated risk of malignant tumors would become prevalent consequences of constant exposure to air pollution (Epa 2004). Empirical studies have detected a substantial increase in neonatal-related diseases in areas with persistent air pollution (Chay and Greenstone 2003). Additionally, air pollution could escalate the incidence of asthma (Neidell 2004) and reduce life expectancy (Chen et al. 2013). Furthermore, it adversely affects people's mental health, leading to a significant reduction in overall welfare (Huang and He 2013; Zheng et al. 2019).

Air pollution also exerts a notable influence on people's social behaviors and productivity. For instance, research on Chinese professional football players has demonstrated that air pollution negatively affects individual productivity (Wei et al. 2017). Fu et al. (2021) documents that air pollution has detrimental effects on per capita value added within enterprises, ultimately reducing overall productivity. Moreover, studies by Chen et al. (2017) and Sun et al. (2019) find that elevated PM2.5 levels would propel population migration, thus impacting the distribution of human resources. It is also found that increased exposure to polluted air would significantly elevate adrenal cortisol levels, eventually causing metabolic disorders, reducing the desire for risk-taking behavior, and even changing the public's risk preferences (Nowakowicz-Debek and Saba 2004). The costs of air pollution also extend beyond physical, mental, and behavioral well-being, causing unnecessary expenses derived from disease prevention and treatment. For example, Deryugina et al. (2019) examine the link between particulate matter exposure, mortality, and healthcare use in the U.S. Barwick et al. (2018) show that both short-term (a week) and long-term (3 months) health expenditures are associated with PM2.5 exposure. Xie et al. (2014) have analyzed a specific severe haze pollution event in China and suggested that short-term exposure to high concentrations of PM2.5 would pose great health risks and generate considerable economic burdens on affected individuals.

As individuals become increasingly aware of the adverse effects of air pollution, and confront increased potential medical expenses, many of them would recognize that solely relying on pensions and mandatory medical insurance cannot provide enough support for future risks. Commercial health insurance thus emerges as an effective financial product to spread risk and an essential complement to individuals' asset allocation. With the help of the widespread dissemination of financial knowledge across society, public interest in commercial health insurance shows an increasing trend in China. From 1999 to 2013, China's commercial health insurance premiums exhibited an average annual growth rate of 27.53% (Peng et al. 2017).

Previous research has explored both the supply and demand side of commercial health insurance. It is notable that China's social health insurance system not only failed to replace commercial health insurance but also facilitated its growth instead (Peng et al. 2017; Liu and Wang 2012). In terms of the demand side, Liu and Wang (2012) emphasize the significance of personal risk exposure and purchasing power as pivotal factors affecting individuals' decisions to invest in medical insurance. Moreover, cultural factors and taxation policies suggested by Thomasson (2003) pose remarkable influences on individuals' acceptance of commercial health insurance. This suggests when the risk of harm stemming from environmental factors (e.g., air pollution) escalates, the heightened demand for commercial health insurance will follow.

However, there remains a gap in existing research that directly investigates the effect of air pollution on the demand for commercial health insurance. Moreover, limited attention has been paid to how air pollution can impact consumers' preferences in asset allocation. Chang et al. (2018) unveil that air pollution is positively correlated with individuals' demand for commercial health insurance. Meanwhile, this study also suggests that under changing external conditions, people's decision-making processes are more likely to be affected by biases, also influencing the allocation of commercial insurance. Nevertheless, this study heavily relies on short-term data from a single company which would probably introduce biases and lose precision in estimation, making it not applicable to a more general context. In addition, individual characteristics are pivotal factors influencing decision-making processes, yet the study fails to control for residents' individual characteristics, and the omitted variable issue could possibly arise, thus weakening the reliability of its results. Moreover, this study effectively addresses the gaps in the existing literature and avoids the overreliance on individual-level data. However, it is worth noting that provincial-level data employed in this research lacks the precision featured by lower-level data.

The subsequent sections of this paper will unfold as follows: Sect. 7.2 will elucidate the development of our model, provide a description of data, and present summary statistics. In Sect. 7.3, we will present the empirical results regarding the impact of air pollution on the demand for commercial health insurance consumption and provide several heterogeneity analyses and robustness checks. Finally, we will conclude our study.

7.2 Empirical Strategy and Data

7.2.1 Empirical Strategy

Based on the analyses above, we present the baseline specification as follows:

$$\ln(Health\ Insurance_{it}) = \beta_0 + \beta_1 PM2.5_{i(t-1)} + \beta_2 FI_{it} + \beta_3 X_{it} + \beta_4 W_{it} + \alpha_i + \rho_t + \varepsilon_i t$$

where *ln(Health Insurance)* is the natural logarithm of premium income for commercial health insurance in year t in area i. *PM2.5* is the annual average concentration of PM2.5 in year t in area i. For the control variables, we introduce a vector, denoted as X, comprising the natural logarithm of government fiscal income, the mean total income of residents, the level of foreign direct investment, the ratio of college and university students per thousand people, Health Resources Index (the proportion of hospitals per thousand people), and the insurance industry Herfindahl-Hirschman Index (HHI). We also include a weather vector consisting of three weather-related variables (sunshine, precipitation, and temperature) which are all converted into natural logarithmic forms. α represents the prefecture fixed effects, which control the time-persistent city attributes that could affect the demand for commercial health insurance. ρ denotes the year fixed effects to capture the year-specific shocks to the demand for commercial health insurance.

7.2.2 Variable Description

The dependent variable in this paper, relative to prior research, is the premium income due to its direct reflection of consumer financial behavior and its ability to avoid potential collinearity issues with our control variables. Concerned about the interpretation of the results, the natural logarithm is employed to conduct the regression. In terms of the independent variables, to address the data gaps in historical PM2.5 concentration, we follow the approach brought by Shao et al. (2016) and employ China's annual average PM2.5 concentration dataset gridded by Dalhousie University's Atmospheric Composition Analysis Group (Donkelaar et al. 2015, 2019). Using ArcGIS software, we convert this dataset into specific annual average PM2.5 concentrations (μg/m^3)

at the prefectural city level in China during the period from 2009 to 2017, consistent with the assessments of air pollution by the Chinese Ministry of Ecology and Environment and with trends exhibited in the AQI index issued by the same ministry. Meanwhile, to facilitate robustness checks, we have also gathered AQI data spanning 2009 to 2017 and then aggregated it into a yearly variable. Furthermore, inspired by Yang and Guo (2019), we obtained Baidu index data by searching for the keyword "PM2.5" in numerous cities during the period from 2011 to 2017 and subsequently compiled the acquired information into a yearly variable for later analysis.

Our control variables represent important determinants affecting the propensity to purchase commercial health insurance, as suggested by previous literature. Fiscal revenue is a proxy for the local social health insurance development support which aligns with the findings of Peng et al. (2017), which indicates that the progress of social health insurance is correlated with the development of commercial health insurance. Resident income represents the local economic performance, indicating that a higher level of resident income signifies greater affordability and willingness to allocate personal assets to ancillary commercial insurance. Foreign direct investment, displays a significant positive association with fine particulate matter (PM2.5) pollution, which is measured in million yuan. Education level can reflect a city's cultural education standard, consistent with Suo et al. (2015) who reveal that a higher educational background results in an increased likelihood for individuals to buy health insurance for risk management. The Health Resources Index represents the availability of local medical resources, measured by the number of hospitals per thousand people. This aligns with Peng et al. (2017) assertion that fewer medical resources could increase the burden of medical expenses, thereby encouraging residents to possess health insurance. Furthermore, the insurance industry Herfindahl-Hirschman Index controls the concentration of the insurance industry in a particular area, which is proposed by Suo et al. (2015). A higher industry concentration in a specific location often leads to higher product prices, thus potentially influencing the demand for the product or the service. This index is calculated as the sum of squared market share numbers for all companies within the local insurance market. Eventually, since local weather conditions can also have a significant impact on individuals' financial decisions and have correlations with PM2.5 concentration (Zheng et al. 2019), we also introduce a series of meteorological variables including sunshine, precipitation, and temperature, measured by annual sunshine hours, precipitation (in millimeters), and average temperature (in Celsius). Natural logarithmic transformation is then applied to both total sunshine hours and precipitation in the regression.

7.2.3 Data and Descriptive Statistics

Our research covers the period from 2009 to 2017 and employs data from 278 cities across 29 provinces in mainland China, excluding Tibet and Xinjiang due to data unavailability. Premium income data of commercial health insurance, life insurance, and accident insurance are sourced from the China Insurance Yearbook, while other

Table 7.1 Descriptive statistics

Variable	Obs	Mean	Std. Dev.	Min	Median	Max
Health	2878	4.903	1.441	−1.427	4.840	12.777
Acci.	2876	3.378	1.128	−2.996	3.307	11.415
Life	2879	7.573	1.116	0.010	7.585	15.487
PM2.5	2870	37.396	16.677	4.676	34.809	86.480
AQI	1560	79.663	24.826	27.477	75.241	384.000
Lnindex	1911	3.648	1.177	0.000	3.829	8.099
HR	2828	0.569	0.742	0.000	0.429	11.477
HE	2828	175.653	235.335	0.000	88.345	1311.241
Salary	2805	10.606	0.378	8.509	10.633	11.810
Fiscal	2828	13.655	1.132	10.174	13.592	18.010
HHI	2839	0.244	0.123	0.067	0.215	1.000
Sunshine	2728	7.547	0.278	6.394	7.554	8.402
Rain	2728	6.741	0.642	3.959	6.782	8.078
Temp.	2728	14.833	4.968	0.200	15.700	26.900

control variables derive from the data of the China City Statistical Yearbook, and meteorological variables are obtained from various regional statistical yearbooks. AQI data is sourced from the official website of the Ministry of Ecology and Environment of the People's Republic of China, and collected through web crawling and manual collation. Similarly, Baidu Index data is extracted from the Baidu Index official website. It is noteworthy that the China Insurance Yearbook only offers commercial health insurance premium income data up to 2017, thus setting the temporal scope for all sample data in this study up to that year. Descriptive statistics are detailed in Table 7.1 presented as follows.

7.3 Empirical Results

7.3.1 Baseline Results

Initially, a baseline regression is run to estimate the immediate influence of the independent variable (represented by the previous period's air pollution level measured by PM2.5 concentration) on the demand for commercial health insurance, utilizing a fixed effects model to control for unobservable factors. Our study also assesses the direct impact of the previous period's PM2.5 concentration on the current demand for commercial life insurance and accident insurance. The results are then presented in Table 7.2.

Table 7.2 Results of the baseline specification

Dep. Var.	Health	Acci.	Life
	(1)	(2)	(3)
Lag PM2.5	0.006** (2.02)	−0.003 (−1.33)	0.005*** (2.81)
FI	0.201*** (3.56)	0.219*** (3.40)	−0.094** (−2.53)
SAL	0.067 (0.69)	−0.016 (−0.15)	0.121 (1.36)
FDI	−0.044 (−0.37)	0.316** (2.52)	0.223* (1.91)
HR	−0.006 (−0.39)	0.012 (1.08)	0.004 (0.59)
HE	−0.001* (−1.75)	0.000 (0.16)	0.000 (0.43)
HHI	0.380 (1.06)	0.767 (1.59)	−0.924*** (−5.47)
Sunshine	−0.106 (−1.32)	−0.082 (−1.09)	0.005 (0.09)
Rain	0.033 (0.74)	0.049 (1.29)	0.004 (0.18)
Temperature	0.029 (1.50)	−0.006 (−0.38)	−0.004 (−0.41)
Year F.E.	Yes	Yes	Yes
City F.E.	Yes	Yes	Yes
Observations	2395	2394	2395
Adjusted R^2	0.82	0.63	0.61

Robust t values are in parentheses. *** $p < 0.01$, ** $p < 0.05$, * $p < 0.1$

As demonstrated in Table 7.2, at the countrywide level, the direct influence of air pollution on the demand for commercial health insurance is statistically significant at a 5% significance level. Specifically, a 1 μg/year increase in PM2.5 concentration during the city's previous period results in a 0.006% rise in the demand for commercial health insurance in the current period. However, the impact of air pollution on the demand for commercial accident insurance does not present statistical significance, which aligns with our expectations since most accidents are unrelated to air pollution. This could also eliminate confounding factors and confirm the robustness of our results. Moreover, it is notable that the significance level of air pollution's impact on the demand for commercial life insurance stands at 1%. A 1 μg/year increase in PM2.5 concentration during the previous period in a certain city corresponds to a 0.005% increase in the demand for commercial life insurance. This finding could be attributed to the fact that commercial life insurance serves as a financial instrument for risk-averse individuals. Since air pollution would exert long-term effects on individuals' health, investing in commercial life insurance could bring long-term advantages to these people. It is also worth mentioning that substituting the independent variable in this model with the current PM2.5 concentration level does not affect the demand for any type of commercial insurance. This might be put down to the cognitive lag among the public, despite the objective existence of air pollution, the public's subjective awareness of its impact on health lags behind. Only when the public fully comprehends the relationship between air pollution and health and enhances the accuracy of risk perception, they will be more likely to purchase commercial health insurance ultimately.

Concerning the control variables, factors such as healthcare resources, the proportion of the population with higher education, and individual income on average do not exhibit significant effects on the demand for various types of commercial insurance in our results. The availability of medical resources appears to be more of a foundational prerequisite than a critical determinant in individuals' considerations of future health risks. When medical resources are sufficient, their influence on individual risk-related decisions appears limited. Moreover, since the number of individuals pursuing higher education can serve as an indicator of a city's cultural sophistication, the results suggest that there may still exist a notable deficiency in financial literacy among the public, thus restricting the effect of education on the demand for commercial insurance. Similarly, while an increase in average personal income theoretically encourages individuals to utilize financial instruments to narrow their risk exposure, our data does not yield expected outcomes. This is possibly ascribed to the lack of widespread access to financial education and health risk awareness. Moreover, government fiscal income could indirectly signify the prevalence of social health insurance within a region. In our results, this variable could exert a substantial influence across all three categories of commercial insurance, significant at the 1% confidence level. It also accentuates how the presence of a social health insurance system promotes demand for both commercial health insurance and commercial accident injury insurance, aligning with prior scholarly research findings (Liu and Wang 2012). Meanwhile, this social health insurance system could wield a moderating effect on the demand for commercial life insurance, which can be explained by the overlapping roles of social medical insurance and commercial life insurance in China. Regarding the HHI index, we do not observe a significant effect on commercial health insurance, but when we exclusively examine commercial life insurance, it becomes significant at the 1% level, indicating that a high HHI index could negatively influence the demand for life insurance. This phenomenon emerges because, within Chinese insurance companies, the premium income generated from health insurance is smaller relative to life insurance. Particularly, in our robustness checks adopting instrumental variables, we find that HHI could inflict a significantly negative impact on the demand for commercial health insurance, which is consistent with our expectations.

7.3.2 *Heterogeneous Effects*

In this section, we conduct several heterogeneity analyses to better comprehend the alterations underneath our main results. Initially, it can be assumed that the demand for commercial health insurance exhibits regional variations, given that the purchasing behaviors of commercial health insurance could be influenced by the economic, geographical, and cultural conditions of different areas. Therefore, we first conduct several regressions on regional subsamples. Our regional division is based on the upper boundary of the warm temperate zone, characterized by an annual average temperature of 13 °C, thereby categorizing the country into two general regions: Northern China and Southern China. The Qin Mountains-Huai River boundary is a typical demarcation for this, which also separates out the warm temperate and subtropical zones. Our first heterogeneous results are documented in Table 7.3.

Table 7.3 Heterogeneous results by Northern and Southern China

	Northern (<13 °C)	Southern (≥13 °C)
	(1)	(2)
Lag PM2.5	0.006** (2.26)	0.012** (2.57)
FI	0.210** (2.29)	0.117 (1.42)
SAL	0.049 (0.45)	−0.029 (−0.16)
FDI	−0.021 (−0.09)	−0.061 (−0.41)
HR	0.001 (0.08)	−0.028 (−1.15)
HE	−0.001*** (−3.13)	−0.000 (−0.40)
HHI	1.080 (1.49)	−0.132 (−0.38)
Sunshine	−0.342** (−2.44)	0.075 (0.72)
Rain	0.049 (0.89)	0.011 (0.18)
Temp.	0.058 (1.55)	0.015 (0.55)
Year F.E.	Yes	Yes
City F.E.	Yes	Yes
Observations	686	1709
Adjusted R^2	0.80	0.83

Robust t values are in parentheses. *** $p < 0.01$, ** $p < 0.05$, * $p < 0.1$

According to the results, it is evident that over a long time frame, the direct influence of air pollution on the demand for commercial health insurance in both the southern and northern regions of China is statistically significant at a 5% significance level. If the PM2.5 concentration in a city in the northern region during the previous period increases by 1 μg/year, the demand for commercial health insurance during the current period in that city will rise by 0.006%. In comparison, if the PM2.5 concentration in a city in the southern region in the previous period increases by 1 μg/year, the demand for commercial health insurance in the current period in that city will increase by 0.012%, which is twice the effect captured in the northern region. This difference might stem from the fact that overall, southern China displays a stronger awareness of personal health and better economic conditions, possibly leading to a greater aversion to health risks in the public, thus causing a more significant impact of air pollution on the demand for commercial health insurance.

On top of that, the severe haze event that occurred in central and eastern China in December 2013, spanning from December 2 to December 14, 2013, marked one of the most extensive haze pollution incidents in China. Nearly all areas in these regions were intensively affected. The air quality index in places such as Tianjin, Hebei, Shandong, Jiangsu, Anhui, Henan, Zhejiang, Shanghai, and others all reached the highest level of severe pollution (level 6), according to China's air pollution categorization. Extant research has demonstrated that short-term exposure to high concentrations of PM2.5 pollution can enhance health risks, resulting in various acute respiratory ailments, depleting medical resources, and eventually increasing both short-term and long-term personal healthcare expenditures. It can be presumed that due to the substantial air pollution during this period, residents' perception of health risks may have been elevated. To allay these risks and benefit from avoiding potential harm, more individuals may have recognized the importance of acquiring commercial health insurance, thereby boosting the local demand for it. Based on that, our research also analyzes the subsamples from the central and eastern regions in China respectively, spanning the periods before and after 2013 (beginning in 2014), while constructing a control group encompassing the entire sample across China. The results are displayed in Table 7.4.

As demonstrated in Table 7.4, concerning the central and eastern regions of China, following the severe haze event in 2013, a statistically significant increase in demand for commercial health insurance at a 10% significance level occurs. Specifically, if the average annual PM2.5 concentration of a city in the previous period increases by 1 μg/year, the demand for commercial health insurance in this city during the current period will rise by 0.011%. In contrast, before 2013, there was no significant correlation between air pollution and the demand for commercial health insurance. Likewise, the same regression conducted using the national sample does not reveal a substantial correlation between air pollution and the demand for commercial health insurance. As per the existing literature, public attention tends to exhibit more immersive characteristics in the aftermath of severe pollution events, significantly influencing an individual's perception of air pollution's impact and subsequently their decision to purchase commercial health insurance. This phenomenon introduces an attention bias (Bordalo et al. 2013). Our results reveal that severe haze pollution incidents

Table 7.4 Heterogeneous results of the 2013 haze event in Eastern & Central China

	Eastern & Central		All	
	Before	After	Before	After
	(1)	(2)	(3)	(4)
Lag PM2.5	0.006 (0.93)	0.011* (1.66)	−0.000 (−0.05)	0.002 (0.38)
Controls	Yes	Yes	Yes	Yes
Year F.E.	Yes	Yes	Yes	Yes
City F.E.	Yes	Yes	Yes	Yes
Observations	1097	1042	1307	1088
Adjusted R^2	0.77	0.71	0.63	0.51

Robust t values are in parentheses. *** $p < 0.01$, ** $p < 0.05$, * $p < 0.1$

could cause residents to become significantly more aware of air pollution's health repercussions, motivating a shift in their risk perception and eventually, an enhanced interest in purchasing commercial health insurance.

7.3.3 Robustness Checks

7.3.3.1 Alternative Air Pollution Measures

To ensure a more cautious and comprehensive conclusion, our paper also conducts several robustness tests using the annual average Air Quality Index (AQI) for each city from 2009 to 2017 to replace the annual average PM2.5 concentration employed in the previous section. In the context of China, AQI is a more commonly used air pollution indicator, and it could provide a more intuitive measure of air quality. To further validate our previous findings, we construct a binary variable based on the annual average AQI for each city, which equals 1 when on an observed day, the AQI exceeds 100 (namely slight air pollution) and 0 otherwise. This process is repeated for each day, and we name the resulting variable AQI_H100. Similarly, if the AQI on a specific day exceeds 150 (indicating moderate air pollution), it is recorded as 1; otherwise, it is recorded as 0, and this is summed up for the whole year to create the variable AQI_H150. Apart from that, to examine the influence of public attention to PM2.5 on the demand for commercial health insurance, our study also employs the annual average Baidu index data obtained by searching for the keyword "PM2.5" in each city from 2011 to 2017. The Baidu index is the Chinese counterpart of the commonly used Google index in previous research, which can serve as a useful measure of public interest in a particular concept. Notably, our paper uses "PM2.5" as the search keyword instead of "haze" because "PM2.5" is more of a neutral terminology without derogatory connotations unlike "haze". Hence, individuals concerned about their health risks are more likely to proactively search for "PM2.5." The regression results related to these two newly-constructed variables are presented in Table 7.5.

Our results reveal that the lagged AQI index has no significant impact on the demand for commercial health insurance, which may be caused by the limitation of the AQI index algorithm. Regarding the processed index, no matter whether the AQI_H100 is currently or lagged, there is no significant correlation between the demand for commercial health insurance (relevant results are limited in length and thus are not reported), which may be attributed to concern bias caused by the public's inattention. For AQI_H150, under the conditions of the current period, at a significant level of 10%, the index has a positive correlation with the demand for commercial health insurance. In terms of economic significance, if the number of days that the AQI index exceeds 150 in a city in the current period increases by 1 day, the demand for commercial health insurance will rise to 0.002% correspondingly. Compared with the impact of the annual PM2.5 average, AQI_H150 has no time lag. This may be because the AQI index exceeding 150 usually features more severe pollution conditions, which might draw more attention from individuals. The cognitive bias can thus be weakened.

Nevertheless, concerning human health, there is no clear evidence to suggest that the impact of mild pollution is less harsh than heavy pollution. Particularly for small pollutants like PM2.5, they can ultimately cause irreversible harm. This underscores the need for the authority to improve the current public information systems and visual communication design systems to better alert the public to potential health risks. Besides, our results indicate that at a 1% significance level, when the average Baidu index of a city increases by 1% in a year, the demand for commercial health

Table 7.5 Alternative air pollution measures

	Lag AQI_year	AQI_H100	AQI_H150	Lnindex
	(1)	(2)	(3)	(4)
Lag AQI_year	0.006 (0.93)	0.011* (1.66)	−0.000 (−0.05)	0.002 (0.38)
AQI_H100		0.000 (0.56)		
AQI_H150			0.002* (1.87)	
Lnindex				0.169*** (3.54)
Controls	Yes	Yes	Yes	Yes
Year F.E.	Yes	Yes	Yes	Yes
City F.E.	Yes	Yes	Yes	Yes
Observations	1466	1547	1547	1785
Adjusted R^2	0.85	0.74	0.74	0.80

Robust t values are in parentheses. *** $p < 0.01$, ** $p < 0.05$, * $p < 0.1$

Table 7.6 Instrumental variable strategy

	First-stage	Second-stage
	(1)	(2)
Thermal inversion	24.464*** (11.28)	
Lag PM2.5		0.006* (1.84)
Controls	Yes	Yes
Year F.E.	Yes	Yes
City F.E.	Yes	Yes
Observations	2395	2395
Adjusted R^2	0.48	0.81

Robust t values are in parentheses. *** $p < 0.01$, ** $p < 0.05$, * $p < 0.1$

insurance in that year will rise by 17.8%.[1] This attests to the conclusion that when the public actively follows health risks posed by air pollution, it could significantly correct their perception of risk. Government and relevant agencies can utilize data such as the Baidu Index, Weibo "hot entries," and other indices of public attention as effective indicators during the decision-making processes, as well as promptly sharing them with the public as risk warnings.

7.3.3.2 Instrumental Variable Strategy

The omitted variable issue is another concern in our research. To address these endogeneity concerns effectively, we also attempt to employ an instrumental variable approach in this section as an additional robustness test. Specifically, following the methodology outlined by Chen et al. (2017), we consider the thermal inversion a suitable instrumental variable choice due to its significant impact on PM2.5 concentration while having no effect on human behavior, in line with findings from Arceo et al. (2016) and Chen et al. (2017). Our estimation results, as presented in Table 7.6, reveal that the direction and significance of the influence of air pollution on the demand for commercial health insurance remain consistent with the baseline results, further demonstrating the robustness of our main results. To ensure the adequacy of the instrumental variable, rigorous tests including under-identification and weak identification tests are also conducted, and the results affirm the validity of our instrument variable strategy.

[1] Note that the calculation method of the Baidu Index is confidential, so the exact factors causing it to increase or decrease are unknown to us.

7.4 Conclusion

Utilizing panel data encompassing 278 cities across 30 provinces in China spanning from 2009 to 2017, our study constructs a theoretical framework grounded in behavioral finance. Subsequently, it employs a fixed-effects model to empirically unveil the direct impact of air pollution on the demand for commercial health insurance. Furthermore, robustness tests are conducted by repositioning the independent variable and introducing an instrumental variable. Our findings of are twofold. First, at the city level, it is observed that air pollution significantly stimulates the demand for commercial health insurance. However, this effect exhibits a time lag, implying that the public requires time to fully recognize the health implications of air pollution before making decisions to procure commercial health insurance. Notably, the study employs the Air Quality Index (AQI) and its two derivative indices to demonstrate that individuals' comprehension of these indices directly influences their risk perception and the temporal bias associated with this perception. Moreover, proactive comprehension fosters the rectification of risk perception. Second, by assessing the temporal dimension of air pollution's impact, the research discerns that the direct influence of air pollution on the demand for commercial health insurance in China's central and eastern regions became significant after 2014. This alignment with China's air pollution history underscores that knowledge bias can be mitigated by external factors. Heterogeneity tests further suggest that increased access to information can lead to more rational risk perception, thereby bolstering the resilience of cognitive biases and, consequently, the demand for commercial health insurance.

Based on our conclusion, our paper also offers the following policy implications. Initially, air pollution undeniably fosters the demand for commercial health insurance due to people's inclination to "benefit from avoiding harm." Consequently, it underscores the necessity of addressing the escalating air pollution issue by mitigating or eradicating its health risks at their source. To this end, the government must establish market-oriented environmental regulations, facilitate industrial structural optimization, and institute enduring mechanisms to ensure the consistent enforcement of environmental regulations. Concurrently, augmenting investments in environmental protection and devising a compensation system for ecological and environmental damage is imperative. Second, recognizing that environmental challenges will persist for the foreseeable future, it is crucial to acknowledge that commercial health insurance remains a viable risk-mitigation financial instrument for the general populace, alongside national personal pensions and social medical insurance. Therefore, government initiatives should encompass intensified health risk management education and the cultivation of a sound commercial health insurance consumption ethos. Encouraging insurance companies to diversify their product offerings to align with people's requirements for commercial health insurance products is equally vital. Furthermore, given the public's inaccurate and time-lagged perception of the health impact of air pollution, efforts should be directed toward promoting more intuitive and effective methods of conveying air pollution-related information. This would serve to enhance the accuracy and efficacy of such information, ultimately diminishing comprehension delays and facilitating a broader public understanding of the health hazards stemming from air pollution. In doing so, it would further encourage their adoption of risk-mitigation measures like commercial health insurance.

References

Arceo E, Hanna R, Oliva P (2016) Does the effect of pollution on infant mortality differ between developing and developed countries? Evidence from Mexico city. Econ J 126(591):257–280

Barwick PJ, Li S, Rao D, Zahur NB (2018) The morbidity cost of air pollution: evidence from consumer spending in China (0898-2937)

Bordalo P, Gennaioli N, Shleifer A (2013) Salience and consumer choice. J Polit Econ 121(5):803–843

Chang TY, Huang W, Wang Y (2018) Something in the air: pollution and the demand for health insurance. Rev Econ Stud 85(3):1609–1634

Chay KY, Greenstone M (2003) The impact of air pollution on infant mortality: evidence from geographic variation in pollution shocks induced by a recession. Q J Econ 118(3):1121–1167

Chen H, Goldberg MS, Burnett RT, Jerrett M, Wheeler AJ, Villeneuve PJ (2013) Long-term exposure to traffic-related air pollution and cardiovascular mortality. Epidemiology 24:35–43

Chen S, Oliva P, Zhang P (2017) The effect of air pollution on migration: evidence from China. National Bureau of Economic Research

Deryugina T, Heutel G, Miller NH, Molitor D, Reif J (2019) The mortality and medical costs of air pollution: evidence from changes in wind direction. Am Econ Rev 109(12):4178–4219

Donkelaar A, Martin RV, Brauer M, Boys BL (2015) Use of satellite observations for long-term exposure assessment of global concentrations of fine particulate matter. Environ Health Perspect 123(2):135–143

Donkelaar A, Martin RV, Li C, Burnett RT (2019) Regional estimates of chemical composition of fine particulate matter using a combined geoscience-statistical method with information from satellites, models, and monitors. Environ Sci Technol 53(5):2595–2611

Epa U (2004) EPA air quality criteria for particulate matter [Final Report]. US Environmental Protection Agency, Washington, DC

Fu S, Viard VB, Zhang P (2021) Air pollution and manufacturing firm productivity: nationwide estimates for China. The Economic Journal 131(640): 3241–3273

Huang YM, He LY (2013) Urbanization, environmental pollution and subjective well-being of residents—empirical evidence from China. Soft Sci China 12:82–93

Liu H, Wang J (2012) An empirical analysis of private health insurance ownership in China. China Econ Q 4:359–382

Neidell MJ (2004) Air pollution, health, and socio-economic status: the effect of outdoor air quality on childhood asthma. J Health Econ 23(6):1209–1236

Nowakowicz-Debek B, Saba LHB-W (2004) The effects of air pollutants on the cortisol and progesterone secretion in polar fox (Alopex lagopus). Scientifur

Peng HR, Zheng QY, Tong YH (2017) Does the expansion of social health insurance in China promote the development of private health insurance? J Financ Res 443(5):97–110

Shao S, Li X, Cao JH, Yang LL (2016) Economic policy choices of haze pollution control in China: based on the perspective of spatial spillover effect. Econ Res 51(9):73–88

Sun WZ, Zhang XN, Zheng SQ (2019) Air pollution and spatial mobility of labor: study on the migrants' job location choice. Econ Res J 11:102–117

Suo LY, Wan YY, Chen T (2015) A research on the uneven development of health insurance and its reason. Insur Stud 1:42–53

Thomasson MA (2003) The importance of group coverage: how tax policy shaped US health insurance. Am Econ Rev 93(4):1373–1384

Wei XH, Lin T, Zhang N, Liu HY (2017) Inability to breathe: the impact of faze on individual productivity: micro-evidence from professional football players in China. J Financ Econ 43(7):4–19

Xie YB, Chen J, Li W (2014) An assessment of PM2.5 related health risk and impaired values of Beijing residents in a consecutive high-level exposure during heavy haze days. Environ Sci 35(1):1–8

Yang T, Guo MM (2019) Investor attention and the stock market: a new perspective on PM2.5 concept stocks. J Financ Res 467(5):190–206

Zheng S, Wang J, Sun C, Zhang X, Kahn ME (2019) Air pollution lowers Chinese urbanites' expressed happiness on social media. Nat Hum Behav 3(3):237–243

Chapter 8
Investing in Clean Air: How Air Pollution Is Driving Green Innovation

Abstract Over the past three decades, China's rapid economic growth has been accompanied by significant environmental degradation, making sustainable development a critical national priority. Green innovation has emerged as a key response, though most studies focus on national or regional trends rather than firm-level dynamics. This study seeks to address this gap by conducting empirical research on 1049 publicly traded manufacturing enterprises spanning the years 2000–2017. Our findings reveal that companies are influenced by environmental pollution, prompting them to engage in greater levels of green innovation. Notably, this stimulus has a more pronounced effect on the encouragement of high-value, invention-based green innovation. State-owned enterprises exhibit a greater degree of activity in the realm of green innovation compared to their non-state-owned counterparts. Additionally, large enterprises and technologically advanced companies with stronger financial capabilities exhibit a greater inclination towards pursuing green innovation. Moreover, businesses located in regions characterized by high levels of pollution tend to intensify their green innovation efforts when faced with worsening air pollution conditions.

Keywords Air pollution · Corporate innovation · Green innovation

8.1 Introduction

Over the past three decades since the initiation of reform and opening-up policies, China has witnessed sustained economic growth, but this has come at the cost of significant ecological degradation. This issue has now become a critical challenge that must be addressed in the context of China's social and economic development. The country has faced challenges such as a high level of energy dependency, which, in turn, has led to environmental pollution and ecological deterioration due to excessive energy consumption. As China stands as the world's manufacturing hub, its ecological and environmental concerns have emerged as pivotal factors constraining its socio-economic advancement. The excessive reliance on energy resources has been a

M. Guo et al., *Social-Economic Impacts of Air Pollution*, Climate Change and Energy Transition, https://doi.org/10.1007/978-981-96-7858-7_8

major driving force behind China's pressing ecological issues. From a water resource perspective, in 2017, over 850 out of 1200 monitored rivers in China were found to exceed pollution standards, signifying that approximately 78% of these rivers are unsuitable for use as drinking water sources for residents. Furthermore, over 50% of groundwater sources are contaminated, significantly contributing to water scarcity problems in many Chinese cities. China is also grappling with severe air pollution problems that pose risks to everyday life and social development. Meteorological data reveals that numerous Chinese cities, particularly in the Beijing-Tianjin-Hebei region, the southeast coastal areas, and various other regions, consistently experience elevated levels of suspended particulate matter in the air, as well as periodic acid rain occurrences. Industrial production has generated substantial industrial waste, with China accumulating a total of 6.4 billion metric tons of solid waste to date, and an annual production of approximately 6.6 billion metric tons of industrial solid waste. This figure is growing at an annual rate of 8%, and these waste products have occupied approximately 500 million m^2 of land in China. According to information from the environmental authorities, China incurs direct economic losses of over 40 billion USD annually due to environmental issues.

In the 2005 Copenhagen Conference, nations worldwide crafted explicit emission reduction plans for greenhouse gases. The Chinese government committed to a 40% reduction in carbon dioxide emissions by 2020, based on 2005 standards. Consequently, China redirected its focus towards emission reduction efforts in the recent past, offering comprehensive support for the development of a green and low-carbon economy. This commitment effectively bolstered China's circular economy and intensified research and development efforts in environmental protection technologies. Positive results were achieved in environmental protection, with substantial reductions observed in emissions of pollutants such as sulfur dioxide and nitrogen oxides. Despite these achievements in emission reduction, China still grapples with substantial environmental challenges. According to data from relevant Chinese authorities, out of 338 prefecture-level cities in China, only 99 cities meet the air quality standards, accounting for a mere 29.3% of cities nationwide. Furthermore, approximately 463 cities in China have established water quality monitoring systems, and 18.8% of these cities experience acid rain precipitation, primarily concentrated in more developed cities to the south of the Yangtze River. Even after years of efforts, environmental issues remain the paramount concern in China's economic development.

In the context of the ongoing discourse on environmental issues, efforts to mitigate environmental degradation have been made at the national and individual levels. China has positioned innovation, sustainability, and resource sharing as core principles in governmental work, encouraging all sectors of society to invest more resources in green development. Enterprises, as integral components of the socioeconomic framework, are particularly urged to embrace the path of green development. As China intensifies its environmental protection endeavors, numerous industries face resource constraints, limiting the growth of traditional high-energy consumption and high-pollution sectors. Innovation serves as a fundamental driver for sustained corporate growth and enhancing market competitiveness. Enterprises, as key drivers of national economic development, exert a pronounced influence on societal innovation levels through their innovation capacity. It is imperative for enterprises and relevant stakeholders to recognize the role of innovation in their own development and in achieving environmental protection goals throughout their growth journey. Amid current research on innovation activities, the focus on green innovation behaviors within enterprises has gained prominence. Green technological innovation by enterprises not only aligns with existing legal and regulatory requirements but also effectively enhances energy utilization efficiency, aiding companies in reducing environmental investment costs, optimizing resource utilization, and sustaining their ongoing development. Nations worldwide have underscored green innovation and environmental protection as primary research and investment focal points, making them central areas of academic inquiry. The resolution of environmental issues necessitates an active role for governmental environmental regulations. Environmental regulations aim to stimulate technological innovation within enterprises and address environmental pollution through technological advancements. As air pollution prompts the introduction of new environmental policies, this study seeks to investigate whether Chinese enterprises will adjust their innovation strategies based on the severity of air pollution to maintain their competitive edge in resource-constrained competition. Will air pollution act as a catalyst for green innovation within enterprises? This article will delve into this matter and conduct subgroup analyses based on distinct enterprise characteristics.

This paper makes three significant contributions. Firstly, it employs patents filed by enterprises as its research focus. By screening and categorizing these patents based on their types, the study investigates how enterprises make green innovation decisions in response to evolving environmental conditions. This approach provides a micro-level foundation for researching enterprise green innovation behavior.

Secondly, by examining the impact of the external environment on enterprise green innovation, the paper extends the micro-level research on enterprise innovation in a low-carbon economy. This expansion offers a clearer understanding of enterprise innovation decisions in the current environmental context, which can enhance enterprises' enthusiasm for green innovation research and development. It also assists in establishing sustainable development systems, allowing enterprises to maintain a forward-looking approach to development.

Thirdly, the paper shifts its research perspective from the city-region level to the enterprise level. This shift can offer decision-making support to governments in formulating corresponding low-pollution and low-energy consumption economic policies. It makes policy formulation more targeted and guiding while providing theoretical references for enterprises engaged in green environmental technology research and development.

The following sections of this paper are structured as follows: Sect. 8.2 provides a literature review. Section 8.3 presents the research background and hypothesis. Section 8.4 introduces the data sources. Section 8.5 encompasses empirical analysis. Section 8.6 presents the further analysis. Section 8.7 concludes the study.

8.2 Literature Review

8.2.1 Effects of Air Pollution

Currently, both domestic and international literature has extensively explored the impacts of air pollution, with a predominant focus on its effects on factors such as residents' health, societal welfare, and well-being. For instance, Heutel and Ruhm (2016), after controlling for demographic variables and incorporating state and year fixed effects, identified a significant positive correlation between carbon monoxide (CO) concentration in air pollution and mortality rates. Lavy et al. (2014), through an analysis of Israeli high school standardized exam scores and students' exposure to polluted air during the years 2000–2002, discovered that air pollution leads to reduced academic performance and cognitive abilities among students.

Air pollution also exerts an influence on economic production. Grossman and Krueger (1995) observed a U-shaped relationship between industrial particulate emissions and economic growth, signifying that air pollution intensifies with rising economic levels until it reaches a critical point. Beyond this threshold, as economic levels continue to ascend, atmospheric pollution levels gradually diminish. Additionally, Shafik and Bandyopadhyay (1992), in a study using environmental pollution data from approximately 150 countries, identified an inverted U-shaped relationship between gas emissions and economic growth, while this relationship did not hold for wastewater and solid waste.

From a labor productivity perspective, Neidell (2023) determined that improving environmental quality enhances the health of the workforce, thereby boosting productivity. Research indicates that improved air quality enhances the productivity of workers in a range of sectors, including agriculture, manufacturing, and services. This finding holds true even in countries with the strictest environmental regulations. Examining the impact on factor productivity, Greenstone et al. (2012) found that the United States experienced a substantial improvement in air pollution levels from 1972 to 1993. However, this reduction in pollution caused a decrease of approximately 4.8% in the productivity of businesses within counties in the United States that did not meet climate standards. This resulted in a loss of $21 billion in the U.S. manufacturing sector.

8.2.2 Connotation of Green Innovation and Related Concepts

The concept of green innovation initially emerged in the 1950s. Over a considerable period of development, a unified definition of this concept has not been established, leading to some disparities in its academic interpretation. Academics generally consider "green innovation" to encompass the following key components: green product innovation, green process innovation, and end-of-pipe treatment technology innovation. These innovations are closely linked to environmental, energy-related aspects, and are also influenced by socioeconomic development. Green technological innovation pertains to the technological innovation activities undertaken by enterprises to simultaneously reduce environmental pollution and enhance energy efficiency. Kemp (1997) suggests that green technological innovation primarily involves companies or relevant institutions improving existing processes to mitigate environmental pollution. Kemp further introduces the notion of systemic innovation into this research, asserting that green technological innovation necessitates support from management and institutional innovations. This concept has gained recognition among numerous scholars. For instance, green technological innovation extends beyond traditional environmental and process innovations, encompassing product, organizational, and management innovations. Chen et al. (2006) also contributes to the understanding of green innovation by considering it as the process of innovating both software and hardware on the foundation of green product innovation, aiming to enhance resource utilization efficiency while reducing pollution production. Further, Green innovation as a means to enhance environmental performance and deems it a form of environmental innovation. Kemp (2011) primarily examines green innovation from a product lifecycle perspective, characterizing it as a form of ecological innovation.

Considering the perspectives of the aforementioned scholars, it is evident that the concept of green innovation is continually evolving. With sustained socioeconomic development, the concept of green innovation has expanded to encompass technological, organizational, and management innovations, establishing a comprehensive green innovation framework that spans the entire product lifecycle. This framework enables businesses to manage operational costs at lower levels and achieve the objectives of enhancing economic and environmental benefits. The World Intellectual Property Organization (WIPO) acknowledges the broad application of green innovation, particularly in technologies related to climate and environmental pollution control. It categorizes technology patents based on how these technologies are used, allowing researchers to differentiate green patents using the International Patent Classification (IPC) code.

8.2.3 Influences on Green Innovation

8.2.3.1 Internal Factors of Green Innovation

Management possesses a strong environmental consciousness can significantly influence the choice and execution of the company's environmental strategies. Amore and Bennedsen (2016) conducted a Difference-in-Differences (DID) analysis using anti-takeover statutes as a proxy variable and found that companies with inadequate management are less likely to obtain green patents through innovation. Leenders and Chandra (2013) contends that a company's internal environmental consciousness is the driving force behind green technological innovation. Scholars suggest that several factors impact a company's engagement in green technological innovation: firstly, corporate social responsibility and ethical constraints; secondly, the pursuit of higher profits.

R&D investment intensity. A company's research and development (R&D) investment has a direct impact on its research and development capabilities and serves as a crucial avenue for enhancing its green technological innovation. Romer (1990) discovered that increased R&D investment by companies leads to a substantial improvement in their technological proficiency and economic benefits.

Nature of the enterprise. State-owned enterprises often play a critical role in public services related to people's livelihoods and serve as pillars of the national economy. They are less profit-oriented and assume more significant social responsibilities. When confronted with environmental changes, state-owned enterprises are more inclined to engage in green innovation compared to non-state-owned enterprises. Additionally, state-owned enterprises are more likely to receive support in terms of technology and investment. Furthermore, many Chinese enterprises face varying degrees of financial constraints, and state-owned enterprises experience fewer financial constraints than non-state-owned enterprises, benefiting from a broader range of financing channels. Consequently, they can better manage the costs of green innovation (Ding et al. 2021).

Company size. Green technological innovation is characterized by high costs and significant risks, leading companies to face higher levels of uncertain returns. Small and medium-sized enterprises typically lack the financial strength to undertake innovative research and development. Excessive financial commitments can hamper their development. Only companies with sufficient financial resources and a larger scale can effectively engage in green technological innovation.

In addition to the factors mentioned above, the nature of the enterprise, environmental awareness, R&D investment, and business scale can exert a substantial influence on their green technological innovation efforts.

8.2.3.2 External Factors of Green Innovation

Market factors. As socioeconomic development continues, people's demands for a higher quality of life have increased. With growing concern over air pollution, environmental awareness among the public has risen significantly. More and more individuals have developed a strong appreciation for low-carbon and eco-friendly products. To gain customer approval and enhance their market competitiveness, companies proactively engage in low-carbon green innovation. Kammerer (2009) found through research that customer benefits have a significant impact on whether companies pursue green technological innovation, representing a form of market demand. Narver and Slater (1990) suggest that market demand has a prominent influence on a company's green technological innovation, analyzing the issue from a market competition perspective. They find that industry competition also affects a company's engagement in green technological innovation. Horbach et al. (2012) asserts that the development of green markets and increasing energy constraints are crucial drivers for companies to undertake green innovation.

Environmental regulations. Most scholars agree that the government must fully exercise the role of environmental regulation to promote the development of green technological innovation. There are three viewpoints on the influence of environmental regulations on a company's green innovation. Firstly, strong environmental regulations may hinder green innovation by causing rapid cost increases that companies cannot afford. This obstructs their engagement in green technological innovation. Secondly, appropriate environmental regulations result in increased costs for companies but encourage the development of green products and processes, leading to innovation compensation effects (Porter 1991). Thirdly, the relationship between environmental regulations and a company's green innovation is uncertain or nonlinear. Some scholars found that government inspection activities did not significantly improve the efficiency of a company's green technological innovation, with relatively small impacts resulting from pollution control measures. In contrast, another strand of literature argue that a company's enthusiasm for green innovation can be significantly boosted by government policies promoting green innovation. This heightened enthusiasm can increase a company's environmental investments. Based on these varying viewpoints, it is evident that there is ongoing debate on how environmental regulations influence a company's green innovation, and a unified perspective has yet to be established.

8.2.4 Impact of Air Pollution on Green Innovation

As air pollution exhibits characteristics of external diseconomies, continuous air pollution issues prompt the government to establish related policies and enforce environmental regulations. These measures progressively transition from soft interventions to more stringent environmental protection measures, including the implementation of comprehensive pollution monitoring systems and increased investment in environmental governance. This approach helps alleviate regional environmental pollution to some extent. These measures are employed to regulate business activities, aiming to achieve a harmonious development of the economy and environmental protection. The increased production costs resulting from air pollution will trigger a sense of "loss aversion" among businesses. Faced with higher environmental costs, companies must take effective measures to reduce their operational costs to prevent a decline in profits. This often involves implementing process innovations to obtain compensation. Some scholars, when considering the dynamic relationship between environmental regulations and corporate innovation, argue that the two are not mutually exclusive. Environmental regulations allow companies to adopt cost-effective compensation methods to reduce their operational costs, leading to increased management attention to resource allocation. This, in turn, enables them to obtain greater benefits through technological innovations and similar strategies. Hamamoto (2006) believes that well-founded environmental regulations can effectively enhance a company's innovation capacity without generating negative effects. Horbach (2008) contends that companies consistently prioritize profit generation throughout their development, and government pressure, such as environmental regulations, can compel companies to improve their production processes. By controlling environmental pollution at lower levels and leveraging the benefits derived from process improvements, companies can offset the increased costs associated with environmental regulations. Summarily, while the stalemate in air pollution leads to increased operational costs, companies can address the challenges posed by environmental regulations by pursuing process innovations and other strategies, thus gaining a competitive edge. This process partly promotes technological innovation.

From the perspective of internal pollution control costs, the exacerbation of air pollution prompts the government to adopt more stringent environmental policies. Consequently, companies increase their operational costs to meet the requirements of these environmental regulations, subjecting their production decisions to greater constraints. This compels them to incur higher costs for pollution control measures. From the standpoint of external pollution prevention costs, the escalation of air pollution leads to environmental deterioration in the external natural environment. As a result, companies must allocate resources to address issues stemming from environmental degradation. If a company's production operations are significantly influenced by external environmental policies, their expenditure on environmental governance will substantially rise.

8.2.5 Comments

The preceding text provides an overview of existing domestic and international literature, revealing that scholars are primarily approaching research on green technology innovation from perspectives such as its essence, external coercive forces, and internal drivers. In studies investigating the impact of environmental factors like air pollution, previous scholars have examined their influence on individual performance, business production, and local environmental protection. However, there has been relatively little research focused on green innovation, which has a close relationship with air pollution. While there are ongoing debates about the influencing factors and mechanisms related to green innovation, there is a consensus among scholars regarding the significance of green innovation and its crucial role in contemporary economic development. Based on the existing literature, it is evident that informal factors like air pollution influence people's choices, government regulations, and subsequently, businesses' decisions regarding green innovation. Furthermore, an overview of the literature suggests that domestic research on green innovation has largely leaned towards qualitative or quantitative analysis. Most studies have used survey questionnaires to interview internal company personnel or have reviewed corporate social responsibility reports. Few studies have utilized patent data for analysis.

Moreover, current research on green technology innovation is primarily concentrated at the industry, regional, and national levels. This has resulted in the majority of scholarly output being focused on these areas. Only a small fraction of scholars has delved into research on green technology innovation at the enterprise level.

Consequently, Chinese companies lack corresponding theoretical references for their green technology innovation efforts. The results obtained through the aforementioned research methods may also carry certain biases and may not accurately represent the real situations of micro-level business entities.

8.3 Research Background and Hypothesis

8.3.1 Brief Description of the Current Status of the Air Pollution Situation

Since the late 1990s, China's economy has been on a rapid growth trajectory. This economic boom has brought about a concentration of environmental issues that had previously unfolded in stages over hundreds of years of industrialization in developed countries. Consequently, the conflict between environmental protection and economic development has been intensifying. The development of industrial civilization, driven by the utilization of energy sources represented by coal and oil, has been a pivotal force propelling human industrial history and the course of human civilization. However, this vast array of energy-consuming machinery has also released copious amounts of smoke and dust during the process of energy conversion, placing a substantial environmental burden on people's production and daily lives. Relative resource scarcity, ecological fragility, and insufficient environmental capacity have gradually become major concerns in China's economic development.

Air pollution in China has worsened over time and only in recent years has the government implemented effective measures to contain it within reasonable limits. Nevertheless, it's essential to acknowledge that in some regions, air pollution days remain unacceptably high, with elevated levels of PM10 and PM2.5 pollutants. Moreover, China boasts an expansive land area with varying climatic and environmental conditions across regions, leading to differences in air pollution situations. According to data from China's meteorological department, among 338 prefecture-level cities in China, only 99 cities have good air quality, with a meager rate of 29.3%. These cities with good air quality account for around 78% of all prefecture-level cities, while the average percentage of days exceeding air quality standards is 22.0%. The average number of good air quality days in all 338 prefecture-level and higher cities declined by 0.8% compared to 2016, and the 74 cities implementing the new standards in the first phase experienced a 1.5% reduction in the average number of good air quality days. Most cities with relatively poor air quality are concentrated in the Beijing-Tianjin-Hebei region, whereas cities with relatively better air quality are clustered in the coastal areas and the Yunnan-Guizhou region. This disparity underscores the variations in air quality across different regions of China.

8.3.2 Brief Description of Green Innovation

The "19th National Congress" has incorporated green development into a fundamental aspect of China's development ideology. It emphasizes the urgency of accelerating the construction of ecological civilization to provide a favorable living environment for future generations. This indicates that the Central Committee of the Communist Party of China and the State Council have recognized the vital importance of green technology development, making the increase in China's green patent applications an inevitable trend.

According to data provided by relevant authorities, China has experienced rapid growth in green technology innovation since 2014. The innovation capabilities of enterprises in the field of green technology have significantly improved, leading to a gradual increase in the number of green patent applications. In terms of quantity, in 2017, the domestic green patent applications reached approximately 749,941, nearly 1.8 times the number of applications in 2014. However, in terms of applicants, most domestic green patents are held by universities, indicating a noticeable deficiency in innovation activities within enterprises. Considering that enterprises are the driving force behind socioeconomic activities, it is crucial to stimulate their enthusiasm for green innovation.

8.3.3 Theoretical Analysis and Research Hypothesis

Publicly traded companies, as a crucial component of the overall economy, have always aimed at maximizing their economic performance. Achieving this goal, they have recognized the significance of sustainable development. However, the environmental issues that accompany economic development have become impediments to the growth of these companies. In China, particularly for publicly listed manufacturing enterprises, the intensifying extreme weather conditions and persistent environmental pollution demand higher environmental standards and regulations. Over time, the focus of corporate development has evolved from merely pursuing economic performance to balancing economic performance with green innovation for sustainable business practices. This transformation enables companies to maintain economic performance while harmoniously coexisting with environmental development. The Air Quality Index, a result of air quality monitoring activities associated with environmental regulations, impacts the formulation of these regulations. It also serves as an informal factor influencing a company's green innovation activities, and can be analyzed from the following perspectives:

Firstly, with escalating air pollution, the government tends to implement stricter environmental regulations to control actions that harm the environment or limit resource consumption by businesses. Consequently, this increases the operational costs of companies. To mitigate these cost increases, companies need to engage in green innovation, optimizing processes and management to achieve energy conservation and material recycling, thus lowering expenses. This encourages businesses to transition into environmentally friendly entities, boosting their enthusiasm for green innovation.

Secondly, green innovation ensures that companies gain a competitive edge in the market. Companies that proactively conduct green innovation to create environmentally friendly products not only capture a larger market share but also enhance brand recognition among consumers. This, in turn, leads to a significant competitive advantage in the market and resolves issues related to increased costs due to environmental regulations. Additionally, by applying for patent protection through intellectual property institutions, companies can charge other businesses a patent usage fee to meet government regulatory requirements.

Thirdly, engaging in green innovation necessitates a strong sense of corporate social responsibility. Companies that willingly assume social responsibility can enhance their recognition among various stakeholders, project a better corporate image, and secure a prominent position in the market. This, in turn, provides assurance for companies to achieve sustainable development in a challenging environmental landscape.

Based on these considerations, this paper proposes the following hypotheses:

Hypothesis 1 Air quality is significantly positively correlated with corporate green innovation, implying that companies tend to engage in more green innovation as air pollution worsens.

A nation's industrial technological level is often reflected in the extent of its industrial development, which, in turn, indicates its overall economic development and technological advancement. Similarly, a company's innovative output reflects its technological prowess. Green innovations with lower added value have little competitive advantage in the market, struggle to yield the expected results, form barriers, and are prone to elimination in a changing environment. They cannot guarantee ideal economic outcomes for a company. In contrast, high-value green innovations can sustain a company's competitive edge, allowing it to continuously benefit from the spillover effects of green innovation on production and products. They are more effective in addressing air pollution. Moreover, high-value, invention-type innovations align with the earlier innovation theories, signifying a completely new task or the process of developing such a task. Therefore, the following hypothesis is proposed:

Hypothesis 2 Compared to other green innovations, high-value invention-type green innovations receive the greatest positive stimulus when air pollution intensifies.

8.4 Data

In this study, we utilized a sample of companies listed on the A-share market from 2000 to 2017. We categorized the industries under investigation, including mining, manufacturing, construction, and transportation, based on the industry classification standards provided by the National Bureau of Statistics. To account for variations in environmental impact, these specific production-oriented sectors were chosen for our research. As a result, our dataset included 1049 companies, totaling 16,795 annual observations.

All financial data for the sample companies and city-level data were sourced from the China Stock Market & Accounting Research (CSMAR) database and WIND databases. Air Quality Index (AQI) data were collected from the data center of China's Ministry of Ecology and Environment. Subsequently, we adjusted the collected high-frequency data to the required frequency as per our research needs. The patent data were obtained from the Chinese Research Data Services Platform (CNRDS) company, specifically from the Innovation Research Database (CIRD) within their research series.

8.4.1 Green Innovation

Concerning the assessment of green innovation, we will employ methods commonly utilized in economics, such as those discussed by Griliches (1990). Specifically, we will use patent data to measure a firm's innovation activities. One of the primary reasons for selecting patent data over research and development (R&D) expenditures as our principal research metric is the clarity and wide applicability of patent application numbers across industries and time periods, making it a more concrete measure of innovation. Furthermore, unlike R&D expenditure, which typically involves aggregated accounting categories, patent applications offer detailed information on the critical features of foundational inventions. This aids in classifying innovations based on their technological content and distinguishing between the values of patents according to their application categories.

Additionally, this study will employ a firm's annual count of patent applications to gauge its innovative capabilities. This choice is motivated by several factors. Firstly, patents, as a product of technological innovation, provide a specific representation of resource input intensity and resource utilization efficiency. Hence, using a firm's patent application data as an output of innovation can effectively measure its innovative capacity. Secondly, considering the nature of the research problem at hand, air pollution represents a relatively recent and pressing environmental concern. Innovations addressing such issues are typically at the forefront, making patent data a more apt representation of their value. Thirdly, as China experiences economic growth, its patent protection system has seen continuous improvements and enhancements in various regulations and legal structures. Consequently, more researchers, institutions, and businesses are choosing to protect their innovative achievements by filing for patents. Hence, patent application numbers have strong representativeness. Among various innovation-related data, patent application data is also relatively objective, authoritative, and comprehensive. Fourthly, the majority of patents applied for by businesses are intended for commercial purposes and serve as a potential source of technological innovation value and profitability. Therefore, a firm's number of patent applications can significantly reflect its innovative capacity (Furman et al. 2002). Fifthly, compared to the number of patents granted, the number of patent applications can provide more timely and accurate insights into a firm's innovation level. The granting of patents involves examination and the payment of annual fees, resulting in greater instability and uncertainty. As a result, the disclosure of patent application data tends to be more stable, reliable, and timely compared to patent grant data.

As a significant indicator for evaluating a firm's technological innovation capabilities, patents in China are classified under the Patent Law into three main categories: invention patents, utility model patents, and design patents. Design patents primarily focus on artistic concepts, safeguarding a firm's achievements in aesthetic design. On the other hand, invention and utility model patents pertain to protecting a firm's technological ideas. Although superficially, there may appear to be some correlation between design and practical product patents, their fundamental content differs significantly. Design patents primarily aim to enhance a product's visual aesthetics, making it more appealing to consumers, while utility model patents are designed to address specific technical problems. Hence, when measuring green patents in this study, we focus exclusively on invention and utility model patents, which are closely related to technology. Invention patents entail proposing entirely new technical solutions for products or methods and, compared to utility model patents, hold higher value. In China, invention patents are considered the most challenging in terms of research and development and possess the highest technological level. They are equivalent to utility patents in the United States and fall within the category of high-level technological innovation subjects. For businesses, they represent a critical output and are an embodiment of a company's core competitive strength. Therefore, when considering a firm's overall green innovation level, this study distinguishes between green invention patents and green utility model patents for empirical research.

The rationale for studying green patents lies in their representation of knowledge within the environmental technology domain. They not only reduce pollution but also have the potential to impact an entire trajectory of corporate innovation. Green patents might generate positive externalities in the form of knowledge spillovers, thereby promoting the adoption and dissemination of environmental technology on an industrial and national level. Given the increasing pressure from various stakeholders and regulatory demands, companies are expected to engage in environmentally responsible practices, which may significantly influence their green innovation activities.

China employs the International Patent Classification (IPC) system for patent classification, which is one of the most widely used patent classification methods worldwide. Therefore, this study utilizes the "IPC Green Inventory" published by the World Intellectual Property Organization (WIPO) in 2010 to filter patents from the patent application records of publicly listed companies, based on their IPC classification codes. Because patent research and the process of filing applications require a certain amount of time, and current innovation decisions may be reflected in future patent applications, when studying the impact of air pollution on firms' green innovation decisions, the explanatory variable of air pollution uses data lagged by one period. This approach can also help reduce endogeneity issues.

8.4.2 Air Quality

The central explanatory variable in this study is air pollution. The measure for air pollution is based on daily city-level Air Quality Index (AQI) data obtained from the website of the Chinese Ministry of Ecology and Environment. This data is collected through ground-level air quality monitoring stations and serves as an effective indicator reflecting the air quality conditions within cities. In accordance with the "Ambient Air Quality Standards" (GB3095-2012) approved by the Ministry of Ecology and Environment, the daily data is aggregated into annual data. When AQI exceeds 100, it is categorized as polluted weather, while an AQI exceeding 200 is classified as severely polluted weather. The natural logarithm of the annual average Air Quality Index, the proportion of polluted weather days, and the proportion of severely polluted weather days are used as separate explanatory variables.

8.4.3 Controls

For the sake of the influence of other factors on the study, the relevant economic characteristics of the firms are selected as control variables in this paper, including enterprise scale, firm maturity, corporate Profitability, enterprise social wealth creativity, enterprise financing ability, GDP (Table 8.1).

Table 8.2 provides a descriptive statistical overview of the main variables presented in Table 8.1. The mean annual value for green patent applications (Gpat) is 3.284, with a standard deviation of 26.82. This substantial standard deviation underscores the considerable disparity in green patent application quantities among different enterprises, suggesting significant variations in their attitudes and capabilities regarding green innovation. In contrast, the mean value for invention-type green patents (Gpatinv) is 1.496, which is less than half of the overall green patent count (approximately 1.642). This indicates that Chinese enterprises tend to focus more on lower-value, minor inventive green creations and lack higher-value technological innovations. Overall, the level of innovation is relatively low, and the degree of inventiveness is not particularly strong. Regarding air quality, certain cities experience pollution levels where nearly all recorded days fall under polluted conditions,

Table 8.1 Definition of variables

Variable	Definition
Gpat	The company filed a total of green patents that year
Gpatuse	The company applied for a total of utility-type green patents that year
Gpatinv	The company applied for a total of invention-based green patents that year
AQImean	The average AQI value of the city where the company is located in the current year
Ratio100	Percentage of days with AQI > 100 in the city where the company is located in that year out of the number of days counted
Ratio200	Percentage of days with AQI > 200 in the city where the company is located in that year out of the number of days counted
Lev	Gearing ratio = total liabilities/total assets, which measures a firm's credit rating
Asset	Measure of firm size
ROA	Measuring corporate profitability
Age	Enterprise maturity
Tobin Q	a measure of corporate social wealth creativity
GDP	Controlling for level of urban development

with over half of them being classified as severely polluted. This situation suggests a less than optimistic outlook for air quality in China, indicating that there is a pressing need for intensified efforts to combat air pollution in various sectors. Furthermore, the vast territorial expanse of China, coupled with regional disparities in development, contributes to significant differences in air quality among different areas.

Table 8.2 Summary statistics

Variable	N	Mean	Std. Dev.	Min	Max
gpatuse	16,795	1.7880	14.3300	0	778
gpatinv	16,795	1.4960	13.7200	0	956
lnaqimean	16,795	4.3150	0.2730	3.0450	5.3570
ratio100	16,795	0.1860	0.1610	0	1
ratio200	16,795	0.0210	0.0390	0	0.5270
lev	16,795	0.5550	0.5250	0.0590	3.6740
lnasset	16,795	12.5300	1.3590	3.1040	19.3000
roa	16,795	4.1910	6.4010	−16.530	30.2200
age	16,795	13.6200	5.9570	0	65
tobinq	16,795	2.2810	2.0420	0.2310	11.2100
lngdp	16,795	10.9000	0.6810	8.2450	12.2800

8.5 Main Results

8.5.1 The Impact of Air Pollution on Enterprise Green Innovation

Given that the dependent variable in this study is patent data, specifically non-negative integers related to green patents, it becomes essential to account for the issues arising from the integer constraints in the model. Green patent data exhibits distinct discrete characteristics primarily due to the inherent uncertainty associated with the outcomes of innovation activities. Furthermore, not all research and development outcomes are patented by enterprises, resulting in situations where a company's patent count might include zero values. Linear regression models rely on several assumptions, such as the normal distribution of residuals, which may not always hold true, making them inadequate for such data. When the dependent variable consists of non-negative integers, it is more appropriate to employ a Poisson regression model for analysis. The Poisson model takes the following form: $\log(\mu) = \alpha + x^T\beta$, where μ represents the mean of the dependent variable Y. The mean follows an exponential relationship, $\mu = \exp(\alpha + x^T\beta) = e^{\alpha + x^T\beta}$. The interpretation of the estimated coefficients is that for each unit increase in the explanatory variable x_i, μ is impacted by a factor of e^β. In other words, when $x_i + 1$ is compared to x_i, the mean of Y at $x_i + 1$ is equal to the mean of Y at x_i multiplied by e^β. If β equals 0, then $e^\beta = e^0 = 1$, implying that the mean of Y remains constant as x_i changes. If β is greater than 0, e^β is greater than 1, indicating that the mean of Y increases with an increase in x_i. Conversely, if β is less than 0, the mean decreases as x_i increases.

Assuming that the number of green patents follows a Poisson distribution, we have: $Enpat_{kit} \sim \text{Poisson}(\mu_{kit})$. In this model, even if the count of environmental patents does not strictly adhere to the Poisson distribution, as long as the mean is correctly specified, the maximum likelihood estimation results are robust (Cameron and Trivedi 2005). The Poisson setting assumes that the conditional variance equals the conditional mean, which is a crucial characteristic of this model. Depending on the specific regression setup, when we introduce the core explanatory variable, we can derive the following regression equation:

$$Enpat_{kit} = \exp(\alpha + \beta AQI_{it} + \beta' X_{kit} + \varepsilon_{kit})$$

Here, ε_{kit} is the random error term. $Enpat_{kit}$ is the number of green patent applications for firm k in place i in year t. The overall number of applications, the number of utility patent applications, and the number of invention patent applications, respectively, will be used as explanatory variables. AQI_{it} is the air pollution in year t in place i. X_{kit} are the corresponding control variables. In this paper, the 1% and 99% percentile of continuous variables are winsorized, and the empirical results of the following descriptive statistics are based on the results of the processed data.

Table 8.3 displays the baseline estimates. To elaborate, we assess the impact of air pollution on corporate green innovation, specifically examining three measures:

total green patent applications (Gpat), green utility patent applications (Gpatuse), and green invention patent applications (Gpatinv). When employing the lagged natural logarithm of the annual average air quality index (AQI) as the explanatory variable, the estimated coefficients for all three dependent variables are not statistically significant. This suggests that enterprises might not be sensitive to the annual average air quality index as a measure of pollution. However, pollution weather days (Ratio100), representing the percentage of days with pollution, has significant positive coefficients of 0.1977, 0.0964, and 0.2989 for the three different green innovation variables (Gpat, Gpatuse, Gpatinv) at the 5% level. An increase in pollution weather days leads to an increase in total green innovation by enterprises, particularly in green utility patents, and has the most substantial positive impact on the highest-value green invention patents. Similarly, serious pollution weather days (Ratio200) exhibit coefficients of 0.6772, 0.2618, and 1.0915 for green innovation (Gpat, Gpatuse, Gpatinv) at the 10% level. This implies that a higher proportion of serious pollution weather days significantly promotes green innovation, with the most substantial impact observed in the case of green invention patents. This indicates that as air pollution worsens, enterprises actively engage in green innovation to respond to shifting market demands and various environmental production policies. The worsening air pollution trend in China has compelled the government to implement corresponding environmental regulations based on pollution changes. This results in significantly increased pollution control costs for enterprises, causing them to experience a certain degree of loss aversion. To ensure consistent profits, enterprises innovate in their production processes or product outputs to optimize cost-efficiency and boost profitability.

8.5.2 *Robust Tests*

As mentioned in the literature review, most studies exploring issues related to corporate innovation typically measure a company's innovation level through its research and development (R&D) investment. Moreover, R&D investment is the initial step for companies to achieve patent output. Therefore, to ensure the robustness of the finding that increased air pollution stimulates corporate green innovation, we conducted a robustness test by replacing the dependent variable with the natural logarithm of R&D expenditure. The regression results are presented in the following Table 8.4. The coefficients of the natural logarithm of the annual average air pollution, the percentage of days with pollution, and the percentage of days with severe pollution for the natural logarithm of R&D expenditure are 0.131, 0.190, and 0.596, respectively. All of these coefficients are statistically significant at the 5% level. This indicates that air pollution has a stimulating effect on R&D expenditure, meaning that companies located in regions with more severe air pollution tend to increase their R&D investments. This finding aligns consistently with the previous regression results.

Table 8.3 Model 1: Use of air quality variables with one period lag

	Panel A		
	gpat	gpat	gpat
L.lnAQImean	0.0111 (0.6011)		
L.ratio100		0.1977*** (6.1635)	
L.ratio200			0.6772*** (6.3359)
Observations	16,795	16,795	16,795
R-squared	0.409	0.409	0.409
	Panel B		
	gpatuse	gpatuse	gpatuse
L.lnAQImean	−0.0053 (−0.2033)		
L.ratio100		0.0964** (2.1241)	
L.ratio200			0.2618* (1.7226)
Observations	16,795	16,795	16,795
R-squared	0.392	0.392	0.392
	Panel C		
	gpatinv	gpatinv	gpatinv
L.lnAQImean	0.0272 (1.0384)		
L.ratio100		0.2989*** (6.5869)	
L.ratio200			1.0915*** (7.2635)
Observations	16,795	16,795	16,795
R-squared	0.381	0.381	0.381

Notes The regressions include all control variables, year FE and industry FE. *t* Robust t values are in parentheses. ***1%, **5%, *10%

8.6 Further Analysis

8.6.1 Further Discussion Based on Enterprise Ownership

As China's market economy continues to develop, both state-owned and non-state-owned enterprises play significant roles in the country's economic structure and have a substantial impact on its economic development. These two types of enterprises differ significantly in their operations, ownership structure, technology, and

Table 8.4 Robustness tests

	(1)	(2)	(3)
Variables	lnrd	lnrd	lnrd
lnaqimean	0.1310** (2.5315)		
ratio100		0.1896*** (2.6658)	
ratio200			0.5958*** (2.7580)
Observations	7907	7907	7907
R-squared	0.3195	0.3196	0.3197

Notes The regressions include all control variables, year FE and industry FE. Robust t values are in parentheses. ***1%, **5%, *10%

more, leading to variations in their approaches to and the content of technological innovation. In this study, we conducted empirical research based on the ownership structure of sample enterprises, classifying them as either state-owned or non-state-owned. The results reveal that the coefficient estimate of air pollution, the explanatory variable, for green innovation is positive and statistically significant at the 1% level for state-owned enterprises. In contrast, for non-state-owned enterprises, the coefficient estimate for green innovation is negative and significant at the 1% level. This indicates that increased air pollution has a significantly positive stimulating effect on green innovation in state-owned enterprises but exerts an inhibitory effect on non-state-owned enterprises. Several reasons contribute to this phenomenon. Firstly, green innovation, such as this type of innovation, has strong positive externalities and primarily serves to enhance social responsibility rather than market value. State-owned enterprises often enjoy advantages in policies and institutions, enabling them to secure monopolistic advantages in certain markets. Additionally, they receive government assistance in resource acquisition and international cooperation, leading to more significant support for green technology and investment. Moreover, in the context of an innovation-driven strategy, state-owned enterprises have a close relationship with the Chinese system in terms of technological innovation. Their technological research and development are often influenced by the government, which to some extent promotes technological innovation in state-owned enterprises and affects the allocation of innovation resources and the efficiency of the innovation system. Many enterprises in China still face severe financial constraints, and state-owned enterprises encounter relatively fewer of these constraints. Therefore, concerning innovations with strong positive externalities, such as green innovation, state-owned enterprises are more inclined to engage in green innovation prompted by the impact of air pollution (Table 8.5).

Table 8.5 Grouping according to the nature of the enterprise

	Nationalized business			Non-state enterprise		
Variables	gpat	gpatuse	gpatinv	gpat	gpatuse	gpatinv
L.ratio100	0.6811*** (14.4420)	0.8231*** (11.9325)	0.5741*** (8.8816)	−0.1974*** (−4.4004)	−0.3906*** (−6.3203)	0.0266 (0.4074)
Observations	8026	8026	8026	8769	8769	8769
R-squared	0.476	0.470	0.446	0.330	0.311	0.296

Notes The regressions include all control variables, year FE and industry FE. - Robust t values are in parentheses. ***1%, **5%, *10%

8.6.2 Further Discussion Based on Types of Enterprises

Based on the classification standards for high-tech industries (manufacturing) released by the National Bureau of Statistics, we divided the sample of manufacturing enterprises into two groups: high-tech enterprises and non-high-tech enterprises for group regression analysis. The results reveal that the coefficient of the ratio of pollution weather days, Ratio100, is significantly positive in the group of high-tech manufacturing enterprises and higher than in low-tech manufacturing enterprises. This suggests that when the proportion of pollution weather days increases throughout the year, high-tech manufacturing enterprises experience a stronger positive stimulus for green innovation compared to non-high-tech enterprises. However, for both high-tech and non-high-tech enterprises, the innovation with the most significant promotion effect is the highest-value invention-type green innovation. High-tech enterprises invest significantly in research and development in their production and operations, have a higher proportion of research and development personnel, and engage in activities such as researching, developing, producing, and selling innovative technologies or products, setting them apart from non-high-tech enterprises. High-tech enterprises are inherently more innovative. When faced with changes in the environment and the market, they actively engage in innovation, developing both technological and product innovations, to maintain their competitive edge. Therefore, when air quality deteriorates, high-tech industries are more significantly affected and respond with increased green innovation activities (Table 8.6).

8.6.3 Further Discussion Based on the Profitability of the Enterprise

Using the median of the return on assets (ROA) for all sampled enterprises as the criterion, we divided the companies into two groups: high-profit and low-profit enterprises for empirical research. The regression results after this grouping are presented in Table 8.7. The measure of air pollution levels, namely the ratio of pollution weather days, Ratio100, is only significantly positive in the high-return on assets group. This

Table 8.6 Grouping according to manufacturing technology level

	High-tech enterprises			Non-high-tech enterprises		
	gpat	gpatuse	gpatinv	gpat	gpatuse	gpatinv
L.ratio100	0.7529*** (19.9932)	0.4993*** (9.1023)	0.9832*** (18.9582)	0.1693* (1.8125)	−0.3779*** (−2.9490)	0.7797*** (5.6610)
Observations	8259	8259	8259	4569	4569	4569
R-squared	0.508	0.475	0.487	0.454	0.413	0.427

Notes The regressions include all control variables, year FE and industry FE. Robust t values are in parentheses. ***1%, **5%, *10%

suggests that more profitable companies are more likely to be positively stimulated and exhibit greater green patent output in the face of worsening air pollution. In contrast, companies with lower profitability experience inhibited green innovation under the same circumstances. These findings are influenced by the nature of innovation activities within firms. Innovation activities inherently involve high levels of uncertainty, resulting in a higher risk of losses for companies engaged in green innovation. Furthermore, green innovation is characterized by long investment cycles and substantial capital requirements, which increases the risks associated with innovation. In addition, external investors find it challenging to monitor a company's green innovation activities, which necessitates companies to rely on internal financing to address funding issues. MM theory suggests that when companies engage in innovation financing activities, they primarily rely on internal financing to address funding constraints, followed by debt financing and equity financing. In other words, companies prefer internal financing as their first choice. External financing comes with higher costs compared to internal financing, and companies opting for external financing must bear the burden of higher interest and principal repayments. Companies with high profitability can promote innovation by utilizing internal financing and have the financial capacity to provide ample support for innovation. High-profit companies have a stronger ability to raise funds and maintain substantial risk reserves. Therefore, when confronted with worsening air pollution, highly profitable companies can achieve more green innovation.

Table 8.7 Grouping based on return on assets

	Low-return-on-assets enterprises			High return on assets companies		
	gpat	gpatuse	gpatinv	gpat	gpatuse	gpatinv
L.ratio100	−0.5946*** (−11.5386)	−0.7180*** (−9.7673)	−0.4678*** (−6.4706)	0.6612*** (16.2239)	0.5575*** (9.7245)	0.7616*** (13.1413)
Observations	7054	7054	7054	9741	9741	9741
R-squared	0.427	0.411	0.392	0.421	0.403	0.396

Notes The regressions include all control variables, year FE and industry FE. Robust t values are in parentheses. ***1%, **5%, *10%

8.6.4 Further Discussion Based on Enterprise Size

Based on the asset levels of the enterprises, we divided the sampled companies into large-scale and small-scale enterprises, using the median of the natural logarithm of total assets as the criterion. The regression results, as shown in Table 8.8, reveal that various forms of green innovation activities in large enterprises are significantly positively influenced by air pollution, while small enterprises do not exhibit a significant impact from air pollution.

The scale of an enterprise is considered an essential factor influencing its innovation activities, a notion that has long been integrated into the research on corporate innovation. Scholars have posited several reasons behind this. Firstly, it is widely believed that only large enterprises holding market dominance would utilize innovation as a means to secure greater profits. In other words, these companies can generate more benefits for themselves through technological innovation. In comparison to medium and small businesses, large enterprises possess substantial financial advantages, economies of scale, and market power, which provide ample support for undertaking technological innovation. On a more intrinsic level, expanding an enterprise's scale can effectively enhance its overall strength and reputation, enabling it to gain recognition from a larger consumer base. The heightened reputation, based on an improved overall strength, leads to greater support and resources. Therefore, large enterprises should leverage their financial advantages in the innovation process.

Secondly, regardless of the financing method chosen, companies inevitably face financial constraints when embarking on innovation. They are more inclined to utilize internal funding for innovation activities, resorting to external financing only when internal resources are insufficient. The scale of a company significantly impacts its capacity to access financial resources. Large enterprises not only have a substantial scale advantage but also possess the capability to effectively address the issues stemming from information asymmetry, thus keeping their financing costs at a lower level.

Finally, small and medium-sized enterprises are influenced by their scale and financial constraints, leading to relatively lower R&D investments. This creates a speculative nature in their innovation activities, accompanied by limited risk-bearing capacity. From the perspective of large enterprises, they diversify their investments

Table 8.8 Grouping according to enterprise size

	Small-scale enterprises			Large-scale enterprises		
	gpat	gpatuse	gpatinv	gpat	gpatuse	gpatinv
L.ratio100	−0.1107 (−0.7670)	−0.2836 (−1.4953)	0.1311 (0.5900)	0.2276*** (6.9064)	0.1284*** (2.7403)	0.3277*** (7.0701)
Observations	5997	5997	5997	10,798	10,798	10,798
R-squared	0.129	0.116	0.132	0.371	0.363	0.338

Notes The regressions include all control variables, year FE and industry FE. Robust t values are in parentheses. ***1%, **5%, *10%

across different projects, resulting in substantially reduced R&D investment risks. This, in turn, elevates their risk-bearing capacity.

Several scholars have also explored the connection between corporate size and environmental innovation. They concur that larger companies are more likely to achieve green innovation outcomes. The larger the corporate scale, the more financial and human resources it can allocate to green innovation. Etzion (2007) contends that corporate size directly correlates with environmental performance, as larger companies willingly take on social responsibilities. Chen et al. (2006) combines his research to conclude that larger corporations achieve more prominent green innovation outcomes and subsequently establish a greener image, which, in turn, garners social approval. Furthermore, in relative terms, large corporations receive more public attention, bear more social responsibilities, and, as a result, engage in more green innovation. In summary, as enterprises grow in scale, they gain a competitive edge in market capabilities, overcoming financing constraints, and enhancing their risk-bearing capabilities. Therefore, in the face of worsening air pollution, they are better equipped to engage in green innovation.

8.6.5 Further Discussion Based on the Level of Pollution Locally

Using the median of the annual ratio of polluted days to total days as the grouping criterion, we categorized cities into two types: low-pollution cities and high-pollution cities. Specifically, a city was considered a high-pollution city if its annual ratio of polluted days exceeded the median, while it was categorized as a low-pollution city if the ratio was below the median. The results demonstrate that air pollution exerts distinct impacts on enterprises situated in different types of cities. In the high-pollution city group, the coefficient of Ratio100 is significantly positive, signifying a substantial positive stimulating effect on enterprises in highly polluted cities. Conversely, the coefficient of Ratio100 in the low-pollution city group is significantly negative, implying a notable inhibiting effect on companies in lightly polluted cities. The rationale behind these findings lies in the substantial regional disparities in air quality across China. From a spatial distribution perspective, it is evident that the northern cities of China face more severe pollution, while southern cities experience relatively milder pollution. Moreover, developed cities tend to grapple with more pronounced pollution levels than less developed cities. For instance, cities like Beijing, Shijiazhuang, and Luoyang, characterized by high levels of air pollution, have elevated pollution control to a central issue in their urban development plans. Air pollution has become a pressing concern in the process of economic development for these cities. Consequently, various enterprises within these cities are actively engaged in green research and development (R&D) innovations. Implementing green innovation has become a strategy for both corporate sustainability and the sustainable development of the cities. On the other hand, low-pollution cities are

Table 8.9 Grouping according to the pollution level of the city in which it is located

	Low-pollution cities			Highly polluted cities		
	gpat	gpatuse	gpatinv	gpat	gpatuse	gpatinv
L.ratio100	−1.8539*** (−8.9034)	−0.7425*** (−2.6286)	−3.1224*** (−10.1041)	0.8958*** (19.2184)	0.4845*** (7.3100)	1.3136*** (20.0208)
Observations	7685	7685	7685	9110	9110	9110
R-squared	0.326	0.277	0.327	0.442	0.442	0.403

Notes The regressions include all control variables, year FE and industry FE. Robust t values are in parentheses. ***1%, **5%, *10%

often characterized by lower levels of economic development and limited incentives for corporate green innovation. This disparity underscores the fact that enterprises adopt different strategies to respond to environmental changes based on the varying degrees of pollution levels in their respective regions (Table 8.9).

8.7 Conclusion

Air pollution has become a focal point of concern across various sectors in recent years, impacting various aspects of individuals' lives and exerting an informal influence on business operations. Under constraints related to "environmental pollution" and "resource bottlenecks," green innovation has emerged as a critical pathway for transforming economic development, adjusting economic structures, and gaining competitive advantages. To investigate the impact of air pollution on corporate green innovation, this study begins by summarizing the concepts and underlying principles of green innovation based on both domestic and international research literature. It proceeds to compile an overview of the multifaceted effects of air pollution, factors influencing green innovation, and a summary of studies using patent data to examine the impact of air pollution on green innovation. Subsequently, the study formulates hypotheses, grounded in relevant theories, to explore the influence of air pollution on corporate green innovation as measured by patents. Finally, employing a Poisson model on data collected from 1094 companies and 16,795 samples, the study empirically tests the impact of air pollution on corporate green innovation. The following conclusions are drawn:

1. The overall results indicate that air pollution exerts a certain degree of pressure on companies to engage in green innovation, meaning that businesses tend to increase their output of green innovation as air quality deteriorates. This suggests that a majority of enterprises exhibit a strong commitment to sustainable development. Moreover, among different types of green innovations, the most valuable category, namely inventive green innovation, receives the most substantial stimulus, highlighting businesses' focus on long-term economic benefits.

2. State-owned enterprises play a significant role in overall green innovation. When air pollution intensifies, state-owned enterprises are more strongly stimulated compared to non-state-owned ones. Non-state-owned enterprises do not opt for the path of green innovation in the face of worsening air pollution. To trigger green innovation activities in this category of enterprises, informal influences such as air pollution are insufficient.
3. Variations in the impact of air pollution on corporate green innovation are contingent on factors such as company size, technological proficiency, profitability, and the pollution levels of their respective cities. Larger, technologically advanced, and more profitable enterprises have a greater capacity for green innovation when confronted with worsening air pollution. Additionally, when environmental pressure in the form of air pollution is higher, i.e., in cities experiencing more severe overall air pollution, enterprises are more inclined to adopt green innovation as a response.

References

Amore MD, Bennedsen M (2016) Corporate governance and green innovation. J Environ Econ Manag 75:54–72

Cameron AC, Trivedi PK (2005) Micro-econometrics: methods and applications. Cambridge University Press, Cambridge

Chen YS, Lai SB, Wen CT (2006) The influence of green innovation performance on corporate advantage in Taiwan. J Bus Ethics 67:331–339

Ding X, Guo M, Yang T (2021) Air pollution, local bias and stock returns. Financ Res Lett 39:101576

Etzion D (2007) Research on organizations and the natural environment, 1992-present: a review. J Manag 33(4):637–664

Furman JL, Porter ME, Stern S (2002) The determinants of national innovative capacity. Res Policy 31(6):899–933

Greenstone M, List JA, Syverson C (2012) The effects of environmental regulation on the competitiveness of US manufacturing (No. w18392). National Bureau of Economic Research

Griliches Z (1990) Patent statistics as economic indicators: a survey part I. NBER

Grossman GM, Krueger AB (1995) Economic growth and the environment. Q J Econ 110(2):353–377

Hamamoto M (2006) Environmental regulation and the productivity of Japanese manufacturing industries. Resour Energy Econ 28(4):299–312

Horbach J (2008) Determinants of environmental innovation—new evidence from German panel data sources. Res Policy 37(1):163–173

Horbach J, Rammer C, Rennings K (2012) Determinants of eco-innovations by type of environmental impact—the role of regulatory push/pull, technology push and market pull. Ecol Econ 78:112–122

Kammerer D (2009) The effects of customer benefit and regulation on environmental product innovation: empirical evidence from appliance manufacturers in Germany. Ecol Econ 68(8–9):2285–2295

Kemp R (1997) Environmental Policy and Technical Change. Edward Elgar Publishing

Kemp R (2011) Innovation for sustainable development as a topic for environmental assessment. J Ind Ecol 15(5):673–675

Lavy V, Ebenstein A, Roth S (2014) The impact of short term exposure to ambient air pollution on cognitive performance and human capital formation (No. w20648). National Bureau of Economic Research

Leenders MA, Chandra Y (2013) Antecedents and consequences of green innovation in the wine industry: the role of channel structure. Tech Anal Strat Manag 25(2):203–218

Narver JC, Slater SF (1990) The effect of a market orientation on business profitability. J Mark 54(4):20–35

Neidell MP (2023) Air pollution and worker productivity. IZA World of Labor

Porter ME (1991) Towards a dynamic theory of strategy. Strateg Manag J 12(S2):95–117

Romer PM (1990) Endogenous technological change. J Polit Econ 98(5, Part 2):S71–S102

Shafik N, Bandyopadhyay S (1992) Economic growth and environmental quality: time-series and cross-country evidence, vol 904. World Bank Publications

Chapter 9
Clearing the Air for Investors: How Pollution Is Reshaping Corporate ESG

Abstract The significance of ESG factors and related risk management in corporate strategic decision-making is increasingly pronounced today, yet scant literature delves into this subject. This paper, therefore, employs air pollution as a proxy variable for environmental risk, matching air quality data from cities with data from publicly listed companies in China. It examines the relationship between environmental risk and corporate ESG performance. The research findings suggest that regional air pollution significantly enhances a firm's subsequent ESG performance. From a legitimacy perspective, air pollution exacerbates the uncertainty in a company's operations, leading to a heightened perception of external pressures, thereby driving strategic adjustments. These adjustments manifest in sustainable transformations and increased green investments, consequently enhancing ESG performance. Further analysis reveals that the impact of air pollution on corporate ESG performance varies significantly under different regulatory pressures and market attention levels. Economic consequences analysis indicates that, in the face of severe air pollution, improving ESG performance assists in alleviating future financing constraints and securing higher market valuations. This study not only enriches the understanding of factors influencing ESG but also offers a fresh perspective on the relationship between environmental risk and corporate sustainable transformation.

Keywords Air pollution · ESG · Uncertainty

9.1 Introduction

In recent years, prominent environmental and climate issues have sparked profound contemplation on the matter of sustainable development on a global scale. Governments and regulatory bodies worldwide have demonstrated a heightened concern and regard for ESG (Environmental, Social, and Governance) principles and sustainable development. An increasing number of countries and regions have integrated ESG factors into their national strategic frameworks and have introduced regulatory measures and policy guidelines. For instance, in 2014, the European Union

M. Guo et al., *Social-Economic Impacts of Air Pollution*, Climate Change and Energy Transition, https://doi.org/10.1007/978-981-96-7858-7_9

enacted the "Non-Financial Reporting Directive," incorporating ESG regulation into policy and regulations. The 20th Party Congress emphasized the acceleration of green transformation in the development approach, highlighting that driving the green and low-carbon development of economic and social progress is pivotal for achieving high-quality development. The China Securities Regulatory Commission (CSRC) is also contemplating the inclusion of ESG disclosure in regular information reports for publicly listed companies. ESG represents the tangible manifestation of the green sustainable development concept within capital markets, exerting an increasingly profound and extensive impact on corporate operations and development.

Since the initiation of economic reform and opening-up, China has achieved remarkable economic development results. However, this growth model, characterized by its resource-intensive nature, has also given rise to severe environmental issues, notably concerning air quality. Since 2013, China has witnessed severe smog incidents, with air pollution briefly becoming an annual trending topic. On a macro level, air pollution has constrained the high-quality development of China's economy. On a micro level, air pollution not only affects the health of laborers but also exposes businesses to the risk of labor capital outflow (Wang et al. 2021), decreases corporate output (Fu et al. 2021), raises the risk expectations of capital market participants regarding businesses (Krueger et al. 2020), and significantly escalates the uncertainty in corporate operations. Air pollution's wide-reaching impact and enduring duration are the direct consequences of past decades of prioritizing economic interests while overlooking environmental and social performance, representing a specific manifestation of environmental risk. As ESG and sustainable development principles garner increasing attention worldwide, environmental risk is bound to become one of the essential risk factors that businesses cannot afford to disregard. The question of how businesses can enhance their environmental risk management capabilities and transition from a single-minded economic interest-centric model to one that considers both environmental and social factors is a crucial issue that demands contemplation in the new era.

Distinguishing itself from the literature examining environmental pollution control from a regulatory perspective, organizational strategic theory posits that businesses need to adapt to ever-changing external environments, making strategic adjustments to effectively integrate internal and external resources for sustainable development (Boeker 1991; Rajagopalan and Spreitzer 1997). Internationally, sustainable development is the mainstream trend, and China has recently articulated "dual carbon" goals, emphasizing high-quality economic development. These developments will fundamentally alter the external environment of business operations in China, amplifying the impact of environmental risk on business operations. Hence, beyond government environmental regulations, businesses may voluntarily incorporate environmental uncertainty into their considerations and make strategic adjustments.

In light of the aforementioned considerations, this study empirically investigates the impact of air pollution on corporate ESG performance by matching air quality index data from prefectural-level cities from 2013 to 2019 with the cities where companies listed on the Shanghai and Shenzhen stock exchanges are headquartered.

The research reveals a significant enhancement of corporate ESG performance due to air pollution. Specifically, for each one-standard-deviation increase in the air quality index in the city where a company's headquarters is located, the average ESG rating score of the company increases by 2.78%. The perception of environmental risk by companies serves as a crucial channel through which air pollution affects ESG performance. In other words, air pollution exacerbates the uncertainty in corporate operations, leading to a heightened sense of operational pressure, which, in turn, drives strategic adjustments and impacts ESG rating scores. To account for potential endogeneity issues, this paper employs inversion days as an instrumental variable for air pollution in robustness tests. Furthermore, it conducts robustness tests, such as Heckman two-stage modeling, changing core variables, and employing dynamic panel models. The results from these tests are consistent with the main findings.

Further heterogeneity analysis indicates that the impact of air pollution on corporate ESG performance is more pronounced under higher regulatory pressure and greater market attention, underscoring ESG as a vital means of communication with stakeholders. Lastly, the paper examines the tangible consequences of businesses enhancing their ESG performance in the face of severe environmental risk. The study finds that in areas with high air pollution, improving ESG performance significantly reduces future financing constraints and enhances a company's valuation in capital markets. This further underscores the intrinsic alignment between corporate ESG actions and corporate value, demonstrating that sustainable development not only yields social benefits but also generates economic value.

This research contributes to three main areas: First, it enriches the study of factors influencing corporate ESG behavior by approaching the topic from the perspective of regional air quality, a critical external environmental factor. While existing literature predominantly focuses on factors such as institutional environment (Ioannou and Serafeim 2012), ownership characteristics (Li et al. 2021), and executive traits (Tan et al. 2021a, b), this paper explores the impact of environmental pollution in the region where a company operates, thus expanding the scope of research into ESG influencing factors. Second, the paper's findings extend the domain of environmental governance research. Most existing literature primarily examines the influence of top-down government environmental regulations on businesses, neglecting the proactive strategic adjustments made by companies in response to changing external environmental risks. By considering a company's perception of environmental risk, this study delves deeper into the relationship between external environmental risks and micro-level corporate behavior, complementing the literature on environmental governance. Third, this research enriches the theory and literature on corporate strategic choices. Corporate strategic adjustments are influenced not only by internal factors but also by external environmental conditions and corporate perception. Within the analytical framework of legitimacy theory and organizational strategic theory, this paper investigates companies' strategic responses to air pollution, further analyzing potential mechanisms and underlying economic consequences, offering empirical evidence to better understand and comprehend micro-level corporate strategic adjustment behavior.

The remainder of this paper is structured as follows: Sect. 9.2 formulates research hypotheses based on theoretical analysis. Section 9.3 introduces the data sources and research design. Section 9.4 presents the primary empirical research results. Section 9.5 includes mechanism tests and heterogeneity analysis. Section 9.6 concludes the research and provides insights.

9.2 Literature Review, Theoretical Analysis and Research Hypotheses

9.2.1 Literature Review

9.2.1.1 Air Pollution-Related Studies

Existing research has extensively and deeply examined the impact of air pollution. Studies indicate that air pollution directly affects individual health from both physical and psychological perspectives. It increases the likelihood of individuals suffering from respiratory diseases, raises their medical expenses, and elevates mortality rates (Deryugina et al. 2019). Furthermore, it negatively affects individuals' well-being by inducing poor moods and pessimistic emotions. Building on the framework of behavioral economics, scholars have further analyzed how air pollution affects individuals' health and emotions, consequently influencing businesses and capital markets. Previous research has revealed that air pollution affects labor force participation, impairs individual work efficiency, and diminishes a company's human capital supply, ultimately leading to reduced productivity and poorer performance (Fu et al. 2021; He et al. 2019). Besides its adverse effects on human capital within firms, air pollution indirectly influences the quality of corporate financial reporting. For instance, air pollution, by exacerbating investors' pessimism, heightens stock market risks, impairs analysts' cognition and information processing capabilities, reduces the timeliness of their reports, and decreases the accuracy of earnings forecasts (Dong et al. 2021), consequently affecting the information efficiency of capital markets.

Another branch of literature focuses on examining the strategic behavior of individuals and firms in the context of severe air pollution. Tan et al. (2021a, b) discovered that companies operating in regions with high air pollution exhibit a stronger preventive motive, tending to hold more cash to address the operational uncertainties stemming from air pollution. Cho et al. (2021) found that businesses located in cities with more severe air pollution engage in more aggressive earnings management practices to cope with the operating losses caused by air pollution.

9.2.1.2 ESG Drivers and Their Economic Consequences

ESG, an acronym for Environmental, Social Responsibility, and Corporate Governance, represents the amalgamation of sustainable development principles with modern management. It extends and broadens the concept of corporate social responsibility. Diverging from traditional financial rating systems, ESG focuses on a company's risks across the dimensions of the environment, social responsibility, and corporate governance. It has become a pivotal decision-making factor for market participants (Pedersen et al. 2021). Traditionally, under the perspective of maximizing shareholder value, companies were expected to prioritize shareholders' interests, with the sole social responsibility being the utilization of all resources for profit growth (Friedman 1970). However, extreme climate issues, environmental pollution, and social conflicts have raised questions about this viewpoint and prompted reconsideration of corporate boundaries. Corporate social responsibility now encompasses not only economic responsibility but also new or yet undefined responsibilities related to actively improving the social environment. From a stakeholder perspective, a company's non-financial activities, including ESG initiatives, are no longer seen as value-irrelevant activities. Instead, they are viewed as part of the process of aligning a company's value maximization goals with the interests of different stakeholders to achieve long-term sustainable development. This theory implies that the demands of different interest groups are essential factors influencing a company's ESG efforts. Companies formulate corresponding ESG strategies based on their business objectives and perceptions of external environmental changes (Clementino and Perkins 2021), affecting the attitudes and perceptions of major stakeholders toward the company. As a result, non-financial activities such as ESG are often considered tools for corporate strategic management and risk control (Kim et al. 2021). They help companies convey positive signals, build a corporate image, and cultivate intangible moral capital. For instance, Huang et al. (2022) found that after natural disasters occur in the areas where companies operate, corporate managers strategically disclose more ESG information to address changes in investor risk perception. Liao et al. (2023) discovered that local companies are more willing to disclose social responsibility information and enhance disclosure quality after the opening of capital markets to improve the information environment and attract foreign investors.

Regarding economic consequences, numerous studies have found that proactive ESG activities can bring several operational benefits to companies. For example, ESG activities alleviate competitive pressures in product markets (Flammer 2015) and help optimize financing channels while reducing a company's cost of capital (Dhaliwal et al. 2011). Moreover, ESG can assist companies in risk reduction. Reber et al. (2022) found that companies that disclose more ESG information before their IPOs can mitigate severe information asymmetry issues between insiders and potential investors, reducing non-systematic stock market risks faced by companies after their IPOs. ESG is also related to a company's credit ratings and default risk in the bond market. Studies such as Seltzer et al. (2022) suggest that a company's bond credit rating is associated with environmental performance risk.

9.2.2 Theoretical Analysis and Research Hypotheses

Organizational strategic theory posits that organizations are not static entities; changes in the external environment prompt internal adaptations and adjustments within organizations (Haveman 1992). In the realm of business operations, the external environment is always in a state of dynamic flux. Successful business operations require vigilant attention to environmental changes, striving to find a balance, and making timely strategic adjustments and organizational transformations in response to these dynamics. For transient or reversible changes, companies may only need to make temporary adjustments. However, when faced with irreversible changes with long-term implications, profound transformations are necessary (Rajagopalan and Spreitzer 1997).

From a strategic management perspective, companies are embedded within social network structures, directly or indirectly influenced by social norms, and need to engage in activities or behaviors that align with the institutional norms and values of the society in which they operate to gain legitimacy (Suchman 1995). However, companies guided by profit maximization objectives face a trade-off between satisfying external legitimacy and incurring potential efficiency losses. Companies must strategically choose between legitimacy and efficiency (Jeong and Kim 2019). In this context, China's heightened emphasis on high-quality economic transformation and sustainable green development fundamentally alters the external environment in which companies operate. Changes in mainstream norms compel companies to reconsider the external environment on which they rely for survival and the corresponding legitimacy management (Jackson and Apostolakou 2010).

For business management, the extent to which an organization recognizes and understands changes in its environment significantly impacts the company's strategic decisions and behavioral patterns (Kaplan 2011). Air pollution increases a company's perception of environmental risks through various channels. When facing substantial external pressures, companies must consider how to meet stakeholder expectations to maintain business legitimacy, such as engaging in green transformation, increasing environmental investments, and ensuring employee protection, among other actions. From a profit perspective, the environmental uncertainty brought about by air pollution also amplifies the potential benefits of ESG practices. ESG-related activities are regarded as a company's efforts to enhance social welfare, transcending legal requirements and economic interests, aiding in the formation of moral capital, and facilitating trust-building between the company and its stakeholders (Godfrey 2005). When confronted with the uncertainty resulting from air pollution, stakeholders are more likely to attribute deteriorating business conditions to external factors rather than solely blaming the company. In the face of severe environmental issues, companies that prioritize ESG factors will gradually develop a distinct competitive advantage and gain more resource support (Dhaliwal et al. 2011).

Based on the above analysis, this study asserts that air pollution significantly increases the environmental uncertainty of business operations. Companies operating in areas with severe air pollution are more likely to experience pressures from both the market and non-market forces. Balancing the costs and benefits of ESG activities, they strategically adjust their business operations and engage in more proactive ESG practices. Thus, this study proposes the research hypothesis:

H1: Under the same conditions, air pollution has a positive impact on a company's ESG performance.

9.3 Data and Research Design

9.3.1 Sample Selection and Data Sources

This study focuses on examining the impact of air pollution on corporate ESG performance using data from companies listed on the Shanghai and Shenzhen stock exchanges from 2013 to 2019. Daily air quality index data for the cities where these companies are headquartered is obtained from the National Urban Air Quality Daily Report and serves as a proxy for urban air pollution. In China, air pollution disclosure was divided into two periods, with the year 2013 serving as the dividing point. Before 2013, air pollution data was reported using the Air Pollution Index (API). After 2013, in accordance with the newly enacted 'Environmental Air Quality Standards,' monitoring and disclosure of PM2.5, CO, and O_3 were incorporated into the existing API, creating the Air Quality Index (AQI). PM2.5, which represents fine particulate matter with a diameter equal to or less than 2.5 micrometers, is known for its ability to carry various toxic substances and can persist in the atmosphere for an extended period, making it a primary contributor to air pollution. Consequently, this study employs the AQI as its core variable, starting the sample from the year 2013.

Following the approach used by Huang et al. (2022), this study uses ESG rating data provided by Bloomberg to assess corporate ESG performance. Company-level data, including variables such as company size, profitability, and financial leverage, are sourced from the National Institute of Financial Research (NIFR) and China Stock Market & Accounting Research (CSMAR) databases. Per capita GDP data for cities is derived from the 'China City Statistical Yearbook.' Adopting a similar methodology as He et al. (2019), this study matches corporate data with the city's air quality indicator (AQI) and city-level variables based on the name of the city where a company's headquarters is located, resulting in a panel dataset with annual, city, and company dimensions. Subsequently, the original sample is subjected to the following processing steps: (1) Removal of observations from the financial industry; (2) Exclusion of companies with abnormal financial conditions (ST and *ST); (3) Elimination of missing values; (4) To mitigate the influence of extreme values, truncation is applied to all continuous variables at the 1st and 99th percentiles. Ultimately, this study compiles a dataset comprising 6179 observations for the years 2013 to 2019 in the form of annual-city-company panels.

9.3.2 *Definition of Main Variables*

9.3.2.1 Air Quality

In this study, the air quality index (AQI) is employed as a measure of the air quality in the cities where the companies' headquarters are located. Using daily air quality index data for cities at the prefectural level and above, the annual average AQI is computed and logarithmically transformed. A higher value of this index signifies more severe air pollution in the city. To ensure the robustness of the findings, this paper also conducts robustness checks using various alternative measures, such as PM2.5.

9.3.2.2 Corporate ESG Performance

The corporate ESG rating data is sourced from Bloomberg, which has been at the forefront of monitoring and assessing environmental, social, and governance issues for global companies. The database covers approximately 13,000 companies across more than 100 countries and regions, representing around 88% of global market capitalization. This database employs a combination of quantitative and qualitative methods to rate companies on their ESG performance and provides an overall ESG rating score.

The overall ESG rating score is calculated as the sum of equally weighted (33.33%) scores across the three dimensions: environmental (E), social (S), and governance (G). The rating ranges from 0 to 100 and reflects a company's ESG disclosure and quality, with higher scores indicating better ESG performance. Within the environmental (E) dimension, the themes and weights include: air quality (4.78%), climate change (4.70%), ecological and biodiversity impact (4.79%), energy (4.73%), materials and pollutants (4.74%), supply chain (4.79%), and water resource use and protection (4.79%). The social (S) dimension encompasses themes and weights such as community and customers (5.53%), diversity (4.70%), ethics and compliance (5.57%), health and safety (5.58%), human capital (5.55%), and supply chain (5.54%). Finally, the governance (G) dimension covers themes and weights including audit risk and oversight (4.17%), board (4.16%), compensation (4.16%), diversity (4.17%), independence (4.18%), nomination and governance oversight (4.18%), sustainability governance (4.18%), and tenure (4.18%).

9.3.3 *Research Model*

To examine the impact of air pollution on corporate ESG performance, following the approach employed by Wang et al. (2021), this study establishes the following empirical model:

$$ESG_{i,j,t+1} = \beta_0 + \beta_1 AQI_{j,t} + \gamma Contols_{i,t} + CityFE + IndustryFE + YearFE + \varepsilon_{i,j,t} \quad (9.1)$$

where $ESG_{i,\,j,\,t\,+\,1}$ represents the ESG performance of enterprise i headquartered in city j in year t + 1. $AQI_{j,\,t}$ signifies the air quality in city j in year t, serving as a metric for air pollution. β_1 captures the effect of air pollution on corporate ESG performance. $Contols_{i,\,t}$ encompasses company- and region-level control variables. To account for causality over time, ESG variables are measured in period t + 1, while other variables are at time t. Additionally, the model includes city and industry fixed effects to control for time-invariant unobservable factors, and it introduces annual fixed effects to control for factors that do not vary at the individual level. Robust standard errors are used for all regressions, with clustering at the company level.

Drawing from the studies by Huang et al. (2022) and Wang et al. (2021), the model incorporates a set of enterprise-level variables that may influence ESG performance, aiming to mitigate the omission of variables. These variables include: company size (SIZE), where larger companies attract more attention and place greater emphasis on their social image and reputation, resulting in increased investment in social and environmental initiatives; company profitability (ROA) and operating cash flow (OCF), strong profitability and sufficient cash flows provide financial support and assurance for ESG activities; financial leverage (LEV), companies with higher debt burdens may reduce their ESG investments due to financial pressure; company age (AGE), which can affect a company's focus on ESG; ownership type (SOE), where state-owned enterprises face more stringent environmental assessment requirements and prioritize ESG investments.

Considering the influence of management on corporate ESG decision-making, the model also controls for a set of executive team characteristics, including the proportion of women in the top management team (FEMALE_TMT), the average age of the top management team (AGE_TMT), and the proportion of overseas backgrounds in the top management team (OVERSEA_TMT). Existing research suggests that older managers may be more sensitive to air pollution and pay greater attention to corporate ESG practices (Tan et al. 2021a, b). Finally, considering the role of regional macroeconomic development in city air pollution and corporate social responsibility practices, the model includes the per capita gross domestic product (GDP) of the city. Detailed variable definitions are provided in Table 9.1.

9.4 Main Results

9.4.1 Air Pollution and Corporate ESG Performance

Table 9.2 presents the baseline regression results of the impact of air pollution on corporate social, environmental, and governance (ESG) performance. Column (1) reports the results without the inclusion of control variables, where it can be observed

Table 9.1 Definition of variables

Variables	Definition	Data sources
ESG	Corporate ESG performance rating score	Bloomberg
E	Corporate environmental performance rating score	Bloomberg
S	Corporate social performance rating score	Bloomberg
G	Corporate governance performance rating score	Bloomberg
AQI	Logarithm of the annual average air quality index of the city where the enterprise is located	National Urban Air Quality Daily
SIZE	Logarithmic total assets of the enterprise	CSMAR
ROA	Net profit of the enterprise divided by total assets	CSMAR
LEV	Total liabilities of the enterprise divided by total assets	CSMAR
OCF	Net operating cash flows of the enterprise divided by total assets	CSMAR
AGE	Logarithmic number of years of business establishment	CSMAR
SOE	Dummy variable, if the nature of the enterprise's equity is state-owned, 0 otherwise	CSMAR
FEMALE_TMT	Number of women in the executive team divided by the total number	CSMAR
AGE_TMT	Logarithmic average age of the executive team	CSMAR
OVERSEA_TMT	Number of executive team members with overseas backgrounds divided by total number of members	CSMAR
GDP	Logarithmic GDP per capita of the city where the firm is located	China Urban Statistical Yearbook

that the regression coefficient for the Air Quality Index (AQI) is 1.831 and significantly positively associated with corporate ESG performance at a 5% significance level. After incorporating enterprise characteristic variables, column (2) shows that the regression coefficient of AQI is 1.899, and it remains significant at the 1% level. Finally, after adding executive team characteristic variables and city-level macroeconomic variables, column (3) reveals that the regression coefficient for AQI is 1.961, still significant at the 1% level. At this stage, the model's adjusted R-squared increases from 0.200 to 0.371, signifying an improved model fit and enhanced explanatory power.

The regression results in these three columns all indicate a significant positive impact of air pollution on corporate ESG performance, corroborating Research Hypothesis 1. This suggests that severe air pollution prompts companies to adjust their business strategies, leading to improved ESG performance. Furthermore, considering that a company's financial situation may also influence its response to air quality in terms of ESG performance, the study conducted further tests by controlling for interaction terms between air quality (AQI) and financial variables. The results of this test align with the baseline regression.

Table 9.2 Air pollution and corporate ESG performance: benchmark regression results

	(1)	(2)	(3)
	ESG_{t+1}	ESG_{t+1}	ESG_{t+1}
AQI	1.831**	1.899***	1.961***
	(3.185)	(3.428)	(3.520)
Observations	6179	6179	6179
Adj.R^2	0.200	0.367	0.371

Notes Robust t-values are in parentheses and standard errors are clustered at the firm level. The regressions include all control variables, year FE, industry FE, city FE. ***1%, **5%, *10%

The results from the baseline regression not only hold statistical significance but also carry substantial economic implications. Specifically, for column (3), for every one standard deviation increase in the Air Quality Index (0.321), the composite ESG performance score of companies increases by an average of approximately 2.78% (=0.321*1.961/22.65). The sign and significance of the control variables in the model are broadly consistent with expectations, where factors such as company size, cash flow, ownership structure, and executive overseas backgrounds have a positive impact on corporate ESG performance.

Furthermore, the study proceeds to investigate whether air pollution's impact on corporate ESG is consistent across the three individual dimensions. The dependent variable in Model (9.1), the ESG rating score, is replaced with corporate Environmental (E), Social (S), and Governance (G) scores, and separate regressions are conducted for each, as presented in Table 9.3. Column (1) reports the effect of air pollution on corporate environmental performance, revealing that the regression coefficient for the Air Quality Index (AQI) is 2.910 and significantly positive at a 1% significance level. In column (2), the impact of air pollution on corporate social performance is found to be significant at the 10% level. In column (3), air pollution also exhibits a significant positive effect on corporate governance performance at a 5% significance level. These findings suggest that the impact of air pollution on different dimensions of corporate ESG varies. While there are positive effects on the social and governance aspects, air pollution's influence is notably more pronounced in enhancing corporate environmental performance.

9.4.2 Robustness Testing

9.4.2.1 Endogenous Issues

As a city-level variable, air quality is generally not expected to be related to firm-level characteristics. However, as pointed out by Fu et al. (2021), some omitted time-varying variables at both the city and firm levels can lead to OLS models underestimating or overestimating the impact of air pollution. Additionally, measurement

Table 9.3 Air pollution and corporate ESG performance: three dimensions tested separately

	(1)	(2)	(3)
	E_{t+1}	S_{t+1}	G_{t+1}
AQI	2.910***	2.041*	1.255**
	(3.781)	(2.429)	(2.709)
Observations	6179	6179	6179
Adj.R^2	0.342	0.264	0.341

Notes Robust t-values are in parentheses and standard errors are clustered at the firm level. The regressions include all control variables, year FE, industry FE, city FE. ***1%, **5%, *10%

errors in the core variables can potentially introduce endogeneity issues. Therefore, this study follows the approach of Fu et al. (2021) and Wang et al. (2021) by using the number of temperature inversion days in a year in the city where the company is located to construct an instrumental variable (Thermal Days) and re-estimate the baseline model using two-stage least squares (2SLS).

Instrumental variables must satisfy strict conditions, and the number of temperature inversion days in a city where a company operates in a given year serves as an appropriate instrumental variable for the following reasons. Firstly, temperature inversion is a meteorological concept. Normally, temperature decreases with height in the atmosphere's convection layer, but temperature inversion represents the opposite phenomenon. Temperature inversion conditions lead to higher concentrations of air pollutants near the surface, causing severe air pollution, thus meeting the relevance condition. Secondly, temperature inversion conditions meet the exclusivity requirement. Currently, there is no direct theoretical or empirical evidence to suggest that temperature inversion days directly affect a company's ESG performance. In other words, temperature inversion can only influence a company's ESG performance through its effect on air quality.

Table 9.4 reports the results of the two-stage least squares regression based on the instrumental variable. Column (1) presents the first-stage results, indicating a significant positive correlation between the number of temperature inversion days (Thermal Days) and air pollution, with a significance level of 1%, as expected. The KP F-statistic is 59.55, well above the critical value of 16.38 at the 10% level, suggesting the absence of a weak instrument problem. Column (2) reports the results of the second stage, showing that even after using the instrumental variable for estimation, the air quality index remains significantly positively correlated with corporate ESG performance, confirming the reliability of the baseline model regression results.

9.4.2.2 Sample Selection Bias

Whether companies receive ESG ratings is a self-selection process by rating agencies, which may introduce sample selection bias. To address this issue, this study conducts robustness tests using the two-stage model proposed by Heckman (1979).

Table 9.4 Air pollution and firms' ESG performance: instrumental variables regression

	(1)	(2)
	AQI	ESG_{t+1}
Thermal days	0.001***	
	(7.717)	
AQI		10.723**
		(2.434)
Observations	6179	6179
Adj.R^2	0.909	0.356
KP F-statistic	59.55	

Notes Robust t-values are in parentheses and standard errors are clustered at the firm level. The regressions include all control variables, year FE, industry FE, city FE. ***1%, **5%, *10%

Specifically, in the first stage, a Probit model is used to estimate whether companies receive ESG ratings. The percentage of companies within the same industry receiving ESG ratings (ESG_IND_P) is included as an exclusion restriction variable. Since the first stage does not involve city-level air quality (AQI), the model only controls for industry and year fixed effects. Based on the regression results in the first stage, an inverse Mills ratio (IMR) is constructed and included in the second-stage model to account for selection bias.

From the results in Column (1) of Table 9.5, it can be observed that the estimated coefficient of the exclusion restriction variable is significantly positive, aligning with expectations. Column (2) reports the results of the second stage, showing that the IMR is significantly positive, indicating the presence of some selection bias. However, after controlling for the impact of selection bias, the relationship between air pollution and corporate ESG performance remains significantly positive. The estimated coefficient of 1.829 in the second stage is only 0.132 lower than the coefficient of 1.961 in the baseline regression, suggesting that selection bias has a limited impact on the main results and their corresponding economic implications in this study.

9.4.2.3 Replacement of Core Variables and Estimation Models

Considering that different ESG rating agencies may provide rating scores with discrepancies, which may lead to measurement errors, this study conducts robustness tests using alternative indicators. ESG rating data from Huazheng (a Chinese ESG rating agency) obtained from the Wind database is used as an alternative measure. The results in Column (1) of Table 9.6 report the regression results using Huazheng's ESG rating data. It is observed that the coefficient of the variable AQI is 0.095, and it is significantly positive at a 5% significance level, consistent with the results of the baseline regression.

Table 9.5 Heckman two-stage model

	(1)	(2)
	ESG_D	ESG_{t+1}
AQI		1.829***
		(3.337)
ESG_IND_P	1.110*	
	(2.240)	
IMR		6.985***
		(6.302)
Observations	18,989	6179
Pseudo/Adj.R^2	0.343	0.391

Notes Robust t-values are in parentheses and standard errors are clustered at the firm level. The regressions include all control variables, year FE, industry FE, city FE. ***1%, **5%, *10%

Table 9.6 Replacement of core variables and estimation model

	(1)	(2)	(3)	(4)	(5)
	Replacement of ESG metrics	Replacement of air pollution metrics			Dynamic panels
	ESG_HZ_{t+1}	ESG_{t+1}	ESG_{t+1}	ESG_{t+1}	ESG_{t+1}
AQI	0.095**				2.596*
	(3.056)				(2.107)
AQI_RATE		0.983**			
		(3.180)			
PM25			1.461***		
			(3.521)		
PM10				1.319**	
				(2.696)	
Observations	18,504	6179	6179	6179	6179
Adj.R^2	0.166	0.371	0.371	0.371	–
Dependent variable lag	–	–	–	–	Phase 1

Notes Robust t-values are in parentheses and standard errors are clustered at the firm level. The regressions include all control variables, year FE, industry FE, city FE. ***1%, **5%, *10%

Additionally, this study explores alternative ways to measure regional air quality. Following the approach of Cho et al. (2021), the average air quality index rate (AQI_RATE) is calculated based on the daily air pollution levels, which represent air quality from 0 (good) to 5 (severely polluted) to avoid aggregation errors. Furthermore, considering that air pollution is primarily caused by fine particulate matter, the concentrations of PM2.5 and PM10 in cities are used as alternative air quality variables. The results in Columns (2) to (4) of Table 9.6 present the regression results using these alternative indicators to measure air quality, demonstrating the robustness of the findings.

Finally, considering the strong autocorrelation in ESG rating scores provided by Bloomberg between the current and lagged periods, this study includes the lagged value of the dependent variable, ESG rating score one period behind, on the right-hand side of Eq. (9.1). Dynamic panel models are employed for estimation. Column (5) of Table 9.6 reports the corresponding results, showing that the impact of air pollution on corporate ESG remains significantly positive, consistent with the results of the OLS regression, further confirming the robustness of the main findings.

9.4.2.4 Replacement of Samples

For large publicly listed corporations, their corporate headquarters are primarily responsible for marketing and management, while the production facilities may be located in different regions. Using the air quality index (AQI) of the city where the corporate headquarters is located as the core explanatory variable could introduce some bias. To address this issue, two tests were conducted: Firstly, based on information about the cities where the companies primarily operate, the air quality data at the city level was re-matched to construct the variable AQI_OPER, which was then used for robustness testing. The results in Column (1) of Table 9.7 show that the estimated coefficient of AQI_OPER is 2.171 and significantly positive at a 1% significance level, consistent with the baseline regression results. Secondly, Observations in the sample where the location of the corporate headquarters and the primary operational locations differed were excluded, and the analysis was re-run, as reported in Column (2) of Table 9.7. After removing observations with inconsistent corporate headquarters and primary operational locations, the main results remained unchanged.

Table 9.7 Replacement samples

	(1)	(2)
	ESG_{t+1}	ESG_{t+1}
AQI_OPER	2.171***	
	(3.784)	
AQI		2.052***
		(3.427)
Observations	6179	5583
Adj.R^2	0.357	0.368

Notes Robust t-values are in parentheses and standard errors are clustered at the firm level. The regressions include all control variables, year FE, industry FE, city FE. ***1%, **5%, *10%

9.4.2.5 Placebo Testing

Finally, drawing inspiration from Wang et al. (2021), this study conducted 1000 placebo tests to control for the influence of unobservable factors on the estimation results. Specifically, a pseudo-variable, False_AQI, was created by randomly assigning air quality index values to each city in the sample. False_AQI was then used to replace the actual air quality variable, AQI, in the baseline model, and this process was repeated 1000 times. Figure 9.1 illustrates the distribution of T-values based on estimates using False_AQI. The figure shows that the T-values from the 1000 placebo tests are centered around zero in a normal distribution, with only a few results close to the actual T-value (represented by the solid black line). This suggests that unobserved macro-level or time-varying factors are unlikely to affect the primary findings of this study.

9.5 Further Research

9.5.1 Analysis of Transmission Mechanisms

The empirical analysis above has confirmed the positive effect of air pollution on a firm's ESG performance. In the theoretical framework, this study posits that air pollution can alter the external environment faced by firms, heighten their awareness

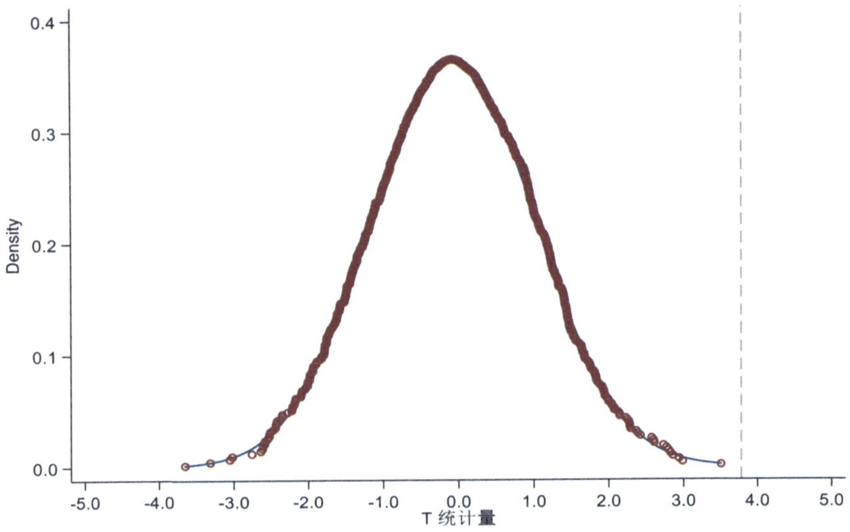

Fig. 9.1 Placebo test

of environmental risks, and subsequently promote adjustments in their ESG strategies. Firms operating in regions with severe air pollution confront more substantial external pressures, such as public opinion impacts, media attention, and government environmental regulations. These factors significantly increase the uncertainty in a firm's operations and prompt them to take measures to maintain their legitimacy. To directly validate the impact of this mechanism, this study constructed two indicators to measure a firm's degree of sustainable transformation and their environmental investment intensity. Firstly, using text analysis, keywords related to green sustainable development were extracted from annual reports, such as "energy conservation and emissions reduction," "environmental protection strategy," "sustainability," "environmental protection and governance," among others, to construct the Sustainable Transformation Index (SUS). A higher value of this index indicates a higher level of sustainable transformation for the firm. Secondly, detailed information related to environmental pollution prevention, environmental governance, green investments, etc., was obtained from the notes to the financial statements of firms. The Environmental Investment Index (EPI) was then constructed by multiplying the total environmental investment amount for the year by 100 and dividing it by the firm's total equity.

Columns (1) and (2) of Table 9.8 report the regression results for the Sustainable Transformation Index (SUS) of firms for the following period and the Environmental Investment Intensity (EPI) for the next period, respectively, as dependent variables in the mechanism tests. The results indicate that the coefficients of the air quality variable, AQI, are both significantly positive at the 5% significance level. This suggests that the more severe the air pollution, the more likely firms are to engage in sustainable transformation and increase their environmental investments. In other words, air pollution encourages firms to pursue sustainable transformation and boost green investments, thereby enhancing their ESG rating performance.

Table 9.8 Air pollution and firms' ESG performance: a mechanism test

	(1)	(2)
	SUS_{t+1}	EPI_{t+1}
AQI	1.281**	0.352**
	(2.757)	(2.883)
Observations	6179	6179
Adj.R^2	0.228	0.243

Notes Robust t-values are in parentheses and standard errors are clustered at the firm level. The regressions include all control variables, year FE, industry FE, city FE. ***1%, **5%, *10%

9.5.2 *Heterogeneity Analysis*

9.5.2.1 Regulatory Pressures

Given that air pollution has a positive promoting effect on a firm's ESG performance, does this effect vary with changes in regulatory pressure? The escalating environmental pollution issue has led governments and markets to increasingly focus on and emphasize sustainability. Compared to conventional firms, those in industries with pollution attributes face greater regulatory pressure, resulting in higher operational uncertainty (Berrone et al. 2013). Therefore, the impact of air pollution on a firm's ESG performance might be more pronounced in heavily polluting companies. To validate this prediction, this study divides the sample companies into heavily polluting and non-heavily polluting industries for subgroup analysis. Columns (1) and (2) of Table 9.9 report the results of subgroup regressions. It can be observed that the regression coefficient for air pollution's effect on a firm's ESG performance is significantly positive in the heavily polluting group, while in the non-heavily polluting group, it is not significant, consistent with the expectations.

Furthermore, media serves as a crucial external overseer in capital markets. Its wide-reaching communication connects investors, corporate management, regulators, analysts, and numerous other capital market participants. Increased media coverage makes firms more exposed to the public eye, not only increasing the market's demand for specific information about the firm (Drake et al. 2012) but also altering and influencing the attitudes, decisions of stakeholders, and the focus of regulatory authorities (Snyder and Stromberg 2010). Companies that receive more media attention face greater external supervision pressure. This may intensify the negative impact of air pollution on firms, prompting them to adopt more proactive ESG strategies. To verify this impact, we obtained web media news report quantities from the China Research Data Service platform (CNRDS) and calculated the logarithm of the total number of annual web media news reports for the firm (COVERAGE) to measure the firm's media attention. Based on the median value of this index, the sample was

Table 9.9 Regulatory pressures

	(1)	(2)	(3)	(4)	(5)	(6)
	Heavy pollution	Non-heavy pollution	High media attention	Low media attention	Institutional holdings are high	Low institutional ownership
	ESG_{t+1}	ESG_{t+1}	ESG_{t+1}	ESG_{t+1}	ESG_{t+1}	ESG_{t+1}
AQI	2.469**	1.049	2.845***	0.973	3.160***	0.858
	(2.884)	(1.483)	(3.380)	(1.316)	(3.495)	(1.020)
Observations	2715	3464	3086	3093	3089	3090
Adj.R^2	0.468	0.344	0.440	0.250	0.353	0.435

Notes Robust t-values are in parentheses and standard errors are clustered at the firm level. The regressions include all control variables, year FE, industry FE, city FE. ***1%, **5%, *10%

divided into high media attention (equal to or greater than the median value) and low media attention groups (less than the median value) for subgroup testing. As shown in columns (3) and (4) of Table 9.9, the impact of air pollution on a firm's ESG performance is significant only in the high media attention group, as expected.

Finally, considering the supervisory and governance role played by institutional investors in promoting ESG and sustainable development, this study further conducts subgroup tests using the number of shares held by institutional investors (INST). Existing literature has found that institutional investors actively engage in corporate ESG management by using their voting rights, thereby promoting a firm's positive ESG behavior (Li et al. 2021). Thus, when institutional investors hold more shares, firms may face greater supervisory pressure and thus place more emphasis on environmental and sustainable development issues. Similarly, this study uses the median value of this index to divide the sample into two groups for testing. Columns (5) and (6) of Table 9.9 show the regression results, indicating that the impact of air pollution on a firm's ESG performance is more significant when institutional holdings are higher, suggesting that institutional investors play a certain role in this regard.

9.5.2.2 Market Concerns

According to the salience theory, capital market participants are often drawn to significant issues in a given context, and these issues are reflected in their decision-making processes. Capital markets are characterized by foresight and guidance, and in the context of sustainable transformation and high-quality economic development, environmental issues and the associated corporate risks are more likely to be incorporated into stock prices, increasing the demand for ESG information among investors. Krueger et al. (2020) note that with the global prevalence and widespread acceptance of the ESG concept, investors increasingly consider environmental and climate-related risks when making decisions. The level of attention that market participants pay to ESG is an important factor affecting the supply of ESG by companies. Depending on the degree of attention from market participants, air pollution may have a heterogeneous effect on a firm's ESG performance.

To test this, the study employs the number of analysts tracking a firm (ANALYST) and the analysts' reports' focus on environmental issues (ATTENTION) as measures of capital market participants' attention. Analysts are vital information intermediaries in the capital market, utilizing their expertise to unearth and analyze information in the market, and their opinions or attitudes significantly influence the direction of the capital market and alter investors' judgments (Huang et al. 2014). The study collected over 400,000 analyst reports for A-share listed companies in the Shanghai and Shenzhen stock exchanges and constructed a measure for analysts' attention to environmental issues. Specifically, it started by collecting vocabulary related to environmental issues from government reports such as the "Twelfth Five-Year" Comprehensive Work Plan for Energy Conservation and Emission Reduction and the "Thirteenth Five-Year" Comprehensive Work Plan for Energy Conservation and Emission Reduction. Combining this with the Wikipedia corpus, a natural

Table 9.10 Market concerns

	(1)	(2)	(3)	(4)
	Analyst tracking multi	Less analyst tracking	Analyst environment focuses on high	Low analyst environmental concerns
	ESG_{t+1}	ESG_{t+1}	ESG_{t+1}	ESG_{t+1}
AQI	3.141***	0.869	2.475***	−0.065
	(3.326)	(1.126)	(3.866)	(−0.051)
Observations	2984	3195	2491	3688
Adj.R^2	0.469	0.284	0.331	0.376

Notes Robust t-values are in parentheses and standard errors are clustered at the firm level. The regressions include all control variables, year FE, industry FE, city FE. ***1%, **5%, *10%

language processing method was used to generate the five most similar phrases for each vocabulary. Unrelated phrases were manually deleted to create an environmental dictionary. This dictionary was then used for text analysis of analyst reports. The environmental attention of each report is calculated as the number of words related to environmental themes divided by the total number of words. Finally, the mean environmental attention in annual analyst reports was calculated to generate the ATTENTION variable.

Based on the median values of these two variables, the sample was divided into groups with high capital market attention (greater than or equal to the median) and low capital market attention (less than the median) and subjected to separate tests. Table 9.10 reports the regression results, showing that the positive impact of air pollution on a firm's ESG performance is more pronounced when there is a higher number of analysts tracking the firm and greater environmental attention among analysts. This is likely because with higher attention, air pollution has a greater impact on a firm's operational uncertainty, prompting the adoption of more proactive ESG strategies as a response.

9.5.3 Analysis of Economic Consequences

The pressing issue of severe air pollution drives companies to enhance their ESG performance to counter the increased operational uncertainty. However, a crucial question is whether improved ESG performance can yield tangible benefits to their production and operations. Financing is a critical challenge in a firm's operations, and existing literature suggests that ESG can offer firms a financial advantage by mitigating information asymmetry, establishing a responsible corporate image, improving access to financing channels, and enhancing their environmental credentials, which is favored by capital market participants (Krueger et al. 2020).

Table 9.11 Analysis of economic consequences: dynamic panel model estimates

	(1)	(2)	(3)	(4)
	High air pollution group		Low air pollution group	
	SA_{t+1}	P/B_{t+1}	SA_{t+1}	P/B_{t+1}
ESG	−0.003**	0.088**	−0.007	0.095
	(−3.044)	(2.608)	(−0.627)	(0.002)
Observations	2380	2836	2624	3033
Adj.R^2	Phase 1	Phase 1	Phase 1	Phase 1

Notes Robust t-values are in parentheses and standard errors are clustered at the firm level. The regressions include all control variables, year FE, industry FE, city FE. ***1%, **5%, *10%

With this backdrop, the study divides the sample into high and low air pollution groups based on the annual and city-level median air quality values. This division is used to examine the impact of enhanced ESG performance on financing constraints and price-to-book (P/B) ratio for companies operating in regions with high air pollution levels. The study calculates the financing constraint SA index to measure the severity of financing issues faced by firms. Following Pedersen et al.'s (2021) work, the study uses the price-to-book ratio (P/B) as a measure of market valuation of companies. Due to the potential endogeneity of a company's operational and ESG performance, the study employs a dynamic panel model to analyze the economic consequences.

Table 9.11 reports the empirical results, revealing that in the high air pollution group, a firm's ESG performance significantly alleviates their financing constraints in the subsequent period and increases their market valuation. This suggests that actively fulfilling ESG responsibilities can yield substantial returns, helping firms cope with external environmental uncertainties.

9.6 Conclusion

This study examines whether severe air pollution prompts companies to adjust their ESG strategies, focusing on A-share listed companies in the Shanghai and Shenzhen stock markets. The research uncovers a significant positive correlation between the air pollution in the city where a company's headquarters is located and its ESG performance in the following period. Further mechanistic analysis suggests that air pollution enhances a company's sustainable transformation and increases green investments, ultimately enhancing its ESG rating. Heterogeneity analysis indicates that the impact of air pollution on ESG performance is more pronounced when companies face greater regulatory pressure and higher market attention. Finally, the study conducts an economic consequence analysis, revealing that companies adjusting their ESG strategies based on air pollution conditions help mitigate financing constraints and improve market valuation in regions with high air pollution levels. This implies that actively fulfilling ESG responsibilities can result in substantial returns and aid in coping with external environmental uncertainties.

Based on the aforementioned research findings, this study offers the following insights. First, for regulators, it is essential to recognize the proactive role that enterprises can play in environmental governance. In regional environmental governance, both "command-based" and "guidance-based" policies should be employed, considering that businesses are the primary creators of environmental issues. The nature of regional air pollution is, in essence, an economic externality stemming from companies' extensive development practices. As opposed to government's top-down environmental regulations, which serve as a direct deterrent to enterprises, companies that proactively undergo sustainable transformation, internalizing green sustainable development within their actual production and operations, bringing about fundamental organizational changes, are better suited to address most of the regional environmental pollution issues from the source, with greater efficiency. Nevertheless, businesses are bound to encounter difficulties during this transformation, such as financial, technological, and managerial challenges. Therefore, regulators, when crafting environmental governance policies, should consider the hardships that businesses face when assuming environmental responsibility, and provide adequate support. Regulators can integrate ESG factors into their evaluation and assessment systems and, according to the characteristics and transformation difficulty of each enterprise, offer targeted incentive policies, such as increasing green subsidies or reducing taxes. Policy initiatives can act as guiding and incentive measures, capitalizing on multiple efforts, collectively driving the transformation of business operations to optimize regional air quality and facilitate high-quality economic development.

Second, for enterprises, there is a need to shift away from traditional management paradigms and proactively incorporate ESG factors into their strategic management systems to enable sustainable green transformation. High economic development inevitably prompts a reevaluation of the relationship between the environment and the economy, as well as corporate business ethics. China's 'Dual Carbon' goals and high-quality development are products of this reevaluation, which has fundamentally changed the external environment in which enterprises operate, increasing the adverse impact of regional environmental risks on their operations. Consequently, enterprises should rethink their strategic planning, eschew the exclusive pursuit of economic interests, and place greater emphasis on environmental, social, and governance performance in their strategic decisions. This shift is not only in line with the trend of the times but is also an effective way for enterprises to confront external uncertainties. The economic consequence analysis in this study demonstrates that ESG investment and improved economic performance are not inherently contradictory. For companies operating in areas with severe air pollution, proactive sustainable green transformation that enhances ESG performance can result in legitimacy advantages, enabling these companies to access more resources and increase their value. This underlines that stakeholders are willing to support companies with strong ESG performance. For companies operating in regions with more severe environmental pollution, proactive ESG investment will yield even greater returns. Furthermore, companies should prioritize ESG communication and disclosure, enrich the content of ESG disclosures, enhance the quality of ESG information disclosure, convey signals of sustainable development, earn the trust of stakeholders, and establish the foundation for long-term value realization.

References

Berrone P, Fosfuri A, Gelabert L, Gomez-Mejia LR (2013) Necessity as the mother if "green" inventions: institutional pressures and environmental innovations. Strateg Manag J 34(8):891–909

Boeker W (1991) Organizational strategy: an ecological perspective. Acad Manag J 34(3):613–635

Cho CH, Huang Z, Liu S, Yang D (2021) Contaminated heart: does air pollution harm business ethics? Evidence from earnings manipulation. J Bus Ethics 1:22

Clementino E, Perkins R (2021) How do companies respond to environmental, social and governance (ESG) ratings? Evidence from Italy. J Bus Ethics 171:379–397

Deryugina T, Heutel G, Miller NH, Molitor D, Reif J (2019) The mortality and medical costs of air pollution: evidence from changes in wind direction. Am Econ Rev 109(12):4178–4219

Dhaliwal DS, Li OZ, Tsang A, Yang YG (2011) Voluntary nonfinancial disclosure and the cost of equity capital: the initiation of corporate social responsibility reporting. Account Rev 86(1):59–100

Dong R, Fisman R, Wang Y, Xu N (2021) Air pollution, affect, and forecasting bias: evidence from Chinese financial analysts. J Financ Econ 139(3):971–984

Drake MS, Roulstone DT, Thornock JR (2012) Investor information demand: Evidence from Google searches around earnings announcements. J Account Res 50(4):1001–1040

Flammer C (2015) Does product market competition foster corporate social responsibility? Evidence from trade liberalization. Strateg Manag J 36(10):1469–1485

Friedman M (1970) The social responsibility of business is to increase its profits. New York Times Magazine

Fu S, Viard VB, Zhang P (2021) Air pollution and manufacturing firm productivity: nationwide estimates for China. Econ J 131(640):3241–3273

Godfrey PC (2005) The relationship between corporate philanthropy and shareholder wealth: a risk management perspective. Acad Manag Rev 30(4):777–798

Haveman HA (1992) Between a rock and a hard place: organizational change and performance under conditions of fundamental environmental transformation. Adm Sci Q 37:48–75

He J, Liu H, Salvo A (2019) Severe air pollution and labor productivity: evidence from industrial towns in China. Am Econ J Appl Econ 11(1):173–201

Heckman JJ (1979) Sample selection bias as a specification error. Econometrica 153:161

Huang AH, Zang AY, Zheng R (2014) Evidence on the information content of text in analyst reports. Account Rev 89(6):2151–2180

Huang Q, Li Y, Lin M, McBrayer GA (2022) Natural disasters, risk salience, and corporate ESG disclosure. J Corp Finan 72:102152

Ioannou I, Serafeim G (2012) What drives corporate social performance? The role of nation-level institutions. J Int Bus Stud 43(834):864–864

Jackson G, Apostolakou A (2010) Corporate social responsibility in western Europe: an institutional mirror or substitute? J Bus Ethics 94(3):371–394

Jeong YC, Kim TY (2019) Between legitimacy and efficiency: an institutional theory of corporate giving. Acad Manag J 62(5):1583–1608

Kaplan S (2011) Research in cognition and strategy: reflections on two decades of progress and a look to the future. J Manag Stud 48(3):665–695

Kim S, Lee G, Kang HG (2021) Risk management and corporate social responsibility. Strateg Manag J 42(1):202–230
Krueger P, Sautner Z, Starks LT (2020) The importance of climate risks for institutional investors. Rev Financ Stud 33(3):1067–1111
Li Z, Wang P, Wu T (2021) Do foreign institutional investors drive corporate social responsibility? Evidence from listed firms in China. J Bus Financ Acc 48(1–2):338–373
Liao L, Pan Y, Yao T (2023) Capital market liberalization and voluntary corporate social responsibility disclosure: evidence from a quasi-natural experiment in China. Account Finance 63(2):2677–2715
Pedersen LH, Fitzgibbons S, Pomorski L (2021) Responsible investing: the ESG-efficient frontier. J Financ Econ 142(2):572–597
Rajagopalan N, Spreitzer GM (1997) Toward a theory of strategic change: a multi-lens perspective and integrative framework. Acad Manag Rev 22(1):48–79
Reber B, Gold A, Gold S (2022) ESG disclosure and idiosyncratic risk in initial public offerings. J Bus Ethics 179(3):867–886
Seltzer L, Starks LT, Zhu Q (2022) Climate regulatory risk and corporate bonds. NBER Working Paper, (29994)
Snyder J, Stromberg D (2010) Press coverage and political accountability. J Polit Econ 118(2):355–408
Suchman MC (1995) Managing legitimacy: strategic and institutional approaches. Acad Manag Rev 20(3):571–610
Tan J, Tan Z, Chan KC (2021a) Does air pollution affect a firm's cash holdings? Pac Basin Financ J 67:101549
Tan Z, Tan J, Chan KC (2021b) Seeing is believing? The impact of air pollution on corporate social responsibility. Corp Soc Responsib Environ Manag 28(1):525–534
Wang L, Dai Y, Kong D (2021) Air pollution and employee treatment. J Corp Finan 70:102067

Chapter 10
Breathing Freely: A Vision for a Future with Clean Air

10.1 Summary

Throughout this book, we have highlighted the many dimensions in which air pollution influences economic and social systems. Chapters 2 through 9 delve into specific mechanisms through which air pollution exerts its effects—ranging from its influence on stock market performance and the behavioral responses of consumers and investors, to its effects on health insurance markets and the strategic decisions of corporations striving to cope with pollution-related risks. By connecting environmental degradation to economic performance across a variety of sectors, we aim to present a comprehensive overview of the complexity and urgency of this global challenge.

This concluding chapter synthesizes the key findings from the preceding chapters and reflects on their broader implications. It also outlines future directions for research, policy, and business practice—emphasizing the need for resilient systems and sustainable solutions to mitigate the adverse effects of air pollution and safeguard long-term socio-economic well-being.

In Chap. 2, *Choking Returns: Air Pollution and Stock Market Performance*, we examined the relationship between air pollution levels and corporate financial performance. The empirical findings indicated that firms located in regions with higher levels of air pollution tend to experience lower stock returns and reduced trading volumes. This relationship was more pronounced in firms with lower institutional ownership and less analyst coverage, suggesting that regional investors and those less informed about the broader market dynamics are particularly susceptible to the effects of air pollution. The chapter also highlighted a gradual adaptation among investors, who have become increasingly aware of the financial implications of air pollution, leading to shifts in trading behavior over time.

In Chap. 3, *Trading on Thin Air: Pollution, Behavior, and Market Efficiency*, we explored how air pollution affects individual investors' decisions and challenges

M. Guo et al., *Social-Economic Impacts of Air Pollution*, Climate Change and Energy Transition, https://doi.org/10.1007/978-981-96-7858-7_10

market efficiency. The findings revealed that pollution negatively influences the likelihood of investors making purchases, but paradoxically, it increases their propensity to sell stocks. This finding challenges the efficient market hypothesis by suggesting that environmental factors like air pollution can induce irrational behavior, particularly in less experienced investors or those living in areas of severe pollution. This insight adds another layer to our understanding of how environmental factors can shape market outcomes and investor behavior, raising concerns about the efficiency and fairness of financial markets.

Together, Chaps. 2 and 3 offer a robust assessment of how air pollution distorts financial markets, particularly for retail investors and companies in heavily polluted regions. These findings imply that environmental policies aimed at reducing air pollution could also enhance stabilize financial markets and restore investor confidence.

Shifting focus to investor behavior on the IPO market, Chap. 4, *A Breath of Fresh Capital? Air Pollution and the IPO Market*, demonstrated that air pollution negatively impacts IPO performance, with environmental firms being more affected than non-environmental stocks. This observation underscores the growing role of environmental concerns in investment decisions, particularly as public awareness of air pollution rises. The chapter shows that air pollution not only affects the pricing of individual stocks but also shapes broader capital market trends, including the success of new public offerings. These insights are crucial for both policymakers and businesses, indicating that environmental stewardship may foster market stability and promote green innovation.

In Chap. 5, *Hazy Perceptions: How Air Pollution Colors Customer Ratings*, the impact of air pollution on consumer reviews was explored, revealing a negative relationship between poor air quality and the ratings of restaurants. Consumers in areas with higher pollution were more likely to leave lower reviews, particularly when pollution levels exceeded certain thresholds. This phenomenon reflects broader shifts in consumer behavior, where individuals are increasingly sensitive to environmental conditions, particularly in industries related to hospitality, retail, and tourism. The chapter also highlighted the nonlinear effects of air pollution, where its influence on consumer satisfaction grows stronger with more severe pollution levels.

Chapter 6, *The Unseen Cost of Travel: Air Pollution and the Tourism Industry*, further builds on this theme, showing that air pollution negatively affects domestic tourism in China. A rise in pollution levels leads to a significant reduction in tourism revenue and the number of visitors, with more severe effects in areas with high public concern over air quality. This finding is significant for the tourism industry, which is a major economic driver in many countries. Tourism businesses must adapt by promoting cleaner, more sustainable travel options and improving air quality in tourist hotspots.

Chapter 7, *Breathing Easier? Air Pollution and the Health Insurance Sector*, investigated the effects of air pollution on health insurance markets, specifically in China. The study found that increases in air pollution levels, measured by PM2.5 concentrations, led to greater demand for commercial health insurance. This chapter emphasizes the link between environmental factors and health-related economic behavior.

As pollution contributes to higher incidences of respiratory diseases and other health issues, the resulting financial strain on individuals and families prompts increased spending on health insurance, thereby shifting the landscape of the insurance market.

These chapters collectively underscore the pervasive impact of air pollution on consumer decisions, public health, and industries that rely on consumer spending. They highlight the need for businesses to consider environmental risks in their strategic planning and to adapt to changing consumer preferences for cleaner, healthier products and services.

Chapters 8 and 9 focus on the corporate sector and how businesses are responding to the challenges posed by air pollution. Chapter 8, *Investing in Clean Air: How Air Pollution is Driving Green Innovation*, revealed that high levels of pollution incentivize businesses to invest in green innovation, particularly in the manufacturing sector. The findings suggest that companies located in regions with high pollution levels are more likely to engage in green innovation, especially in the development of high-value, invention-based technologies. State-owned enterprises, larger firms, and technologically advanced companies are particularly inclined to pursue green innovation, indicating that the economic incentives for innovation in response to pollution are stronger among more resource-rich companies.

Chapter 9, *Clearing the Air for Investors: How Pollution is Reshaping Corporate ESG*, examined how air pollution influences corporate ESG (Environmental, Social, and Governance) performance. The research found that regional pollution significantly enhances a company's ESG performance, as companies adjust their strategies to mitigate environmental risks and improve their sustainability credentials. This chapter highlights the growing importance of environmental factors in corporate governance and the pressure companies face to demonstrate their commitment to sustainability, particularly in the face of rising public and regulatory scrutiny. Companies that improve their ESG performance in response to pollution may also benefit from better financing conditions and higher market valuations, further emphasizing the economic incentives for adopting more sustainable practices.

These chapters underscore the important role of businesses in responding to the economic challenges posed by air pollution. By embracing green innovation and improving their ESG performance, companies can not only mitigate the direct risks associated with environmental degradation—such as regulatory penalties, reputational damage, and operational disruptions—but also unlock new opportunities for growth. In an increasingly sustainability-conscious market, firms that demonstrate a commitment to environmental responsibility are more likely to attract investment, build consumer trust, and strengthen stakeholder relationships. Moreover, proactive engagement with environmental challenges can foster long-term resilience and agility, enabling businesses to navigate evolving policy landscapes and shifting consumer expectations.

10.2 Policy Implications and Future Directions

Air pollution, as a multifaceted and global issue, requires a comprehensive and strategic response from both policymakers and businesses. The findings from this book underline the critical need for coordinated actions across various levels to mitigate the economic, social, and environmental costs of air pollution. This section expands on the policy implications drawn from the research and outlines potential future directions, focusing on regulatory measures, market-driven solutions, and the broader implications for sustainability and economic development.

10.2.1 Strengthening and Expanding Regulatory Frameworks

The first step in tackling the economic impacts of air pollution is strengthening and expanding regulatory frameworks. Historically, air quality management policies have focused primarily on improving public health outcomes, such as reducing the incidence of respiratory diseases and limiting particulate matter (PM) emissions. However, as this book has shown, the economic consequences of air pollution are just as significant, influencing market behavior, consumer confidence, corporate strategy, and investment flows. It is essential for governments to adapt their regulations to consider these economic dimensions and enforce stricter air quality standards that not only protect human health but also incentivize cleaner industrial practices. Several key regulatory measures could be enacted:

Tighter Emissions Standards: Governments should implement and enforce stricter emissions standards for industrial activities, transportation, and energy production. Setting ambitious targets for reducing CO_2, PM, and other air pollutants will push industries toward cleaner technologies, reducing their environmental footprint and mitigating the broader economic impacts of air pollution.

Carbon Pricing and Pollution Taxation: One of the most effective market-driven approaches to reducing pollution is carbon pricing, including carbon taxes and cap-and-trade systems. By putting a price on carbon emissions, governments can incentivize businesses to reduce their pollution levels and invest in cleaner alternatives. The revenues generated from such taxes can then be reinvested in public health initiatives, pollution-reduction programs, and research into green technologies.

Urban Air Quality Initiatives: In urban areas where pollution is most concentrated, local governments should focus on creating air quality zones, mandating the use of low-emission vehicles, and improving public transportation infrastructure to reduce vehicular emissions. These policies could have a direct positive impact on the health and productivity of urban populations while simultaneously supporting green technologies and industries.

Enhanced Transparency and Accountability: Governments must enforce greater transparency on air quality and its economic impacts, encouraging businesses to disclose their environmental footprints and the strategies they are implementing to reduce pollution. Transparent environmental reporting will not only raise awareness among consumers but also drive companies to adopt better practices.

10.2.2 Encouraging Green Innovation Through Incentives

This book has demonstrated that air pollution serves as both a challenge and an opportunity for green innovation. Businesses located in highly polluted areas have a compelling economic incentive to develop cleaner technologies, particularly in the manufacturing sector. Therefore, policies should encourage green innovation through a variety of financial incentives and support programs.

R&D Tax Credits and Subsidies: Governments should provide tax credits and subsidies for companies investing in research and development (R&D) of environmentally friendly technologies. This can help offset the initial costs of innovation and encourage companies to prioritize green technologies. Additionally, investing in renewable energy technologies, electric vehicles, and sustainable agriculture practices could stimulate new industries and job creation, reducing both environmental and economic costs.

Green Technology Partnerships: Public-private partnerships can be highly effective in fostering innovation. Governments could collaborate with businesses, universities, and non-governmental organizations (NGOs) to fund and promote research in air pollution control technologies, carbon capture and storage, and cleaner production methods. Such partnerships can drive the development of cutting-edge technologies that not only reduce air pollution but also provide economic returns in the long term.

Innovation Incentives for Pollution-Heavy Sectors: The most polluting sectors, such as coal, oil, and chemical industries, need targeted policies to drive innovation. Governments could implement policies that require these sectors to invest in pollution reduction and environmental innovation, including setting long-term clean-tech goals that push the industries to diversify and invest in low-emission technologies.

10.2.3 Promoting Corporate Responsibility and ESG Standards

As outlined in Chap. 9, corporate behavior is also a crucial determinant in mitigating the economic impacts of air pollution. Companies must recognize that addressing environmental risks is not just a moral obligation but also a key component of long-term financial success. This book highlights how air pollution can drive green innovation, and how companies are increasingly motivated by both regulatory pressure and consumer preferences to improve their environmental performance. To support these trends, policymakers must promote corporate responsibility through:

Strengthened ESG (Environmental, Social, and Governance) Regulations: Governments can introduce mandatory ESG disclosures for companies, ensuring they report their pollution levels, sustainability practices, and the economic impact of their environmental strategies. Transparency is essential for investors, as well as for consumers, in making informed decisions about where to invest and which companies to support.

Corporate Tax Incentives for Environmental Performance: Providing tax incentives to companies that meet high environmental standards or achieve significant reductions in pollution can encourage businesses to invest in cleaner practices. Companies that achieve exemplary environmental performance should be rewarded through preferential tax rates or access to government contracts.

Aligning Executive Incentives with Sustainability Goals: Corporations should link executive compensation to sustainability targets, encouraging leaders to prioritize long-term environmental and economic goals over short-term profits. This shift will require changes in corporate governance but could be a game-changer in driving systemic changes within industries.

10.2.4 Strengthening the Role of Local Governments in Air Quality Management

Local governments play a pivotal role in air quality management, as air pollution often varies significantly from one region to another. As evidenced in the chapters discussing the tourism and consumer markets, air quality has a direct impact on regional economic activities, such as tourism, hospitality, and local businesses. Therefore, policy recommendations include:

Decentralized Air Quality Regulations: Local governments should have the authority to set air quality standards tailored to the specific pollution challenges of their regions. This could include introducing stricter regulations for cities with severe pollution levels, developing localized action plans, and engaging with local communities to promote pollution-reduction behaviors.

Community-Based Monitoring and Reporting: Empowering local communities to monitor and report air quality levels can help ensure that air quality regulations are being enforced at the grassroots level. Community engagement programs can also raise awareness about the importance of reducing personal carbon footprints and participating in local pollution-reduction efforts.

10.2.5 Enhancing International Cooperation and Standards

As air pollution is a transboundary issue, global cooperation is essential to address it effectively. Several countries, especially in developing regions, face severe challenges in managing pollution due to limited resources, weak regulatory frameworks, and insufficient technological know-how. To address these issues, international cooperation is critical.

Global Air Quality Standards: International organizations, such as the World Health Organization (WHO) and the United Nations (UN), should work together to establish global air quality standards. These standards would guide national governments in setting pollution thresholds and offer technical assistance to countries that lack the resources to address air pollution effectively.

Technology Transfer and Financial Assistance: Wealthier nations and international development banks should provide financial assistance and technology transfer to developing countries to help them tackle air pollution. This could include funding for pollution monitoring, cleaner industrial technologies, and capacity-building programs for local governments.

Climate Change and Air Pollution Synergies: The global community should leverage the synergies between climate change mitigation and air pollution reduction. Many of the strategies to combat climate change, such as transitioning to renewable energy and reducing carbon emissions, can also help improve air quality. Policies aimed at reducing greenhouse gas emissions should simultaneously focus on reducing air pollutants such as sulfur dioxide (SO_2) and nitrogen oxides (NOx), which contribute to both climate change and air pollution.

10.2.6 Future Directions

Air pollution remains one of the most pressing global challenges, with far-reaching consequences for public health, economic stability, and environmental sustainability. While the problem is complex, the future of air pollution governance is not without hope. A combination of innovative strategies, including energy transition, green finance, technological advancements, and behavioral changes, offers a multifaceted approach to mitigating air pollution. This chapter explores these pathways, highlighting their potential to create a cleaner, healthier, and more sustainable future.

10.2.6.1 Energy Transition: Shifting to Cleaner Energy Sources

The Role of Renewable Energy The transition from fossil fuels to renewable energy is a cornerstone of air pollution governance. Fossil fuel combustion is a major source of air pollutants, including particulate matter (PM2.5), nitrogen oxides (NOx), and sulfur dioxide (SO_2). Renewable energy sources such as solar, wind, and hydropower offer a cleaner alternative, significantly reducing emissions and improving air quality.

Countries worldwide are increasingly investing in renewable energy infrastructure. For example, China, the world's largest emitter of greenhouse gases, has become a global leader in solar and wind energy production. Similarly, the European Union has set ambitious targets to achieve carbon neutrality by 2050, with a strong emphasis on renewable energy deployment. These efforts not only reduce air pollution but also contribute to global climate goals.

Electrification of Transportation The transportation sector is a significant contributor to air pollution, particularly in urban areas. The shift toward electric vehicles (EVs) offers a promising solution, as EVs produce zero tailpipe emissions. Governments and private sector players are supporting EV adoption through incentives, subsidies, and infrastructure development. For instance, Norway has achieved over 50% EV penetration in new car sales, thanks to policies such as tax exemptions and toll discounts. Other countries, including the United States and India, are also ramping up efforts to promote electric mobility.

Energy Efficiency and Conservation Improving energy efficiency and promoting conservation are critical components of the energy transition. Energy-efficient technologies and practices reduce the demand for fossil fuels, thereby lowering emissions. For example, energy-efficient buildings, appliances, and industrial processes can significantly cut energy consumption. Governments are implementing policies such as building codes, energy performance standards, and public awareness campaigns to drive efficiency improvements.

10.2.6.2 Green Finance: Mobilizing Capital for Clean Air

The Rise of Green Bonds Green finance has emerged as a powerful tool to fund environmental projects, including those aimed at reducing air pollution. Green bonds, in particular, have gained traction as a financing mechanism for renewable energy, energy efficiency, and pollution control projects. In 2020, global green bond issuance surpassed $270 billion, reflecting growing investor interest in sustainable opportunities.

Sustainable Investment and ESG Criteria The integration of environmental, social, and governance (ESG) criteria into investment decisions is reshaping the financial landscape. Investors are increasingly prioritizing companies and projects with strong environmental performance, driving capital toward sustainable initiatives. This shift not only supports air pollution mitigation but also aligns with the growing recognition that sustainable investments can deliver competitive financial returns.

Public-Private Partnerships Public-private partnerships (PPPs) play a crucial role in advancing green finance and air pollution governance. By leveraging public and private sector resources, PPPs can accelerate the implementation of clean energy and pollution control projects. For example, the Green Climate Fund (GCF) supports PPPs that aim to reduce emissions and improve air quality in developing countries.

10.2.6.3 Technological Innovations: Harnessing the Power of Innovation

Air Quality Monitoring and Data Analytics Advancements in air quality monitoring and data analytics are transforming air pollution governance. Real-time monitoring systems, powered by IoT (Internet of Things) devices and satellite technology, provide accurate and timely data on air quality. This information enables policymakers to identify pollution hotspots, implement targeted interventions, and track progress over time. For instance, cities like Beijing and Delhi have deployed extensive air quality monitoring networks to inform their pollution control strategies.

Carbon Capture and Storage (CCS) Carbon capture and storage (CCS) technologies offer a promising solution to reduce emissions from industrial sources. CCS involves capturing carbon dioxide (CO_2) emissions from power plants and industrial facilities, transporting them, and storing them underground. While still in its early stages, CCS has the potential to significantly reduce emissions from sectors that are difficult to decarbonize, such as cement and steel production.

Smart Cities and Urban Planning Smart city initiatives and sustainable urban planning can play a pivotal role in reducing air pollution. By integrating technology, data, and infrastructure, cities can optimize energy use, reduce traffic congestion, and promote green spaces. For example, Barcelona's smart city program has implemented measures such as smart lighting, waste management, and public transportation systems, contributing to improved air quality and quality of life.

10.2.6.4 Behavioral and Cultural Shifts: Changing Mindsets for a Cleaner Future

Public Awareness and Education Raising public awareness about the health and environmental impacts of air pollution is essential for driving behavioral change. Educational campaigns can encourage individuals to adopt sustainable practices, such as using public transportation, reducing energy consumption, and supporting clean energy initiatives. For example, the "Clean Air for All" campaign in India has successfully mobilized communities to take action against air pollution.

Corporate Responsibility and Green Practices Businesses have a critical role to play in air pollution governance. By adopting green practices, such as reducing emissions, using renewable energy, and implementing sustainable supply chains, corporations can significantly contribute to cleaner air. Many companies are also setting ambitious sustainability goals, such as achieving net-zero emissions, to align with global climate targets.

Policy and Regulatory Frameworks Strong policy and regulatory frameworks are essential for driving systemic change. Governments can implement measures such as emissions standards, carbon pricing, and pollution taxes to incentivize cleaner practices. For example, the European Union's Emissions Trading System (ETS) has successfully reduced emissions by putting a price on carbon and creating a market for trading emissions allowances.

The future of air pollution governance lies in a multifaceted approach that combines energy transition, green finance, technological innovation, behavioral change. By transitioning to renewable energy, electrifying transportation, and improving energy efficiency, we can significantly reduce emissions. Green finance mechanisms, such as green bonds and sustainable investments, can mobilize the necessary capital to support these initiatives. Technological advancements, including air quality monitoring and carbon capture, offer innovative solutions to tackle pollution at its source.

The manufacturer's authorised representative in the EU is Springer Nature Customer Service Centre GmbH, Europaplatz 3, 69115 Heidelberg, Germany. If you have any concerns regarding our products, please contact ProductSafety@springernature.com

Printed and bound by CPI Group (UK) Ltd, Croydon, CR0 4YY
01/10/2026
02225923-0002